SEVEN FALLEN FEATHERS

SEVEN FALLEN FEATHERS

RACISM, DEATH, AND
HARD TRUTHS IN A
NORTHERN CITY

TANYA TALAGA

ANANSI

Published in Canada and the USA in 2017 by House of Anansi Press Inc.
www.houseofanansi.com

House of Anansi Press is committed to protecting our natural environment. As part of our efforts, the interior of this book is printed on paper that contains 100% post-consumer recycled fibres, is acid-free, and is processed chlorine-free.

21 20 19 18 17   4 5 6 7 8

Library and Archives Canada Cataloguing in Publication

Talaga, Tanya, author
Seven fallen feathers : racism, death, and hard truths in a northern city
/ Tanya Talaga.

Issued in print and electronic formats.
ISBN 978-1-4870-0226-8 (softcover).—ISBN 978-1-4870-0227-5 (EPUB).—
ISBN 978-1-4870-0228-2 (Kindle)

1. Native children—Ontario—Thunder Bay—Social conditions. 2. Native peoples—Canada—Social conditions. 3. Native peoples—Canada—Government relations. 4. Canada—Race relations. 5. Native peoples—Civil rights—Canada.
I. Title.

E98.S67T35 2017   305.897'071312   C2016-906674-6
                         C2016-907020-4

Library of Congress Control Number: 2016958341

Book design: Alysia Shewchuk

 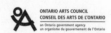

We acknowledge for their financial support of our publishing program
the Canada Council for the Arts, the Ontario Arts Council, and the Government of
Canada through the Canada Book Fund.

Printed and bound in Canada

For the next generation, Natasha and William

For strong mothers, Sheila and Margaret

And for Jethro, Curran, Robyn, Paul,
Reggie, Kyle, and Jordan

CONTENTS

NISHNAWBE ASKI NATION

MANITOBA

Fort Severn

Weenusk
(Peawanuck)

Sachigo Lake

Bearskin Lake

Muskrat Dam

Wapekeka

Kasabonika Lake

Wawakapewin

Sandy Lake

Koocheching

Kingfisher Lake

Keewaywin

North Caribou Lake

Attawapiskat

Deer Lake

Wunnumin Lake

Webequie

North Spirit Lake

Nibinamik

Poplar Hill

McDowell Lake

Kashechewan

Pikangikum

Neskantaga

Cat Lake

Fort Albany

Eabametoong

Moose Cree

Mishkeegogamang

Marten Falls

MoCreebec
Council of the
Cree Nation

Slate Falls

Lac Seul

Whitewater Lake

Aroland

50°   50°

Long Lake #58

Constance Lake

Flying Post

Ginoogaming

Taykwa Tagamou

Hornepayne

Wahgoshig

Missanabie Cree

Mattagami

Beaverhouse

Brunswick House

Matachewan

Chapleau Cree

Chapleau Ojibwe

⚪ Independent Bands

△ Independent First Nations Alliance

▢ Keewaytinook Okimakanak

⚫ Matawa First Nations

⬭ Mushkegowuk Council

⬚ Shibogama First Nations Council

▲ Wabun Tribal Council

⬛ Windigo First Nations Council

THUNDER BAY

TORONTO STAR GRAPHIC

The Anishinaabe are guided by seven principles:

Zah-gi-di-win (love): To know love is to know peace.
Ma-na-ji-win (respect): To honour all of creation is to
 have respect.
Aak-de-he-win (bravery): To face life with courage is to
 know bravery.
Gwe-ya-kwaad-zi-win (honesty): To walk through life
 with integrity is to know honesty.
Dbaa-dem-diz-win (humility): To accept yourself as a
 sacred part of creation is to know humility.
Nbwaa-ka-win (wisdom): To cherish knowledge is to
 know wisdom.
De-bwe-win (truth): To know of these things is to know
 the truth.

> — *Bakaan nake'ii ngii-izhi-gakinoo'amaagoomin*
> (*We Were Taught Differently: The Indian*
> *Residential School Experience*)

❧ ❧ ❦ ❦

Cultural genocide is the destruction of those structures
and practices that allow the group to continue as a group.
States that engage in cultural genocide set out to destroy
the political and social institutions of the targeted group.
Land is seized, and populations are forcibly transferred
and their movement is restricted. Languages are banned.
Spiritual leaders are persecuted, spiritual practices are
forbidden, and objects of spiritual value are confiscated
and destroyed. And, most significantly to the issue at
hand, families are disrupted to prevent the transmission
of cultural values and identity from one generation to the
next. In its dealing with Aboriginal people, Canada did
all these things.

— Honouring the Truth, Reconciling for the Future:
Summary of the Final Report of the Truth and
Reconciliation Commission of Canada

PROLOGUE

YOU SEE, THE GIANT NANABIJOU MADE A DEAL.

The giant spent his days lumbering around Gichigami, the colossal body of water that looked like a sea. He stomped and he stomped and he stomped. His noisy footprints created massive valleys and rock faces, cut from the granite and the slate that surrounded the water.

But he never bothered the Ojibwe, who lived with him in the gorges and forests that he left standing. They had a close existence, full of happiness and peace. On the smooth rock walls near Gichigami's shores, the Ojibwe drew pictographs, telling the stories of their lives for later generations to see.

Nanabijou had a secret only the Ojibwe knew: embedded in the rock there was a shiny metal that twinkled like the starry sky. The giant didn't want anyone to take something of such beauty away from him. So he told the Ojibwe never to tell the white man where he had hidden his silvery stash. If they kept his secret, Nanabijou promised to always protect them. If they did not, if they told the white man, who was beginning to settle in wooden houses near Gichigami, something catastrophic would happen and he would never be able to protect the Ojibwe again. The Ojibwe listened and they agreed to keep Nanabijou's secret safe.

For many moons, the giant and the Ojibwe lived in peace. Then one day, the Ojibwe found a Sioux man who said he was lost and in need of help. They took him in. But the Sioux man was a secret sneak. He had heard stories of the precious glittery metal and he wanted some to take back to his people. He befriended the Ojibwe and lived with them so he could gain their trust and find out where the silver was hidden.

The Sioux man waited patiently. Then one day he overheard the Ojibwe talking about where the silver could be found. Armed with this knowledge, he snuck away in search of the loot.

He slipped into a canoe and manoeuvered down the waters and into the crevice where the silver lay. When the Sioux man saw the treasure, he could not believe his eyes or his good fortune. He filled his pockets and stole away in the canoe.

The Sioux man was not as clever as he thought. As he made his escape down the river, he ran into travelling white men who captured him and took him prisoner. He tried to barter for his freedom with a piece of the stolen silver. But the greedy white men took his loot and asked for more. The Sioux man refused to tell them where he had found it but the white men would not take no for an answer. They knew how they could get him talking. They sat by the fire and brought out the firewater. The firewater calmed his fears, made him feel happy, made his lips loose. When he was full of drink, the white men asked again where the silver was stashed and the Sioux man spilled out the secret.

A falcon flying overhead watched the whole scene unfold. When he heard the betrayal, he quickly flew to warn Nanabijou. But Nanabijou had known as soon as the Sioux man's words were spoken. Suddenly, he began to feel heavy, so heavy he could barely move. His limbs seized and all he could do was lie down.

He turned from warm flesh and blood to solid stone.

The Ojibwe were now on their own.

THUNDER BAY HAS ALWAYS been a city of two faces. The Port Arthur side is the white face and the Fort William side is the red face. Port Arthur lies on the north shore. It is built up on the gentle, sloping Canadian Shield. Two-storey brick houses line streets that run up and down the Shield, each with a beautiful view of Lake Superior as far as the Sibley Peninsula, where the stone-cold Sleeping Giant Nanabijou sleeps.

The red side is located down by the Kaministiquia (known locally as the Kam) River, on the Ojibwe's traditional lands near the base of Mount McKay in the flatlands known as Fort William. Except for one tiny enclave of grand homes near Vickers Park, built by the affluent of another time, the residential streets of Fort William are staunchly working class, small bungalows or two-storey homes in various stages of repair, most with a pickup truck parked out front.

For more than ten thousand years, the Indigenous people built a thriving society along the banks of the Kam and of Gichigami, or Lake Superior, and points north and west. Gichigami is the stuff of legends. It is the largest freshwater lake in the world. The sheer vastness of Superior controls the unpredictable weather in the bay, and all who live near her bow and bend to her moods — the jet streams, the unexpected gusts of wind, the torrential rain, and the brilliant sun. In an instant, bright, sunny skies can turn black and ominous, leaving those who are on the water wishing they were not. Hundreds of rivers and streams pour into her from all points north, including the Kaministiquia, the McIntyre, the Nipigon, the Pigeon, and the St. Louis. These rivers were the Indigenous thoroughfares of the past — families followed them either on foot or in their canoes, travelling all over the north. From time immemorial, the junctures of these rivers have provided meeting places for the Ojibwe and their Cree cousins.

Before the white face came to town, this area was where the action was. The rivers were the highways of the traders. It was the hub of the fur trade and the place where the French coureurs de bois and the Indigenous trappers and traders met. The Ojibwe called this place Animikii, or Thunder, the place where the sky rumbled and pounded with Superior's immense power. The French agreed and quickly called it Baie de Tonnaire, or Thunder Bay.

The Kaministiquia, an Ojibwe word meaning "river with islands," is the largest river in Thunder Bay. Beginning at Dog Lake, it gains its mighty strength over the rugged rocks of Kakabeka Falls, a raging wonder of nature standing forty-seven metres in height. Powered by Kakabeka's flow, the Kam snakes into Fort William and commands its way around Mount McKay, where the descendants of Nanabijou's people, the Ojibwe of Fort William First Nation, still live.

Today, the Kam is dotted with industry. The white faces have tried to capture and use its speed and force. There are two generating stations on the Kam owned by Ontario Power Generation, which is owned by the provincial government. Resolute Forest Products mill, formerly AbitibiBowater, sits on the fir-lined banks. Logging trucks flow in and out of the mill all day long. A massive Bombardier assembly plant that builds sleek streetcars for southern cities is also on the Kam's banks.

The colonials have marked their territory here on the red side by constructing their important buildings of power and governance. In 2009, a new 3,995-square-metre City Hall opened at the corner of May and Donald Streets, a modern building made of shiny glass and smooth concrete. More than one hundred people can gather in the first-floor lobby and hundreds more can mingle outside on the landscaped front entranceway, complete with waterfalls and plenty of seating areas. Its wide-open spaces have also made it a popular transit hub. The streets in front of City Hall are populated by stops for buses that can take you around the city.[1] Just down the street from City Hall, the architecturally revered Thunder Bay Courthouse, which opened in 2014, occupies nearly an entire city block. The 18,580-square-metre building is six storeys high, with fifteen courtrooms, an open atrium, signs posted in English, French, and Ojibwe, and security provided by the Thunder Bay Police.

The Kam still draws people to its shores. Teens come down to the river's gummy banks to take cover under bridges or in bushes to drink and party. Here they have privacy, a space of their own, beside the giant pulp and paper mill that spews smelly, yellow, funnel-shaped clouds into the air. Here they are close to nature. They sit on the rocks and listen to the rush of the water, and they are reminded of home.

Beside the mill's entrance, there is a green provincial road sign that says *Chippewa Road*. Some bureaucrat must have had a sense of humour because this is the entrance to Fort William First Nation, one of the 133 Indigenous reservations located in the province of Ontario. Chippewa Road is now the only way onto the rez. There used to be another entrance, the James Street swing bridge, but somebody set fire to it in 2013. The CN-owned bridge connected the reserve to the city. There was always something special about crossing the old, rickety bridge into Fort William. Cars were forced to slow down, tires creeping over every bump. Always at the back of your mind was the subtle fear that maybe, just maybe, this time you'd fall right through. Now, the blackened burned-out wood-and-steel shell sits there, unrepaired, as the Kam River moves swiftly underneath. Three levels of government — the city, the province, and the federal government — can't decide on who should pay for the repairs. The reserve won't pay and neither will the railway company. The finger of blame points in all directions so nothing gets done.

OLD MONEY FROM VICTORIAN times built Port Arthur. The white face is the face of business and commerce and the rule of law. It wears button-down shirts, eats at the Keg, and lives in a cookie-cutter house in a brand-new subdivision with a Kia parked in the driveway. The people who live there are the doctors, the lawyers, and the proprietors of the twin city. On Saturdays they zip around in their cars to the big-box stores on the way to their cottages, or "camps," so they can play with their powerboats and Jet Skis.

In 1870, the British Army's Colonel Garnet Wolseley named the settlement Port Arthur to honour one of Queen Victoria's sons. Wolseley had been passing through the area with 1,200 men under orders to replace Métis leader Louis Riel's provisional government in what is now the province of Manitoba. It was from here, the north shore of Superior, where the nation building of Canada began. Railways and roads were plotted from this point west. The grand old Prince Arthur Hotel was conceived and constructed by rail barons, who needed a comfortable place to stay and dine while they expanded their growing business in the north. Deals were spun to acquire land from the Ojibwe and the Hudson's Bay Company so the young country of Canada could grow.[2]

The prospectors, labourers, and immigrants with

dreams of owning their own farmland followed the railway, which in turn brought the movement of goods and grains from the fast-growing west. A series of tall grain elevators — massive concrete silos standing sentry — were built on the red side, including the Western Grain elevator, down by the Kaministiquia River, on the Ojibwe's traditional lands near the base of Mount McKay. This port still has the largest grain-storage capacity in North America with eight functioning terminals along the river.[3]

As Port Arthur prospered, settlers arrived, bringing their families, their churches, and their own creed. Victorian ladies set up church societies and school boards, and Finnish labourers settled by the hundreds. Hospitals were constructed. The Church, in its infinite wisdom, sent harbingers of faith to administer the word of God to the masses of half-breed sons and daughters of French coureurs de bois, and to educate and convert the pagans and savages coming in from the bush.

In the name of all that is pure and Victorian, Port Arthur society began to flourish. But by the turn of the twentieth century, the fur trade had all but dried up and disappeared, leaving many Indigenous people destitute yet dependent on the goods and the lifestyle they had become used to being able to afford thanks to sales of beaver pelts. As the fur trade waned, many Indigenous families lived on the outskirts of town, in ramshackle cabins or houses, most with no heating or plumbing. They were not schooled in Western culture or education and did not fit into what was fast becoming the dominant British society in Port Arthur.

So if the "Indians" were to become proper English-speaking Canadians loyal to the Crown, they needed to be assimilated. Already in 1870, the Sisters of St. Joseph had opened a Catholic orphanage on the Fort William side. As soon as the orphanage became operational, complete with a school, it swelled with little Indigenous girls. The nuns, desperate to care for more souls, began to admit boys. They also appealed to the federal government's Department of Indian Affairs for money to help them expand. And the money came. The more children they had, the more funding they got. The Sisters of St. Joseph would eventually morph into the St. Joseph's Indian Residential School (also known as the Fort William Indian Residential School).

The school, which in 1907 moved to a new building on Franklin Street, took in thousands of Indigenous children who were either abandoned or dropped off by their poverty-stricken parents, who bought into the idea that if their kids were given an English education, they could adapt to this emerging colonial society. Others were rounded up from reserves and communities by the Royal Canadian Mounted Police and delivered to the sisters. The red-coated police were sent in to apprehend children by Indian Agents or agents of the Crown whose job it was to make sure all the Indians were kept in line.

Not every child went willingly to residential school. There are reports of runaways in different numbers and frequencies scattered throughout historical archives. Also catalogued are reports from parents who did not want to send their kids away because they had been told by their children and others what was going on at the schools.

Children who did not return to school were duly noted and local Indian Agents would send the Royal Canadian Mounted Police to fetch them. For instance, the family of a boy named Joseph Piska, living in Savanne, west of Thunder Bay, tried to keep their boy at home. The RCMP was dispatched by Indian Agent James Burk to bring Joseph back to school. RCMP constable D. K. Andersen kept meticulous notes of his attempt to apprehend Joseph on October 25, 1930. He left the Fort William train station at 7:20 a.m. with orders to retrieve Piska and to see if any other children were hiding. But when Andersen arrived at Savanne, he found that he could not cross the water due to the unpredictable late-fall weather.

"I found that the lake was frozen over to the extent of 2 inches in depth, and all navigation stopped. As the only way of reaching the reserve is by water, there being no overland trail, and the ice not yet being safe, I wired Sgt. Mann for instructions and he wired that I return by the next train," Andersen later wrote in a report to his superiors. He was forced to abandon his search for Piska and the other children possibly hiding in Savanne.[4] But others would not be as lucky as Piska was on that day.

In 1966, St. Joseph's Indian Residential School was finally demolished. At least six students lost their lives at St. Joseph's and another sixteen are unaccounted for. One of the school's famous residents was the acclaimed Ojibwe painter Norval Morrisseau. His grandson Kyle Morrisseau is one of the seven students who are the subject of this book. Sitting on the site of the former residential school now is a Catholic elementary school, Pope John

Paul II. No special plaque or monument was mounted to remember Thunder Bay's complicity in this dark chapter in Canada's history, until June 19, 2017, when a mural was unveiled, depicting the old school and its students. Now every September 30, Indigenous people in Thunder Bay and across Canada commemorate all residential school survivors on Orange Shirt Day, the national day of remembrance. Folks first congregate at City Hall and then walk together to the site of the old school. When they get there, they perform a ceremony at Pope John Paul II.

To understand the stories of the seven lost students who are the subjects of this book, the seven "fallen feathers," you must understand Thunder Bay's past, how the seeds of division, of acrimony and distaste, of a lack of cultural awareness and understanding, were planted in those early days, and how they were watered and nourished with misunderstanding and ambivalence. And you must understand how the government of Canada has historically underfunded education and health services for Indigenous children, providing consistently lower levels of support than for non-Indigenous kids, and how it continues to do so to this day. The white face of prosperity built its own society as the red face powerlessly stood and watched.

All this happened as Nanabijou slept.

NOTES FROM A BLIND MAN

ARTHUR STREET RUNS EAST TO WEST IN A LONG, STRAIGHT ribbon through the downtown area of the Fort William region of Thunder Bay. Arthur Street is devoid of charm — it's a stretch of drive-thru restaurants, gas bars, and grocery stores, and cars in a hurry to get anywhere but here.

Turn off Arthur, north onto to Syndicate, and you'll find the Victoriaville Centre, a poorly planned shopping mall with a 1970s vibe. The mall is riddled with empty stores and stragglers having a cup of coffee before heading over to the courthouse across the street. Parts of the mall have been taken over by mental health clinics, an art gallery, and an Indigenous health centre. Upstairs is the main administration office of Nishnawbe Aski Nation (NAN), a political organization representing forty-nine First Nations communities encompassing two-thirds of the province of Ontario, spanning 543,897.5 square kilometres.[1]

There is one elevator and it behaves like an old man. It grumbles as the door shuts, and it shakes and heaves its way slowly upstairs. A sign posted near the buttons says, "When the elevator breaks down, call this number..." "When," not *if.*

This was where I found myself one grey day in April 2011. I was there to see Stan Beardy, NAN's grand chief.

The 2011 federal election was in full swing. The incumbent Conservative candidate, Prime Minister Stephen Harper, was largely loathed by the Indigenous community. During his five years as prime minister, he had stripped away environmental protections, built pipelines, and continually underfunded the 634 First Nations across Canada.[2] Harper was duking it out with Jack Layton, a former Toronto city councillor and leader of the left-leaning New Democratic Party. Layton was a guitar-playing socialist whose mandate was to tear down highways and build bike lanes and parks.

The receptionist ushered me into a large common meeting room to wait for Stan. Everything in the room was grey — the walls, the tubular plastic tables, the carpets. The only splash of colour was a white flag with a red oval in the middle. Inside the oval — a traditional symbol of life for Indigenous people — is the Great White Bear. The red background is symbolic of the Red Man. The bear is stretched out, arms and legs open wide. His feet are planted firmly on a line, which represents the Earth, while his head touches another line, which is symbolic of his relationship to the Great Spirit in the sky. The circles forming the bear's rib cage are the communities, and the lines of the rib cage are Indigenous songs and legends, cultures and traditions that bind all the clans together.

Stan walked in and greeted me warmly. His brown eyes twinkled as he took a seat.

Stan is a quiet, pensive man. He said nothing as he wearily leaned back in his chair and waited for me to explain why exactly I had flown 920 kilometres north from Toronto to talk about the federal election.

I launched into an explanation of what I was writing about, trying not to sound like an interloper into his world, someone who kind of belongs here and kind of doesn't. This is the curse of my mixed blood: I'm the daughter of an Eastern European and Ojibwe mother who was raised in the bush about one hour's drive west of Thunder Bay, and a Polish father from Winnipeg.

I rattled off abysmal voting-pattern statistics among First Nations across Canada, while pointing out that in many ridings Indigenous people could act as a swing vote, hence influencing the trajectory of the election.

Stan stared at me impassively.

I started firing off some questions, but every time I tried to engage him, he talked about the disappearance of a fifteen-year-old Indigenous boy named Jordan Wabasse.

It was a frustrating exchange. We were speaking two different languages.

"Indigenous voters could influence fifty seats across the country if they got out and voted, but they don't," I said. "Why?"

"Why aren't you writing a story on Jordan Wabasse?" Stan replied.

"Stephen Harper has been no friend to Indigenous people, and if everyone voted they could swing the course of this election," I countered.

"Jordan has been gone for seventy-one days now," he said.

I tried to ask about Layton. Surely the policies of the left-leaning New Democratic Party would be more focused on Indigenous issues, I pressed.

But to this, Stan said, "They found a shoe down by the water. Police think it might have been Jordan's."

This standoff went on for a good fifteen minutes before I gave up and we sat in silence. I was annoyed. I knew a missing grade nine Indigenous student in Thunder Bay would not make news in urban Toronto.

Then I remembered my manners and where I was. I was sitting with the elected grand chief of 45,000 people, and he was clearly trying to tell me something.

"Jordan is the seventh student to go missing or die while at school," Stan said. Since 2000, Jethro Anderson, Curran Strang, Paul Panacheese, Robyn Harper, Reggie Bushie, and Kyle Morrisseau had died. Now Jordan Wabasse was missing.

Stan's message finally sank in. Seven students. Seven is a highly symbolic number in Indigenous culture. Every Anishinaabe person knows the prophecy of the seven fires. Each prophecy was referred to as a fire. Each fire represents a key time in the history of the people on Turtle Island, the continent of North America. The first three fires outline the story of what life was like before first contact with Europeans in 1492, of the peaceful existence along the Atlantic coast and the migration west to find food and water.

The fourth fire predicts the coming of the light-skinned race and what happens once they arrive. This prophecy warned that the Anishinaabe would be able to tell the future by reading the faces of the light-skinned race.[3] There were two predictions based on this reading. In this first, if the face was one of happiness and brotherhood, a time of change would come for everyone on Turtle Island. Two nations would join as one, resulting in the growth of a mighty nation full of knowledge and understanding. This would be a time of harmony and peace.

But the second prediction said that if the light-skinned race wore a face of darkness, the Anisihinaabe must be very careful. This face would bring extreme suffering and death. This face might be hard to see in the beginning. It might resemble the first face, but in fact behind the second face the hearts of the light-skinned race are dark and want nothing more than to take for themselves what the land has to offer. This face would bring forth destruction, filling the rivers and waters with poisons and causing the animals to begin to die.

By the fifth fire, war and suffering would grip the people. There would be promises of salvation by one who would assure them that there would be joy if the Indigenous people accepted his teachings. But if the people listened to this prophet, they would be lost for generations. They would forget the ways of the past and have no direction for the future.

By the sixth fire, the light-skinned face would wear the mask of death. The people would have been deceived. Sickness of the spirit and body would overwhelm the people and the children would be taken away. The teachings of the Elders and the past would be forgotten, and families would be torn apart and stripped bare. The people would be gutted, their purpose in life forgotten — and the "cup of life will almost become the cup of grief."[4]

By the time of the seventh fire, young people would rise up and begin to follow the trails of the past, seeking help from the Elders, but many of the Elders would have fallen asleep or be otherwise unable to help. The young would have to find their own way, and if they were successful there would be a rebirth of the Anishinaabe nation. But if they were to fail, all would fail.

Stan told me the seven students were from communities and families hundreds of kilometres away in the remote regions of Northern Ontario, where there are very few high schools. All of them were forced to leave their reserves to pursue their education.

More than seventy-five northern First Nations from NAN territory and from Grand Council Treaty #3 near the Manitoba border are isolated reservations spread across a vast area of forests full of birch trees, sweet-smelling cedars, and the rock of the Canadian Shield. Indigenous people move to Thunder Bay out of necessity to complete their high school education, to find a job, to access health care, and to escape the poverty of the rez.

About 108,000 people live in the city, and according to Statistics Canada more than 10,000 are Indigenous.[5] But that number is only going up. Near 2030, 15 percent of the City of Thunder Bay's estimated population is expected to be Indigenous.[6]

The city couldn't be any more different from the communities they have left. Back home, there are no traffic lights or crosswalks. No McDonald's or Loblaws. Most communities have only one shop — the Northern Store, a catch-all selling everything from high-priced groceries to batteries and rubber boots. These goods are all flown in via charter airplane, making the prices prohibitive — often three or four times the price of food in southern cities.

Food insecurity in the north isn't just about prices. Vegetables, fruit, and fresh meat are often so expensive that people rely on cheaper food items such as bread, pop, and processed meat to fuel their diet. Poverty forces these choices and a host of food-related problems plague Indigenous people as a result. Diabetes, high blood pressure, heart disease, and dental problems are all consequences of diets high in carbohydrates and sugar. There is a strong push to return to traditional foods — such as moose, rabbit, fish, partridge, and goose — to reduce dependence on pricey, flown-in groceries and to learn the ways of the ancestors.

The communities are surrounded by the largest concentration of freshwater lakes in the world, but the First Nations often have no access to clean running water and sewage systems. If power goes down, water can't be filtered. Access to strong, sustainable power is a constant issue in the north — many communities rely on carbon-spewing diesel generators to supply them with electricity. Lines can freeze in the winter. Nearly half of Ontario's Indigenous communities have a boil water advisory at any given time. People can't drink what comes out of the taps, and parents can't bathe their children in water that isn't laden with bacteria. Sometimes what water they do have is stolen by bigger southern cities. For nearly a century, the Manitoba city of Winnipeg has used an aqueduct to suck away water from the Northwestern Ontario Indigenous community of Shoal Lake 40 to provide the city of nearly 700,000 people with drinking water. Meanwhile, the water left for the residents of Shoal Lake 40 is laced with bacteria and a boil water advisory has been in place for nearly twenty years.[7]

The communities have virtually no hospitals — there is one in Moose Factory — no professional fire departments, and very few functional schools. Almost all of the schools located in fly-in reserves end at grade eight, with only a handful going to grade twelve. If students want to go to high school, they have to move to an urban centre such as Timmins, Sioux Lookout, or Thunder Bay.

The last residential school in Canada was shut down in the 1990s. The federal government, through Indian and Northern Affairs Canada (INAC), was then supposed to fund and maintain schools for Indigenous children. But across Canada, this promise has never been properly fulfilled. The quality of teaching standards and equipment at reserve schools varies widely from coast to coast. Fundamentals that other school jurisdictions take for granted, such as libraries, gymnasiums, and science labs, are routinely absent.

"Going to high school is the right of every Canadian child," Stan said. But these children have been treated differently, their needs forgotten in a country that prides itself on having one of the best education systems in the world.

He looked at me. "Let me take you on a drive."

We left the NAN office and climbed into his beat-up old pickup truck. He popped a CD of gospel music into the player. Listening to gospel music soothed Stan's soul. He felt closer to his son when he thought about God.

Daniel Beardy was nineteen years old when he was found beaten and unconscious at a house party on Fort William First Nation. He was just finishing up at Dennis Franklin Cromarty (DFC) High School in Thunder Bay, the school for Indigenous students run by the Northern Nishnawbe Education Council (NNEC). Most of the kids who attend Dennis Franklin come from reserves several hundred kilometres away from Thunder Bay. The students have to live in boarding houses and the boarding parents are paid by the school to look after the kids. Six of the seven students in this book went to DFC.

The Beardys are from Muskrat Dam First Nation, an isolated community of about three hundred people, deep in Ontario's north, accessible only by air. But because Stan, Daniel's father, was the grand chief, he had to move to Thunder Bay. His wife, Nellie, joined him and so did Daniel, who lived with his parents while he was attending high school.

Daniel was Stan and Nellie's only son, their pride and joy, a gregarious teen who loved life, his friends, and hockey. The Beardys' son fell in love with the game when he was five years old and later ranked second as a goalie in the Ontario Junior A League. The move to Thunder Bay meant he could play for more professional teams that were once home to NHL greats like the Staal brothers, Patrick Sharp, and goalie Matt Murray.

Daniel's NHL dream was beaten out of him on a late July night. After spending thirty hours in intensive care, he succumbed to his wounds on August 1, 2004.

Stan cannot let Daniel go. And he would not let the seven go. When Stan talked about losing his son, the pain of the lost seven was closely tied to him. The loss of Daniel and the loss of the seven represented the loss of hope, the failure of one generation to take care of the next. Their disappearances and deaths signified everything wrong in the relationship between Canada and the Indigenous people.

Stan was telling me that Jordan, the boy who was missing, was a goaltender like Daniel, when he stopped the car.

I looked around and saw the James Street swing bridge that crossed the Kaministiquia River. He parked near the shore, behind a couple of buildings that looked like they were abandoned.

"What are we doing here?" I asked as I stepped out of the truck.

A feeling of dread rose within me.

Before us was the Kam's just-thawing, rushing brown water. On the other side of its swollen spring banks loomed Animikii-wajiw, Ojibwe for Thunder Mountain, or what the colonials call Mount McKay, a tourist destination that offers a panoramic view of the city and of the sleeping Nanabijou. Animikii-wajiw, towering three hundred metres over the city, is not just a scenic outlook. It is the spiritual centre for the Ojibwe of Fort William First Nation.

My heart beat fast. Sickness brewed in the pit of my stomach. I knew this place well. This was my grandmother's reserve, where my children have run through the long grass under the glare of the summer sun and have been chastised by patrolling rez police officers for trying to climb the crumbling shale rocks on the side of the mountain.

Stan nodded and then said, "We think Jordan was chased into the river."

Searchers found one of his running shoes right here. Indigenous hunters, experts in tracking animals through the bush, found footprints leading up to the water. It looked like there had been a chase.

The bodies of four boys had already been discovered in the waters and floodways that feed into Lake Superior.

One month later, Jordan would be the fifth.

THESE ARE THE NOTES from a blind man.

The blind man is an Elder.

He had a vision.

So he told Lillian Suganaqueb. Lillian was in charge of the Webequie First Nation community search for Jordan Wabasse, who went missing on February 7, 2011. She had set up a command centre on the Fort William side of the city, in the old Canadian Red Cross office.

When Jordan disappeared, members of the Webequie First Nation community travelled nearly 540 kilometres south to Thunder Bay to search for him. Dozens of them, young and old, relatives, friends, and strangers, because this is what you do when one of your own has gone missing.

Some of the searchers were expert trackers, known for their prowess in the bush. They travelled the winter roads and came with their trucks and their snowmobiles.

Among them was the blind man.

Lillian talked to the blind man. She sat down with him at a table, and with a ballpoint pen she drew out his vision on six sheets of white paper. The drawing starts with a river, running in a squiggle down the centre of the page. This river is the Kam. Beside the river there is a fence and two buildings, side by side, with a note that says they are about a foot apart.

The Elder says that he sees train tracks on the north side of the water. On the south side he sees Mount McKay. He sees a bridge. The blind man sees the pulp mill. He sees buildings, grain elevators. He sees an industrial warehouse, storage. The place is not fenced. It is along the rail tracks. Lillian draws it all.

He tells Lillian that two people met Jordan on the night he vanished. They are young, like him. There is an altercation. A scuffle.

They are "definitely trying to hide," says the blind man.

The blind man sees the spirit of Jordan's body lying down on the ground. The snow is not very deep. Jordan's spirit sits either on top of the water or on the shore.

The blind man sees Jordan's face. His face faces north. His feet face south.

The blind man says the turtle spirit is near. So is the night bird. He says the bear travels at night.

Then he says, "The more you search, the more he vanishes."

IN SEPTEMBER 2010, Jordan Titus Lawrence Wabasse flew down to Thunder Bay where he was enrolled in the Matawa Learning Centre, a brand-new school located in the two-storey brown building that houses the Matawa Tribal Council. The school has no green space or fields for athletics, no track or anything else that might give the appearance of a high school. It is a dated, low-rise office tower that faces a major thoroughfare and a parking lot.

The Matawa Tribal Council represents nine Cree and Ojibwe northern First Nations, including Jordan's home of Webequie. The council chose the name because in both Ojibwe and Cree *Matawa* means "the meeting of the rivers." Matawa's nine communities share a common geographical boundary in the north — they are all connected by major river systems. It is not uncommon for Indigenous tribal councils to come together and form an alliance to offer a variety of services for those from home who find themselves in the city. The councils can help with job training, housing, and even education.

Matawa runs elementary schools in all nine of its First Nations. The council is also keenly aware of and upfront about its failings. In their own 2007 educational report, they note that despite major improvements over the past ten years, Matawa's education system remains "subpar" in comparison with those of other municipalities and falls below provincial standards. The system struggles with low student achievement and "significant grade gaps against provincial standards." There is a lack of classroom facilities, teaching resources, and specialty teachers who can educate children with cognitive, physical, and special needs.[8]

Only thirty students were enrolled at the Matawa Learning Centre. It offers an alternative education program where kids are given an individualized learning plan — students aren't accepted at the school unless they prove they are responsible and able to handle the program. Jordan was both.

Jordan had begged his mom, Bernice, to let him go to Thunder Bay to continue his education. He was a good student, strong in English and in math.

Bernice was hesitant. She wanted her son to stay in Webequie and attend the local high school. She knew it wasn't the best school — the school was made up of portables and had limited choices in courses — but Thunder Bay was so far away and she wouldn't be able to go with him because she had to stay to take care of Jordan's younger siblings.

Jordan had big dreams. He desperately wanted to play hockey in a real house league and eventually play for the Maple Leafs or another NHL team. He knew that would never happen if he stayed in Webequie. The community didn't even have an indoor arena. There was only an outdoor rink, which wasn't always maintained even in the winter, and there were not enough kids for a proper league. Bernice knew what she needed to do — send her son to the city, where he could get a high school education and play for a real league.

Bernice had to let Jordan go. She couldn't stand in the way of him wanting to better himself. What mother could? It tore her up inside, but she had to smile, fill him with confidence, and ignore the dull ache of worry that gathered inside her.

In Thunder Bay, Jordan would have to board with his distant cousin Clifford Wabasse and his wife, Jessica, in their two-storey townhouse on a crescent near the airport in Fort William. Boarding parents were given $500 a student, every month, to cover living expenses such as the roof over their head, snacks, and dinner. The "parents" were under no obligation to supervise the kids at night, eat meals with them, help them with their homework, or take them to any after-school activities. Clifford's house was small so Jordan shared a room with another student, Shane Troutlake. Clifford liked Jordan right off the bat. He was a quiet, polite kid who kept to himself. Jordan stood a strapping six foot one, and at two hundred pounds he could easily be mistaken for a man. But he wasn't a man. He was a fifteen-year-old kid who had not yet grown into his adult body.

To get to school, Jordan and Shane had to take public transit. A stop was just a short walk away on Mary Street. On Monday, February 7, 2011, Clifford saw Jordan leave for Matawa at 8:20 a.m. as usual.

It was cold that morning. Northern, freeze-your-ears-off cold, the temperature fluctuating between minus seventeen degrees Celsius during the day and minus thirty-two at night. Like most teenage boys, Jordan wasn't dressed for the weather. He wore white Adidas running shoes, a Maple Leafs baseball cap, a purple Hurley hoodie under a lined, dark-blue denim jacket, a white T-shirt that said *Blink If You Want Me*, and black plastic wind pants.

Jordan met his buddy Desmond Jacob, a fellow student from Webequie, on the bus that morning, and Shane saw Jordan in the hall at Matawa later that afternoon. At any given time, there were about a dozen kids from Webequie at the high school. For many, this was the first time they had ever been to a city — the first time they saw traffic lights or a shopping mall. Thunder Bay was nothing like home.

Webequie is perched up high in the James Bay Lowlands, accessible only by flight or by frozen winter ice roads. From the air, the lowlands look like giant green tiger stripes ripped across the landscape. Pea-green muskeg runs beside long, thin rivers and brown, mushy earth. Underneath the mush lie vast, untouched resources, everything from diamonds and nickel to copper and chromite, the material used to make stainless steel appliances. This area of the north is called the Ring of Fire, named by a prospector with a Johnny Cash fetish.

The people of Webequie try to live traditionally. They hunt, they fish, they skin their animals and use the hides for clothes or as a base for beautifully beaded mitts, moccasins, and other goods. Jordan grew up learning the traditional ways of his people and he was at home in the bush. He was a great help to his family when the seasons were changing and it was time to hunt so they could fill the freezer with fish and meat before the cold set in.

Jordan knew about responsibility. If he needed to be somewhere because he was relied upon for help, he'd be there. So when Jordan didn't show up for supper that night in Thunder Bay, and when he didn't call to say he was going to be late, Jessica found it strange. Jordan had hockey that night. He always came home to eat before practice at 8:45 p.m. Jordan was the goalie for the Current River Comets, a Midget B team. Considering he had not played in any house league growing up, this was a remarkable feat and it showed his blossoming talent. The coaches told him that he should have been placed in the AA League, but he had missed the draft date. They told him to keep playing and that he'd make it the following year.

Jordan had also planned to be home that night because he had promised his girlfriend, Myda O'Keese, that he'd call her at 11:00 p.m. Myda was from Eabametoong (Fort Hope) First Nation, a northern community nearly 350 kilometres north of Thunder Bay. She used to live in Thunder Bay with her aunt while she attended Hammarskjold High School. The two had met a couple of summers before at Webequie's community powwow. They were inseparable, seeing each other after school, with Jordan usually visiting Myda at her aunt's house. She was also a permanent spectator at his hockey games. But in January, Myda's aunt had wanted to return to their community, and Myda had no choice but to go with her because there was no one else to care for her in Thunder Bay. The two had been dating for two years and Jordan was missing her deeply. They had made plans for him to visit her at Fort Hope during the upcoming March Break.

Just after midnight, Myda called Jordan's boarding house. The phone rang and rang but no one answered. The only way to reach Jordan was on the land line or through his computer. Jordan had lost his cell phone the month before.

Jessica would lie awake until 2:00 a.m., wondering where Jordan could be.

THE LAST TIME JORDAN was seen alive, he was getting off a white-and-blue Thunder Bay Transit bus, not more than one block away from his boarding house.

He had been at the Intercity Shopping Centre, a popular hangout for teenagers. The Intercity is in the no man's land of Thunder Bay, that nondescript middle part of the city down by the Kam and the railway tracks that links Fort William to Port Arthur. Some call this area the "demilitarized zone" or the DMZ.

Everybody went to the Intercity. It was the largest and only modern mall in all of Northwestern Ontario, with a food court and trendy, brand-name clothing stores. For northern teens who grow up in communities without any stores or restaurants, the mall is an exotic indoor experience full of hamburgers, doughnuts, and pop, with plenty of free seating. After school, you can run into everybody at the mall.

Jordan later met up with more friends, Jared Sugarhead and Michael Semple, and they decided to do a bit of drinking. Besides hanging out at the mall, indiscriminate drinking was a common way to pass the time for some of the teens from the north, who suddenly found themselves unsupervised and in the playland of the city. Drinking was the great social equalizer for lonely kids lacking self-confidence or friends or who just wanted to fit in with the crowd. Where the alcohol came from that night or what it was Jordan was drinking is anyone's guess.

After a while, Jordan split from Jared, tipsy but coherent. His image was captured at 8:15 p.m.; he was walking alone through the mall hallways near the bathrooms, his Maple Leafs baseball cap sitting backwards on his head, a Subway cup in his hands. At that point he would have had to bolt home if he wanted to pick up his equipment and make it back out again in time for his 8:45 p.m. hockey practice.

To make his way home, he had to get from the Intercity to City Hall, where all the buses converge and veer off to other, far-flung parts of the city. City Hall was a central meeting spot for teens who were on their way home to their boarding houses after school. It was also a meeting point for all sorts of travellers trying to keep warm while they waited for buses.

High school students Julie Mequanawap, Victoria Moonias, and Ashley Keeskitay remember seeing Jordan on the 1 Mainline. It was then around 9:30 p.m. and they rode the bus together for nearly half an hour. Jordan was sitting alone near the centre doors, holding a clear bottle in his left hand. The girls were laughing in their cluster, but they knew Jordan and Myda so they decided to get out their smart phones and make a funny video, and in it Jordan told Myda he missed her.[9]

Ashley could tell Jordan had been drinking. She watched him get off at his stop on Mary Street and walk toward his boarding home on Holt Place and she sent the video off to Myda, who she would speak to later that night. The last image of Jordan was caught by Thunder Bay Transit video footage at 10:00 p.m.

The blind man told Lillian about the girls on the bus.

He said the taller one's spirit knew more than she was saying.

JORDAN'S BOARDING PARENT, CLIFFORD, called the Thunder Bay Police on February 8, the day after he last saw Jordan, to report him missing. He told the police that Jordan had left the house at 8:20 the morning before and that he never came home. That night, at 10:00 p.m., Detective Constable Robert Main went to the house and did a thorough check for Jordan. Based on the missing persons report he had received, Main thought that Jordan had gone missing that evening, when in fact it had already been a full twenty-four hours.[10] The detective asked for a photo of Jordan, and Jessica showed the detective an image of him on her desktop computer.[11] Jordan's last post on his Facebook page had been on February 5. Like many northern kids, he was a heavy Facebook user, with 4,300 messages on his page.[12] Over the next forty-eight hours, Main was made aware of, but did not immediately interview, Matawa students who had information about Jordan's last whereabouts.[13]

On February 11, the first article on Jordan's disappearance appeared in the *Chronicle-Journal*. It was a news brief, no longer than four sentences, stating that Thunder Bay Police were asking for the public's help to locate a missing fifteen-year-old: "Jordan Wabasse is Native Canadian and was last heard from on Monday. He is six-foot-one and weighs 200 pounds. Police said he may be in the Victoriaville area and he has been known to frequent the south core area."

That same day, the Thunder Bay Emergency Task Unit conducted its first ground search for Jordan. They had waited three days to search for a fifteen-year-old boy. No Amber Alert was issued — contrary to common practice by Canadian law enforcement when a child goes missing or is believed to have been abducted and police feel the child is in grave danger and can be found. No K-9 unit was sent out; nor was a forensic identification unit dispatched. Police did a search on foot, knocking on the doors of the mostly Second World War–era homes, just kilometres away from Mount McKay and the railway tracks. They started at the bus stop on Mary Street West, where Jordan was last seen, and fanned out, travelling east to Holt Place, then west to Neebing Avenue, and then to the most easterly portion of Georgina Bay. Then they went south back to Mary Street West and north to a bike path. They showed Jordan's picture to every household, every person they encountered, and they came up with nothing. No one had seen him.

The next day, police made up missing persons posters of Jordan and distributed them to every uniformed officer on patrol. Jordan's image was entered into the computer system and widely circulated. The Emergency Task Unit headed out again, expanding the search geographically. On foot, the officers began a grid search, canvassing every single residence and combing through everyone's yard. A plea went out in the newspaper for residents of the area to check their garages and sheds.

Again, there was nothing.

SIX DAYS AFTER JORDAN was last seen, a community search team from Webequie found a baseball cap and footprints in the river snow, running toward the James Street swing bridge.[14] The cap wasn't in the water or half-frozen in ice or buried in the snow. It was lying on top of the ice, near a wooden lean-to that had been constructed right below the bridge, on the east side of the Kam River. To the south was Mount McKay. To the north were the train tracks, and in the distance the two grain elevators that had been in the blind man's visions. The distance from the closest bus stop on Mary Street to the swing bridge was 2.2 kilometres. It was like someone had set the cap down, for just a moment.

The hat looked brand new. It was dark blue with a white Maple Leafs logo. It still had the gold sticker on the brim that indicated the size and authenticated it as official National Hockey League merchandise. The cap was sent to the Centre of Forensic Sciences in Toronto for tests, and the Ontario Provincial Police (OPP) sent up an aerial drone to take photos of the area. Police said they weren't ruling out foul play.

As soon as the Webequie searchers found the hat and the footprints, they contacted the Nishnawbe-Aski Police Service (NAPS), an Indigenous police force, as well as Jordan's parents, Bernice and Derek Jacob.

Bernice and Derek had flown to Thunder Bay on a small charter flight as soon as they heard their son was missing. They rented a block of rooms at the Airlane Hotel on Arthur Street, just across from the airport, for searchers coming in from Webequie and surrounding communities.

Police visited Bernice at the hotel and asked her for a DNA sample.

Then they called in the dive team.

Ontario Provincial Police divers conducted extensive underwater searches in the openings of the ice where the hat had been sitting. The divers scoured the area for nearly two days, working in frigid conditions, deep under solid, thick ice.

But they found nothing.

Calls were flooding in to the police by people who thought they had seen Jordan, at the mall or a Mac's Convenience Store or near a bank or a grocery store, begging for change. By February 18, the police had followed up on nearly twenty different possible sightings of Jordan but had come up empty every single time. They also paid a visit to the security guards at the Intercity mall. One of the guards had torn down a missing persons poster of Jordan that was posted in the mall and thrown it into the trash.[15]

HERE'S THE THING ABOUT the north: Everybody knows everyone else. If you ask Jennifer Wabano, who lives in Attawapiskat First Nation on the coast of James Bay, if she knows Sam Hunter in Weenusk First Nation near Hudson

Bay, she'll most likely say, "Of course I know Sam. He's my cousin."

The north may stretch out over a huge, underpopulated geological land mass of boreal forest, but the people who live there are all connected. They are connected through the land and the rivers and each other. Traditionally hunters and gatherers, Indigenous people travelled vast distances by foot or on water, tracking animals to hunt them or to trap them, then bring them home.

So when a child goes missing from an isolated community like Webequie, Cat Lake responds. So does Marten Falls, and Sioux Lookout, and a whole lot of communities in between. And if the band councils fall short of money to help pay for the search effort — lodging, food, time off work — the Anish start fundraising. They hold bingo nights, community events, and walks to raise funds. In March 2011, one month after Jordan went missing, Peggy and Danny Sakakeep started a five-hundred-kilometre walk from Kitchenuhmaykoosib Inninuwug First Nation in Ontario's northwestern corner, along winter roads made of rock-solid frozen lakes and snow, to Webequie, to raise awareness and money. If a community is in need, the northern Anish organize and they hit the road.[16]

It was a team from Cat Lake First Nation that found Jordan's right Adidas running shoe on March 20, 2011, the first day of their search. Cat Lake is inside the Treaty No. 9 territory, about one hundred and seventy-five kilometres north of Pickle Lake and about three hundred kilometres away from Webequie. The day before, thirteen members of the community arrived in Thunder Bay to help look for

Jordan, who had now been missing for one month. They came in a convoy of vans and checked into the brand-new Holiday Inn. Cat Lake searchers have a reputation for being among the best in the north. Once, they found someone after he had been missing for forty-five days.[17]

Besides searchers, they brought with them loads of food — moose and fresh fish — to feed everyone coming and going from the search headquarters.

The Cat Lake search team put together a mission statement, which they printed out on a piece of paper and handed to everyone:

We will start our search with a prayer and end with
   one as well.

We will all work as one team, mind, body and spirit.

We will search together as a team on one and only one
   location at a time.

We will absolutely not have any use of alcohol or drugs
   during our time in Thunder Bay.

We will not stray from the team.

We will focus only and solely on our mission of locating
   Jordan. This means our personal endeavours will be
   placed aside; we will use the daylight given to us by
   the Creator to search the grounds of Thunder Bay.

We will not leave a member behind and will always
   know the whereabouts of each person.

We will rest when others get tired.

If any member in our team locates Jordan, we will not
   touch but only confirm and block off the area with
   ribbons.

Take pride of your strength and courage in offering yourself to help another.

The Cat Lake searchers went to the shores of the Kam River, guided by the map of the blind man's visions. They brought hooks, ropes, and bars to poke through the ice at the shoreline. Four members — Tom, Maggie, Paddy, and Daisy — found Jordan's shoe. It was a new white Adidas running shoe, size 10.5. The laces were tied behind the tongue of the shoe. They picked the shoe up with a stick, put it in a box, and brought it to the search centre. The searchers also recognized something else near the shoe — drag marks in the snow. They notified the police, who dismissed the marks as "probably kids sliding."[18]

At the searchers' headquarters, which was located in a former Canadian Red Cross office, Bernice took one look at the right shoe and knew it was her son's. Jordan tied his laces behind the tongue. The Thunder Bay Police were called in. They took the shoe as evidence, then went with Tom and Lillian to where it had been found. Tom explained its exact location, which way it had been facing.

Once the police left, the Cat Lake searchers finished for the day. They went to Walmart to unwind and then grabbed something to eat at McDonald's. By the time they got back to the hotel, it was late, but Tom, Daisy, Paddy, and a searcher named Delia Oombash couldn't sleep. At 1:30 a.m., in the freezing March night, they grabbed some tobacco and food and made their way down to the loading docks by the Kam River to make an offering for Jordan's spirit.

The next day, another Cat Lake searcher found blood in the snow. He scooped it up and put it in a ziplock bag. They called Thunder Bay Police, who took the blood away. Later that day, the searchers found two teeth. They got another ziplock bag, put the teeth in it, and called the police again.

They would wait weeks to find out that the blood wasn't human and the teeth weren't Jordan's. But there was a positive match between Bernice Jacob's DNA and a sample of genetic material taken from Jordan's goalie mask and the cap that was found sitting on the ice. The possibility that someone else had the same genetic profile was eleven trillion to one.

THE BLIND MAN WASN'T the only one to have had a vision about Jordan. So did Meredith Anderson from Kasabonika First Nation. Meredith didn't really know Jordan, but she dreamed of him. She told her friend Rose, who took notes on foolscap.

I had another dream of Jordan, the note begins in Rose's loopy letters.

"Really?" Rose asked.

"He was standing," said Meredith.

"Where was he standing?"

"By the fence by the shore," Meredith said.

"On the bridge side?"

"Where we heard a voice before. Just down by the river where the stumps stick out from the lake. He was standing there," Meredith said.

"Left or right?" Rose asked.

"I'm not sure, but I know he was standing somewhere there so he's got to be there somewhere," Meredith insisted.

"Who were you with when you heard the voice?"

"Anita, she heard it too."

"Is it near the grain elevator? That area?" Rose asked.

"Yeah," said Meredith. "Just by the fence where the stumps are. Do you know where I am talking about?"

Meredith had seen Jordan in the exact same area as the blind man had, by the swing bridge and the grain elevators.

SOMETIMES THE SEARCH FELT endless. Every day a community member would post the number of days Jordan had been missing on a white piece of bristol board by the entranceway of the upstairs search headquarters. The tally was a dismal reminder — every single day added was a day of hope lost. Day after day, after the cap was found, there was nothing. But the searchers did not give up. They stood outside by the James Street swing bridge wearing placards with Jordan's face, asking people in cars driving by to donate to the Find Jordan fund. And every day, as the searchers carefully walked along the Kam riverbanks and organized searches of the streets, rumours began to fill the void of information.

Two stood out.

First, somebody told Lillian that a guy named Darren Oliver Beaver had heard that a man named Jordan Waboose, originally from Fort Hope, owed a drug dealer $8,000. Beaver believed that Jordan Wabasse might have been mistakenly kidnapped by Native Syndicate street gang members who believed him to be Waboose. The Syndicate, based out of Manitoba, expanded into Thunder Bay at least two decades ago. The gang has a strong foothold in the city's drug trade, supplying teens with their fix and then sending them home with drugs to sell on the northern reserves.

Second, Sharon Angeconeb, the vice-principal of Dennis Franklin Cromarty High School, called police to say that one of her students, Angela Rae, had spoken to another student, a boy who talked tough. He told Angela that he and his friends had chased Jordan from Mary Street, and that Jordan tried to get away by running across the ice on the river and fell through. Angela said she was with her friends Glen Kwandibens and Amber Angeconeb when she heard the story. The police questioned Glen and Amber, who claimed they didn't know what Angela was talking about. They said she was lying.[19] There is no indication Thunder Bay Police continued to follow up on this lead.

Police also called Liz Waboose, Jordan Waboose's mother, who told them her son was afraid of the Native Syndicate; she feared members of the gang had killed Jordan Wabasse, believing him to be her son.

On March 18, Bernice Jacob gave police a copy of a Facebook chat between Jordan Waboose in Fort Hope and his friend Lawrence Mekanak in Webequie, which had taken place earlier that same day.

WABOOSE: Rumours saying I am the reason Jordan Wabasse is missing.

MEKANAK: I haven't heard anything like that.

WABOOSE: Oh. K. Kool. Because I have.

WABOOSE: Who are the boys parents?

Mekanak responded that it was Bernice Jacob and Derek.

WABOOSE: Oh. K. I think I have information on that shit.

MEKANAK: Yea, should get that info to some1 soon.
Parents getting tired and its lots of money too for
Webequie costing. They just want to find their boy.

Waboose said he knew and that he was waiting for someone to come and talk to him.

Thunder Bay Police called the Nishnawbe-Aski Police Service in Fort Hope and told them they were looking for Jordan Waboose, who was wanted for questioning in Thunder Bay. But NAPS told Thunder Bay Police that the OPP had already spoken to Waboose and given all the information they had to a Thunder Bay detective.[20]

IN EARLY MAY, THE Kam River started to show signs of spring. The ice and snow were beginning to melt. Breaks could be seen in the frozen surface, where the water rushed underneath.

Three boaters called police after they thought they saw a body floating in the river by the Western Grain terminal, in the area of the swing bridge. Thunder Bay Police arrived at 7:05 p.m. and spoke to the three fishermen. Then the fire and rescue trucks arrived. The police called the coroner. About twenty searchers were in the area and had arrived at the scene. They "smoked cigarettes, talked on cellphones, and comforted each other while waiting to hear from police," wrote one reporter in the *Chronicle-Journal*.[21] The search had run for ninety-two days.

Dale Smith stood on the Kam's banks with his wife, Martina. The two had been searching for Jordan since he was first reported missing.

"If it is Jordan," Dale said, "it will put the family at ease, because it could have been the other way around. They might not have found him. If he'd gone on to Lake Superior...Lake Superior doesn't give up its dead."[22]

It was the fire crews that pulled the bloated body from the river. The body was badly decomposed, but the physical description, along with the blue jacket, hoodie, and the white Adidas running shoe on the left foot, matched the description of Jordan.

Waiting funeral home workers, who were standing sentry at the shore, took the body to the morgue.

Bernice had returned home briefly to Webequie in early May. She had been in Thunder Bay for long stretches of time and wanted to see her young sons. On May 10, she flew back to the city, arriving in the early evening. She was met at the airport by a group of volunteer searchers. They told her a body had been found in the river. They drove Bernice down to the water and she met with police, who told her they were not sure it was her son. She went back to her hotel to wait.[23]

At 9:00 p.m., Thunder Bay Police sergeant Don Lewis went to the hotel to speak with Lillian and Bernice about what they had found.[24]

The post-mortem would be conducted the next morning. But the dental records would tell them what they already knew. It was a match. They had found Jordan.

THREE DAYS AFTER HIS body was found, police received a call from a staff member of the Churchill Group Home, a coed residence for teens run by Children's Aid. One of their residents, Josee Charbonneau, said she had heard from someone that a man named Steven Cole and another man had pushed Jordan off the James Street swing bridge. But Josee didn't want to talk to the police or anyone else about it. She fled the group home and told no one where she was going.

Eight days after Jordan's body was discovered, police tracked down an acquaintance of Charbonneau's, Brittany Kakegamic. Brittany said she was speaking to Josee at the Thunder Bay courthouse and that she knew something about Jordan. Josee had said Steven Cole was bragging that he and another, unknown, man were walking to Fort William when Cole pushed Jordan off the James Street swing bridge. Cole had been on his way to Fort William First Nation to buy cigarettes. Jordan tried to fight him.

Police found Josee at the courthouse. She confessed that her friend Arianna Rollin had told her that Steven Cole and a man named Austin Millar, who was also known as Bubbles, saw Jordan and that he was drunk. She said Jordan tried to pick a fight with them and that's when Steven pushed him into the river.

Police tracked down Austin and Steven, who both denied ever having anything to do with Jordan, or even seeing him that night. But five years later, a friend of Cole's, Riley Freeman, admitted in a courtroom that Steven Cole had told him that he did it. Freeman was only thirteen at the time. He said he believed Cole because he was so shaken up.[25]

Freeman knew his friend had a history of being violent and stealing drugs from people. Yet police had not questioned any of Jordan's friends, such as Jared Sugarhead, who saw him that night, to confirm whether Jordan had a bag of pot on him that night and if possibly he was rolled for it.[26]

On June 23, 2011, Thunder Bay Police interviewed Steven Cole. He told them that the last time he saw Jordan was before Christmas. He admitted he knew him but not well; they "hung around with people in the same circle." He said the last he heard anything about Jordan was when his mother told him Jordan's body was found in the river.[27]

Thunder Bay Police also found Jordan Waboose, who was now living in Thunder Bay. He told the police that he had no drug debts, and that if he did he would not be living in Thunder Bay because he would be the target of angry gang members looking for their money. He also said he might have been "high" when he was interviewed by police.

Waboose added that he did not know how the rumour of mistaken identity surfaced on Facebook or where it came from, but speculated it might have been started by another young man named Kenny Wabasse. Then he told the officers his mother probably started the rumour because she was always trying to get him in trouble.

To this day, Jordan's death has no explanation. Police have no idea how Jordan, who had been a stone's throw away from his boarding house on an unforgivingly cold February night, wound up miles away in the frozen river.

The working theory seems to be this: Jordan got off the bus, quite close to his front door, but instead of going home so he could call Myda like he was supposed to, he stumbled 1.2 kilometres down Mary Street, took a 90-degree turn right, and then stumbled another 1.8 kilometres to the bridge. This would have required him to pass all the homes on Mary Street, walk down James Street past an open Robin's Donuts and an open Mac's Convenience Store, continue on past a credit union, and then walk down to an unlit underpass and up to the other side, before taking a sharp turn left to head up to the bridge to Fort William First Nation for a completely unknown reason.

Jordan didn't know anyone at Fort William. Not only that, once he got to the bridge he would have to have walked on massive concrete blocks and industrial garbage discarded by construction crews, down the steep embankment and snow, and then fallen into the water.

The file on Jordan's death was marked "Accidental" by Thunder Bay Police. A final autopsy report on his death was stamped on August 24, 2011, by regional supervising coroner Dr. Michael Wilson. He concluded that Jordan's death was caused by "cold water drowning."[28]

During the inquest into the deaths of the seven Indigenous students, lawyer Chantelle Bryson represented the Office of the Provincial Advocate for Children and Youth, the official provincial voice for children in care and those who are on the margins of society.

"I've driven that route a number of times. I've climbed over the rocks to the river," she said. "I don't buy it. Not for one minute."

WHY CHANIE RAN

THE SLEEK BLACK OFFICE TOWERS AND LUXURY HOTELS that line the Air Canada Centre are the height of modernity in the city of Toronto. This is where multicultural Raptors fans squeeze into the Fan Zone and jump up and down when the network cameras pan over them as legendary Maple Leafs players, with frozen bronze smiles, silently watch over. At the Real Sports Bar & Grill waitresses in tight black T-shirts sell mojitos and Bud Light to badly behaved men on weekend sports getaways with their buddies. Walk up the street and you can climb the CN tower, catch a Jays game, or join the crowds at the aquarium and marvel at stingrays and swordfish as they swim above your head.

Inside the Delta Hotel, in an empty coffee bar, Alvin Fiddler scans the list of herbal teas above the bored-looking cashier's head.

Mint. He'll have the mint.

The cashier has no idea she has just served tea to the grand chief of Nishnawbe Aski Nation, who, after Stan Beardy left, won the support of chiefs encompassing an area roughly the size of France. A man who, two centuries ago, would have commanded the respect of the servants of the Crown as they conspired to carve up the land she is now standing on.

Fiddler looks out of place as he settles down at a small circular table, electric pop tinning out of the café speakers. Small and powerfully built, Fiddler crosses his arms and legs, almost as if he is trying to contain his own energy. He is looking at me with his what's-this-all-about face.

It's Easter weekend and Fiddler has characteristically jammed a number of appointments into three days: a romantic weekend with his wife, Tesa; a Prince concert; a fetal alcohol syndrome conference; the signing of a new treaty between the Cree communities of the James Bay coast and the province of Ontario; and shopping for vinyl on Queen Street.

This weekend is a brief respite from his responsibilities of overseeing the governance of 45,000 people stretched over the immense northern half of the province of Ontario. Most of his Anishinaabe people don't have access to clean water. They can't flush their toilets and many have to haul their shit in pails to dump out in the bush. His youth are experiencing the highest suicide rate in the Western world and he can't stop them from killing themselves.

And God, he has tried.

He arranges baseball clinic weekends, athletic tournaments, and galas in hotel ballrooms to showcase teen talent.

This past spring, Fiddler convinced Prime Minister Justin Trudeau to let a group of his teens travel to Parliament Hill to meet Trudeau in Ottawa, so they could tell Canada's Hollywood-handsome and born-of-privilege prime minister about their lives. Trudeau is sympathetic, but Fiddler knows that he will never truly grasp the enormity of the issues his people live through every single day. History dictates that to be so.

Fiddler runs his hands through his black, spiky hair and fixes his gaze on me.

"How is Raith?" he asks with a laugh.

Raith is a forgotten stop in the bush along the old Canadian Pacific Railway line, about an hour west of Thunder Bay. The town used to be a small settlement of trappers and labourers who lived off the land. There was a well for fresh water because there wasn't any plumbing. A small one-room schoolhouse and a store once stood in the area. Now it is nothing but a handful of rundown houses by the roadside.

Only the Anishinaabe know where Raith is. Ask any white person in Thunder Bay if they've heard of Raith, and they'll screw up their face and look at you as if it sounds kind of familiar but they can't quite place it.

Ask an Indigenous person and, well, it's a different story. They'll tell you exactly how far down the highway it is, how long it will take to get there, and who they used to know there or in Savanne, Upsala, or any points in between.

Raith is where my mother spent much of her girlhood, raised by her maternal grandparents, Liz Gauthier, a residential school survivor, and Russell Bowen (a.k.a. Alphonse Piskey), a trapper and rail worker who was spared from residential school because he was kept hidden from Indian Agents in the bush. Liz and Russ married in Savanne, moved to Graham, and eventually settled in Raith.

When I first told Fiddler my mom was from Raith, he couldn't quite believe it. An urban journalist with roots in Raith. He was fall-off-your-chair astounded.

I tell Fiddler that I'm starting to write a book about the seven students who died while at school in Thunder Bay and that I was troubled that five of those teens died in the waters surrounding Fort William First Nation.

He nods.

I tell him that I have wanted to write this book for five years, since I stood in a former Canadian Red Cross office that had turned into the command centre in the search for Jordan Wabasse. At the time, he had been missing for seventy days. Alvin, a former deputy chief of Muskrat Dam First Nation, was away travelling with the Truth and Reconciliation Commission when Tesa called to tell him that Jordan had gone missing.

The Truth and Reconciliation Commission (TRC) is the Government of Canada's most important attempt to heal the wounds of the past with its 150,000 Indigenous people and their hundreds of thousands of descendants, whose lives were inextricably altered by the residential school system. In 2011, the TRC was travelling across the country, collecting the stories of survivors. Fiddler co-ordinated regional meetings and he oversaw the testimony of all the survivors in Ontario.

He saw first-hand the devastation of intergenerational trauma in Canada's north. He learned about children dying of preventable illness, of how poor nutrition and uncared-for diabetes could ruin the body and the mind, and he became intimately acquainted with suicide epidemics where children as young as ten were killing themselves. He learned about the legacy of sexual abuse and about the ravages of the residential school system. What he saw as grand chief of NAN, what he lived in his own communities, drove him to devote his life to making life better for his people.

Fiddler remembers where he was when Tesa called him again, this time to tell him that Jordan's body had been discovered in the river. He was in Yellowknife, in another hotel, where he had been listening to endless streams of testimony on behalf of the TRC. It had been an emotional day. Each residential school survivor had a witness in the room and an Elder or a health advocate to make sure the survivor received psychological and emotional support while he or she spoke of the most intimate, difficult experience of his or her life. Listening to these stories was both a great honour and a tremendous responsibility. It was also emotionally draining. Some days the pain was unbearable and his head would pound with the weight of remembrance.

Alvin had ducked out into the hallway to take Tesa's call. Tesa told him they had found Jordan in the river.

Alvin started to seethe. He had *told* them. He had *warned* them. He had warned everyone three years ago, in 2008, after another student, Reggie Bushie, was found dead in the water. When he was deputy chief of NAN, he cautioned that the children were dying at school in Thunder Bay and something had to be done to stop it.

I tell Fiddler I didn't write the book back then because life got in the way.

Fiddler nods again.

"You weren't meant to do this book before. You are now," he says. Then he offers some advice: "You need to start with Chanie Wenjack."

I go blank and feel ashamed for not knowing who Chanie Wenjack is. He isn't one of the seven dead students.

Fiddler sees I have never heard his name. He leans forward across the table from me and says, "Chanie Wenjack."

THE WEATHER IN OCTOBER along the shore of Lake Superior can be entirely unpredictable. The birch trees are a brilliant yellow. The crisp cold fall mornings give way to warm sunny days. But at nightfall, the weather turns. The greyness of winter comes fast and the temperature dips to freezing.

This area, dotted along the Canadian Pacific Railway tracks with tiny communities like Savanne and Raith, dances with magic. This is where the Great Spirit, the protector of all living things, ordered the waters on the continent of Turtle Island to split. From this point, the rivers, streams, and lakes begin to turn. Some flow north toward the Arctic. The rest flow south to the Great Lakes and the urban centres that malignantly pock the turtle's shell.

This mystical line, now known as the Arctic Watershed, cannot be physically seen. It can only be felt.

This place has always provided a natural boundary between very different existences. In the seventeenth century, the Hudson's Bay Company used the watershed as a marker to indicate the southern stretch of the land they claimed as theirs. North, west, and east of Superior, they hunted for beaver pelts to make fashionable black top hats for European men. Two centuries later, the area was deemed the northern boundary of lands controlled by the British Crown in the Robinson-Superior Treaty, while the Indians were given their own plot of land near Fort William.

It is vital that people understand how the utter failure and betrayal of the treaties — nation-to-nation agreements First Nations signed with the British Crown — worked in conjunction with a paternalistic piece of legislation called the Indian Act to isolate Indigenous people on remote reservations and to keep them subservient to Ottawa for more than one hundred years.

The treaties covered payments of goods and cash, and the protection of fishing and hunting rights. But they also oversaw the cession of First Nations' traditional land and the creation of the reserves. The reserves are where communities have formed and where traditions are practised, in spite of legislative constraints that have kept Indigenous people isolated in remote areas while the government opened up the rest of the land to white colonial settlers so that the nation of Canada could be formed. Indigenous people have played by the rules of these one-sided deals that did not have their best interests at heart. Canada has not lived up to its end of the bargain.

Fort William First Nation falls under the Robinson-Superior Treaty, which was signed in 1850. From the beginning, the Ojibwe of Fort William were distrustful of the treaty process. In the late 1840s, the Crown had sent scouts up north to check out the shores of Lake Huron and the north shore of Lake Superior. Upper Canada desperately wanted to be in control of these lands so it could eventually expand to the west. The scouts met with Ojibwe spokesman Chief Joseph Peau de Chat, who acted for all the Fort William–area families. Peau de Chat's "original demeanour was hostile," as he thought the scouts had a hidden agenda.[1] In attendance at the meetings was Father Frimeault, a Jesuit priest even the scouts were leery of. A historical interpretation of the 1850 Robinson-Superior Treaty published by Indigenous and Northern Affairs Canada reads:

> The Jesuit here as well as elsewhere tries to influence the Indians with his way of thinking not only as regards his erroneous creed, but also as regards the duties of our mission, not because he fancies he can direct the Indians and thus influence the Government into what he considers a good bargain for the natives and ultimately that he might get their cash to the exclusive benefit of his Priest craft, but of this the Government must be on their guard.[2]

It took days of persuasion, but the scouts, aided by the Church, gained Peau de Chat's trust, paving the way for the visit of William Robinson, who had been given powers to negotiate by Upper Canada's Lord Elgin. Robinson was told he had only £7,500 to cover the entire cost of the negotiation and any annuity payments to come of it. A stumbling block for Peau de Chat was hunting and fishing rights. So Robinson bent over backwards to promise they could enjoy all their hunting and fishing rights as "extensive settlement was unlikely in the barren regions of the Canadian Shield." Essentially, he told Peau de Chat not to worry — no one would move up there anyway. Peau de Chat believed Robinson, so he signed the Robinson-Superior Treaty on September 7, 1850, giving the Crown the entire Lake Superior shoreline, including islands from Batchewana Bay to Pigeon River, and inland "as far as the height of the land." The deal gave the Crown 57,000 square kilometres of land in exchange for meagre annual payments and goods and a reserve that extended 3 kilometres from Fort William inland on the "right bank of the River Kiminitiquia," 9.5 kilometres to the west, 8 kilometres to the north, and "thence easterly to the right bank of the said river, so as not to interfere with any acquired rights of the Honorable Hudson's Bay Company."[3]

This treaty paved the way for the settlement of Thunder Bay and for the expansion of the country. Days later, the Robinson-Huron Treaty was signed, which guaranteed the north shore of Lake Huron to the Crown. Decades later, from 1873 to 1930, in Ontario's far north, 88,500 square kilometres of land along the Manitoba border were taken

by the British Crown in Treaty No. 3. To the east, the signing of Treaty No. 9 delivered 338,000 square kilometres
to the Crown. Finally, Treaty No. 5 yielded a small piece
of land in Northwestern Ontario that opens into eastern
Manitoba. These treaties transformed Upper Canada into
the modern-day province of Ontario.

But it was in 1876 that the Canadian government introduced the Indian Act, administered by the Department
of Indian Affairs. (Today, the department is called
Indigenous and Northern Affairs Canada.) The Indian Act
entrenched even more rules aimed at keeping the Indians
on their reserve land and out of the way of the colonials.

The Indian Act has been described as a form of apartheid, a piece of legislation designed to control and tame
the Indigenous population. The act historically outlined
every aspect of life for an Indigenous person in Canada.
It was through the Indian Act that the Canadian government formed policy surrounding residential schools,
placed bans on religious ceremonies, restricted access to
the courts, limited movement by restricting First Nations
people from leaving the reserve without permission from
an Indian Agent, and prohibited the formation of political
organizations.

To this day, it dictates the terms of who is considered
a real Indian under the federal statute — and hence who
receives treaty rights. The act contains a registry of all
Indigenous people. If a person's name is on the registry,
they get a status card that states which band they are
with and assigns them a number. To limit how many
Indigenous people are granted status, Ottawa has been

careful to dictate the terms of inclusion. In the past, if an Indigenous woman married a white man, she lost her status. Or if an Indigenous person moved off a reserve and bought land, they lost their status. If an Indigenous person joined the Canadian Armed Forces or entered university, they lost their status. If an Indigenous person wanted to vote in an election, they had to relinquish all their status and treaty rights. The right to vote without reprisals wasn't granted to Indigenous people until 1960, when Prime Minister John Diefenbaker was in power.[4] Generations of families have fallen under the oppressive weight of the Indian Act, with its limitations on freedom of movement and even the pursuit of education.

The Indian Act was such a successful piece of legislation for the Canadian government that it was used as a model by white South African legislators when they set up their brutal system of apartheid. These two colonial governments of the British Crown share a dark and racist history. Elder Shannon Thunderbird says the Indian Act created an oppressive regime within a democracy: "It's actually hypocrisy for Canada to stand forward as a kind of bulwark of protest against atrocities going on in other countries while at the same time we turn a blind eye to our own people."[5]

A major difference between the two systems of apartheid was the sheer lopsidedness of white power in South Africa. White South Africans made up only 5 percent of the population of the colony on the southern tip of Africa, yet for decades they held the balance of power under apartheid.

In Canada, the Indigenous population is the inverse, making up roughly 4 percent of the country. As such, the Indian Act has not garnered the national media attention, the international news headlines, or the freedom-fighting rock concerts that aided black South Africans' in their fight for freedom.

The Crown used the treaties not only to take land from the Indigenous people, but also to absorb the next generation into Canadian society. The children were taken from their "savage" families and sent to schools run by the Catholic, Protestant, and Presbyterian churches. In 1883, Canada's first prime minister, Sir John A. Macdonald, described the plan to Members of Parliament:

> When the school is on the reserve the child lives with its parents, who are savages; he is surrounded by savages, and though he may learn to read and write, his habits and training and mode of thought are Indian. He is simply a savage who can read and write. It has been strongly pressed on myself, as the head of the Department, that Indian children should be withdrawn as much as possible from the parental influence, and the only way to do that would be to put them in central training industrial schools where they will acquire the habits and modes of thought of white men.[6]

If every Indigenous child was absorbed into Canadian society, their ties to their language and their culture would be broken. They wouldn't live on reserve lands; they'd live and work among other Canadians and there would no longer be a need for treaties, reserves, or special rights given to Indigenous people. The single purpose, and simple truth, of the residential school system was that it was an act of cultural genocide. If the government of Canada managed to assimilate all Indigenous kids, it would no longer have any financial or legal obligations to Indigenous people. And the Indian Act was designed to be the legislation that would carry out the task.[7]

The Act dictated that students sixteen and under were expected to stay in residential school: "Every Indian child between the ages of seven and fifteen years who is physically able will attend such day, industrial or boarding schools as may be designated by the Superintendent General for the full periods during which such school is open each year."[8]

Across Canada there were one hundred and thirty-nine residential schools.[9] In Ontario there were seventeen: fifteen in Northern Ontario and only two in the south.[10] They opened their doors in the mid-nineteenth century and the last one didn't close until near the end of the twentieth century. In Ontario, seven of the schools were operated by Catholic religious orders, five by the Anglican Church, one by the Presbyterians, one by the United Church, and three others by the Mennonites.[11] Students in residential school would be taught English, mathematics, and science, and they would learn the ways of the Lord.

The schools were often overcrowded. The more students a school had, the more funding they would get from the federal government. Per capita, each student brought in about $140 annually.[12] To increase numbers, Indian Agents were sent out to round up the kids and sometimes they got help. Red-coated Mounties seized children from their homes, thus establishing the long history of suspicion and mistrust that has come to define Indigenous-police relations. The Act allowed for the appointment of any officer or person to be a "truant officer to enforce attendance of Indian children." Truant officers had the power to arrest absentee students and take them to school. The officers also had the power to charge the parents a "fine of not more than two dollars" and to impose "imprisonment for a period not exceeding ten days or both."[13]

Conditions inside the schools were often filthy and unsanitary. Many of the buildings were meant to house a smaller number of kids than were enrolled. The schools were poorly and cheaply constructed. Indian Affairs didn't set aside any regular funds for repairs or upkeep. In 1942, one government visitor to the United Church's Mount Elgin School in Muncey, Ontario, remarked:

> The building is of brick construction and from the outside presents a somewhat imposing appearance, but inside it is one of the most dilapidated structures that I have ever inspected. At the time of my visit the plumbing in the boys' wash-room was in a faulty state of repair, with the result that the wash bowls were full of filthy water and the floor of the wash-room in a filthy condition. The odours in the wash-room and indeed throughout the building were so offensive I could scarcely endure them. Certain parts of this building are literally alive with cockroaches.[14]

Another inspector, at the same school, noted boys used the barn as a bathroom.[15]

The per capita money the institutions received was for clothing, food, and tuition, but there were constant complaints that the children were not properly or warmly clothed and were lacking in proper nutrition. The menu changed at every single school and some supplemented meals with food grown on-site. According to one "official" menu at Cecilia Jeffrey Residential School at Round Lake, northeast of Kenora, the kids ate vegetables three times a week, fruit twice a week, candy three times a week, and had lard served with all meals if no soup or gravy was available. Porridge was the daily breakfast, roast beef was served for lunch on Sunday, and supper generally alternated between bread and soup; beans and prunes; and sometimes there were potatoes. And on Wednesday there was meat pie and bran cake for supper.[16]

In most cases, the schools were hundreds of kilometres away from the children's homes. Instruction was in English, but most of the kids spoke their own dialects of Ojibwe, Cree, and hundreds of other Indigenous languages — languages that are now all nearly lost. Students forgot their culture or had it beaten out of them. They were yelled at, verbally abused, and denigrated for their "heathen" and un-Christian ways. Their hair was chopped off, their clothes and personal belongings taken away. When the kids got sick, many with respiratory viruses or tuberculosis, most were not given proper medical care. They weren't given medicine or timely access to a doctor. Thousands died. While it will never be truly known how many kids lost their lives at these schools — either through sickness or other means — it is believed that the number hovers at nearly 6,000. The exact figure is unknown because most records held by the churches and school authorities were burned or destroyed by other means. Between 1936 and 1944, the federal government destroyed some 200,000 Indian Affairs documents and files.[17] All that remains are fragments of historical truth and none of those fragments tells the whole story of the horrors that happened behind the school walls.

ONE OF THE ONLY traces left of the now demolished Cecilia Jeffrey Indian Residential School at Round Lake are the sidewalks, faded paths so worn out they look like they were used by a legion of Roman soldiers. They start and stop abruptly, taking illogical turns left and right, heading someplace we can no longer see.

What used to stand here, less than a century ago, was a solid four-storey red-brick building, with rows of boxy windows and a chapel attached to its side. The school opened on this site in 1929 and was operational until 1974. Thousands of students passed through the halls before the school was closed, the land given back to the Grand Council of Treaty No. 3, and the building demolished.

A single-storey sky-blue office building now stands where Cecilia Jeffrey once towered. The office, no more than a glorified mobile home, is perched on top of what is left of the school's brick foundation. Beside it lies a derelict parking lot with potholes so big they look more like sinkholes. To the south of the property, near the shore of Round Lake, there is a fence from an old baseball diamond that looks like a bent-over old man. To the west, lying hidden in the brush, directly beside a round stone memorial with a small cenotaph that reads *For the Children*, is a rusted-out swing set. The chains dangle from the steel structure. The seats have rotted away and the metal has twisted into diabolical-looking hooks.

Elder Thomas White is waiting for me inside the blue council building. White is from Whitefish Bay First Nation, about an hour outside of Kenora. He is a residential school survivor but not at Cecilia Jeffrey. He attended St. Mary's Indian Residential School in the Kenora area, which operated between 1897 and 1972. The school, once run by the Catholic Oblate nuns, has been torn down. White is a Grand Council Treaty No. 3 Elder and he spends his days at the council building, reminding people of their past and speaking to survivors about what happened at these schools.

White is spry with a small build. He walks quickly, leading me down the hall to his office. Stopping at the window, he points his finger toward what used to be the baseball diamond.

"See that? Don't go there," he mutters.

He says it is an old burial ground. Already, he had to chase away young staff members at the Grand Council who tried to erect large poles to create a makeshift driving range so they could hit golf balls at lunch.

"They used to hold powwows there," he says.

Powwows are part of the annual summer celebration
of Indigenous life, when generations of families gather for
days, camping and dancing in full feathers, beads, and
headdresses to the steady beat of a drum. It's a time to get
together, honour one another, and remember the teachings
of the Elders.

"Then there were two deaths. Two of the dancers, they
died. Right there. Not together. Both were heart attacks,
they say. Right there," he says, pointing at the neglected
baseball diamond. "Nobody wants to come here."

White's office is inside the mobile home. On the white
wall beside his desk there is a large framed picture, about
a hundred years old, of Indigenous children lined up in
front of St. Mary's, their black bowl haircuts framing
round heads and sullen faces. No one is smiling. Not the
children and not the nuns who stand around them like
black-cloaked spiders.

"There should be a table with all of the books. All the
books we have on the residential schools and the pictures, so people can come and look at them," White says
apologetically.

He wants to set up a display so the survivors and their
families can come and see what is left of Cecilia Jeffrey
and know that their relatives were here.

"But nobody comes. They don't like the feeling when
they come to this place," White says.

He gets up slowly from his desk, shuffles across the
room, then lowers himself onto the floor and crawls
underneath a table. After a few grunts, he re-emerges with
a hard black plastic suitcase covered in dust.

He opens the latches, lifts the lid, and points at the contents inside. "This is all we have left on Cecilia Jeffrey," he says. "If you are looking for Chanie Wenjack, start here."

THERE IS A COLOUR picture of Pearl Wenjack, Chanie Wenjack's older sister. The picture would have been taken in 1965, Pearl's last year at Cecilia Jeffrey. She would have been about seventeen.

The image of Pearl was captured the year before her brother disappeared.

Pearl has curly black hair. She is wearing silver horn-rimmed glasses; a white, high-collared, short-sleeve blouse; and an indigo-blue swing skirt. She is standing on the steps of an unknown building, crushed together on the stairs with eighteen of her female classmates. They all look to be the same age, wear the same uniform, and have the same short haircuts.

It is one of the few photographs in the black suitcase that has the children in the photos actually identified. The other pictures are full of nameless faces.

The number of pictures in the black case is overwhelming. The faces staring back from the photographs all have high cheekbones, brown or black hair, and deep, dark eyes. The students stand solemnly with their teachers in front of the big, old, red-brick school. Nobody looks happy. There are pictures of various school events and holidays. The images of Indigenous children sitting around artificial Christmas trees, full of plastic lights and red and green plastic ornaments, are among the most disturbing. Some of them are passing around gifts. They would have likely been taught about Christmas, but for many of the kids this was the white man's tradition, not theirs.

There is one picture of young boys, no more than eight years old, lined up by the swing set. The photo is haunting. The boys are all dressed alike — blue jeans, plaid long-sleeved shirts, and thin blue jackets. The two boys at the back are shoving each other. The teacher is at the front, wearing a thick, brown, fashionable sheepskin coat buttoned all the way up to the collar. She is handing each student something out of a shopping bag. The grass around them has a yellow, damp, dead appearance.

The boys look miserable: cold and uncomfortable.

There are hundreds of photographs of kids between the ages of six and seventeen in the case. Each new picture I see makes me increasingly uneasy. No one knows who these children are. There are very few names to identify the faces. Hundreds and hundreds of kids are completely anonymous. Looking at these pictures makes me feel as though I am disturbing a gravesite.

There is not one photograph that identifies Chanie Wenjack.

But he could be in here, staring up at me, one of the many nameless boys with black, expressionless eyes, gazing emptily into the camera.

THE CECILIA JEFFREY INDIAN Residential School was named in memory of Cecilia Jeffrey, the secretary in charge of "Indian work" at Rat Portage's Women's Missionary Society.

In those days, Kenora was known by its Ojibwe name, Rat Portage, or "the place where the muskrats congregate."

Jeffrey looks exactly as you would expect. Stout. Stalwart. English. She wore high-collared Victorian dresses with a brooch at her neck and her hair was tied back in a severe bun. A married lady of society and a devout Presbyterian, Jeffrey, along with her women's group, spread the word of God among the Ojibwe scattered throughout the Kenora and Lake of the Woods areas. It was her dream to build a school to teach the children English and to prepare them to live in the white world. The school would "save" the children, Christianizing them and teaching them reading and writing while they lived among the woods and waters.

"The school draws pupils from Sabiscong to White Dog and from North West Angle to the Shoal. It is a far cry from lonely cabins and bush trails, but the primary objective is to train and fit Indian children to take their place in a competitive and new (to them) world," wrote Janet Carruthers, a local woman who was involved with the church and who contributed to the Jaffray Women's Institute's edition of the *Tweedsmuir Community History Book* published in 1945. The Tweedsmuir history series was written by women across Ontario who were active in society. They kept journals and logs from the beginning of the twentieth century onward.

"Training of the Indian child is an undertaking that has to be wide in appeal, deep in understanding," Carruthers wrote. "From far back in their race comes inborn love of freedom and in many still linger superstition and doubt. In moments of extremity such as grave sickness in hospital which the children quickly sensed, a group would gather pails and washing tubs and beat a wild tattoo beneath the window to chase evil spirits away."[18]

The first school was originally located near Shoal Lake First Nation, about seventy kilometres southwest of Kenora near the Manitoba border in the Lake of the Woods area. The United Church–run school was in an incredibly remote area, tucked away in the bush and accessible only by boat. A steamer was used to transport staff, the students, and supplies. The Women's Missionary Society donated the original school building, which was two and a half storeys high. It opened in 1902 and had nine students, most from the nearby Shoal Lake reserve.

By 1905, the school had quickly filled to forty students, thanks to the plethora of Indigenous children in the Treaty No. 3 area and overzealous roundups by Indian Agents in the Lake of the Woods communities.[19] In the twenty-seven years the school was located at Shoal Lake, there was a revolving door to the principal's position — mostly all United Church ministers — and the number of teachers fluctuated depending on enrollment, but there was usually a senior teacher at the school along with a number of junior teachers. The girls were closely watched by a matron and the boys had a dormitory supervisor. The students spent only half the day in class; during the other half of the day they were forced to do chores — everything from gardening to cutting wood to sewing, cleaning, and cooking. The word of the Lord was also drilled into the kids — students were expected to attend worship each morning and night as well as Sunday service, followed by Sunday School and song service in the evening. Every morning, classes started with readings from the Bible.[20]

Many of the Lake of the Woods–area bands were starting to complain about the substandard education their children were receiving, along with the excessive use of discipline. Historical documents show that Chief Sam Kejick of the Shoal Lake Band No. 39 protested the treatment of the eight children from his reserve, but his concerns went nowhere. He was one of a chorus of Shoal Lake members who felt the students were being poorly and harshly treated. Many of the complaints centred around excessive corporal punishment — children were routinely beaten with leather straps — and there was even one complaint that a student died after being severely punished by the principal.[21] From 1912 to 1917, in particular, there were constant complaints of cruel treatment of the students at the hands of the principal, according to *Indian Residential Schools in Ontario*, a residential school history book written by Donald Auger and published by NAN in 2005. From July 8, 1914, to September 1917, the time of heightened abuse claims, the principals of the school were the Reverend Mr. Gandier, J. D. McGregor, and the Reverend F. T. Dodds.[22] While Auger writes that during this period there were "persistent reports of cruel treatment at the hands of the principal," he does not go into great detail as to which principal, or principals, were the perpetrators beyond the mention of Mr. Dodds — who seems to have been both lauded and loathed.[23]

The problems of reported cruelty were so constant, Indigenous families started to actively refuse to send their children to the school. In 1914, one of the Indian Affairs inspectors reported, "Not one pupil, however, could be obtained for the school at any point."[24] The inspector noted that the reason was the corporal punishment used by the principal. Many of the students — both boys and girls — were running away. The Presbyterian Church established a commission to investigate complaints. In their report, they wrote: "We are afraid the School may go wrong… The boys says why they leaves the school that like principal Mr. Dodds isn't very good to them… It is not the Indians fault why all these boys goes away. It is all Mr. Dodds fault why they go away… We always tell him the reason why the boys goes away. And he does not stop when we tell him why."[25] However, Auger also points out that Dodds used to encourage the parents to come and visit their children, and occasionally he'd provide the families with meals.[26]

By 1924, the United Church and the Department of Indian Affairs were actively discussing building another school closer to Kenora. The Shoal Lake school was too far and reliance on boat travel was difficult. The quality and supply of water was also diminishing because the city of Winnipeg had begun to draw water from Shoal Lake, a practice that would continue for nearly a century. Lower water levels were hard on the steamer. Besides, the argument went, if they moved the school to Kenora, they could access and recruit far more students.

The Shoal Lake–area chiefs were angry about the move. The school was filled with many of their children and no one had bothered to discuss with them the issue of relocation. The local chiefs, including Chief Sam Kejick,

protested the removal of their kids to a place seventy kilometres away from home. But their concerns fell on deaf
ears. A new school was going to be built beside Round
Lake outside Kenora on a 169-acre farm. This school would
be big enough to accommodate 125 students, which is the
number of kids that were enrolled when the school opened
its doors in 1929.

For the next decade, the children continued to be
abused at the school, but now they were far away from
home. By the 1940s and 1950s, the government knew the
residential school system was an absolute disaster. The
Indigenous people were not seamlessly assimilating into
Canadian culture and society; in fact, they were actively
resisting assimilation.

Regardless, from the 1940s until 1952, Canadian scien-
tists across the country worked with bureaucrats — who
were in charge of the care of Indigenous children — and
top nutrition experts on what have become notoriously
known as starvation experiments using students at six
residential schools as their subjects. The children were kept
malnourished — milk and dairy rations were held back —
and then given food with experimental additives along
with untested mineral supplements. Doctors wanted to
see how the children's bodies would react to these dietary
changes, especially as they fought off viruses and other
infections. "Many of these children were kept malnourished throughout the experiments... one was a fortified
flour mixture that ended up causing anaemia," historian
Ian Mosby said.[27] The children did not know about or
consent to the experiments, and neither did their parents.

During the time of the experiments, tuberculosis outbreaks were widespread and severe. It is impossible to know how many children actually died of this bacterial infection that attacks the lungs, causing victims to cough up blood, lose weight, and suffer from extreme fatigue. Children were sent to sanatoriums either in Fort William or in Brandon, Manitoba. Some were never seen again. From 1947 to 1952, the infection rate at the school was recorded at 25 percent.[28] There is an unmarked grave at Cecilia Jeffrey where at least fourteen bodies are buried underneath the long slope of grass that leads to the shore of Round Lake. It is unclear what they died of.[29]

IN SEPTEMBER 1966, EIGHTEEN-YEAR-OLD Pearl Wenjack is balancing on the pontoons of a plane floating on the deep, clear water of the Albany River. The pontoons mark the location of the Ogoki Post Airport, which is 3.2 kilometres northeast of Marten Falls First Nation. The Wenjack family lives at Ogoki Post, where the Ogoki River converges with the mighty Albany River that feeds into James Bay. Ogoki is a community of a few hundred people and part of the larger Marten Falls First Nation. Fir trees line the banks as far as the eye can see. On a sunny day, the river acts as a mirror, casting an endless reflection of the forest's edge.

Pearl is small in stature with a slight, agile build. Her brown eyes, set back over high cheekbones, never fail to twinkle with merriment. Pearl has a fun-loving personality and a sharp mind. Her comments are always intelligent and insightful, and she always knows what is going on with whom. She has a knack for bringing levity and ease, no matter how serious the situation, making you feel like everything will be all right.

Pearl's personality would have attracted her twelve-year-old brother, Chanie, like a magnet. He too had that mischievous streak. In their busy house of eleven kids, she held a special spot for him in her heart and he for her.

On that bright, late-summer day, Chanie stood beside Pearl, balancing on the pontoons that were gently swaying back and forth with the flow of the river.

For reasons unknown to her, Pearl's name had been left off the list of kids from the reserve who were being sent to Cecilia Jeffrey Residential School. Her siblings — Annie, Margaret, Daisy, Evelyn, Martha, Lizzie, George, Sam, Emily, and Chanie — were waiting for the plane, but she was the only one who was told she would stay at home that year.

"Why aren't you going?" Chanie asked, looking up at his older sister.

"My name's not on the list," she replied.

"If you aren't going, I don't want to go either," he said.

It was the first time Pearl had ever heard her brother say he didn't want to return to school.[30]

Pearl told him he had to go. Their father wanted him to go to school and all his friends were already on the plane. There was no choice here.

Chanie understood. After a moment of silence, he looked up at Pearl and asked her to promise to do a few things for him. She remembers this is what he said:

"Wash all my clothes and put them away. Put them in a box," he said, referring to the compact cardboard boxes that their cartons of eggs were delivered in. "You can have my burgundy sweater, the one that buttons up the front. Put my red cap on top of the box."

He waited for a moment and then continued. "Look after my dogs, Matches and Anymoosh. Make sure they don't get lost or beaten up."[31]

She agreed but felt a twinge of unease. Then she stood back on the shoreline and watched her brother climb into the the plane and take a seat. She wondered why he had asked her to pack up his clothes in a box. It was odd. That was what they did when someone died.

THREE MONTHS LATER, in November, Pearl went out early in the morning to the corner store to pick up some supplies and the mail. Her father was out trapping deep in the woods and she was in charge at home, looking after her toddler sister and her elderly kokum. Pearl had found out after her siblings left that she had been purposely kept out of school to help her father at home. Her mother was sick with uterine cancer.

There were three letters for her father, James. One was from her mother, Agnes, who had been in the hospital for weeks awaiting surgery to remove two large tumours from her uterus. Pearl couldn't read her their mother's letter because it was all in Ojibwe and she could only read English. Another letter was from Henry, her future brother-in-law, asking for her sister Daisy's hand in marriage. And the last letter was from the principal at Cecilia Jeffrey.

She tore into the principal's letter, eager for the news. The letter was scant on details, just a form-letter update.

It said the Wenjack children were doing "excellent" and were adjusting to the school year well. She returned home to spread the good news.

At 2:00 p.m. she heard the first rumblings from the sky. She was sitting in the main living room by the window overlooking the Albany River. The roar of the twin-engine planes shattered the quiet of the bush.

When a plane came into Marten Falls First Nation, it was an event. And when there was an unscheduled appearance from the sky, excitement mounted. The plane normally came only once a week and was so loud, so unlike anything heard in nature, that people couldn't help but turn their heads to the sky. But on that day, Pearl was astounded: she could see three planes coming in for a landing, a clear mile away.

This must be an occasion, she thought.

She watched the people on the plane disembark onto boats. There were so many people, it took five boats to accommodate them all.

As the boats made their way to the shore, she began to get excited. Those were her brothers and sisters on the boats. They were home!

Ecstatic and laughing, she grabbed her little sister and they ran down to the shore to greet her family. But as she got closer, she noticed no one was laughing. Then she saw Cecilia Jeffrey principal Colin Wasacase disembark with her mother, who was heavily sedated.

Pearl cast a glance at Daisy, her closest sister, and asked what was going on.

Daisy's face was stoic. "Chanie is gone."

CHANIE WENJACK WAS A small boy, about four foot ten, slight with sharp features. He was a sickly child who had battled respiratory illnesses. He had a huge scar around the right side of his torso from lung surgery.

He was nine years old when he started grade one at Cecilia Jeffrey. When he first sat down at his desk, he barely spoke English. Only Ojibwe. The teachers made him repeat grade one. He was labelled a slow learner, but he probably just couldn't understand what was going on around him. In the fall of 1966, Chanie was placed in a senior opportunity class — a remedial class for kids who needed extra help.

The boys and girls were separated inside the school but permitted to play together in the playground. Logs show that intermediate and senior girls, grades four to eight, spent half the day learning and the other half doing housework and crafts; some worked under the nurses in the dispensary. The boys in grades four to eight also attended classes, then worked the other half of the day doing general farm work, interior and exterior decorating and painting, as well as scrubbing, sweeping, and dusting. There were also small cleaning duties and farm work for both boys and girls before and after school.[32]

At recess, Chanie would play marbles with the other boys. Chanie's siblings were usually around when they played, though some of his sisters had to work in the kitchen with the other girls.

A high, barbed-wire fence snaked around the perimeter of Cecilia Jeffrey. At the back of the school there was an opening in the fence, a path to the outside world. It was not unusual for kids to run away from residential school. Officials called them "desertions." It is impossible to know how many students ran away. Many didn't get very far and were brought back to school by truancy officers or the police. They returned to the schools to face harsh punishment. The strap was often used, viciously, in front of other students, to act as a deterrent. Or the children were locked in dark closets without any food besides bread and water. When groups of students ran away, it was because of the abuse they were facing at the school.

The Department of Indian Affairs knew that from the late nineteenth century on, students were being sexually abused in the schools. The students were isolated, vulnerable, and often petrified. Adult kindness often became an entry into sexual assault. Students dreaded being called down to a staff member's office during the night or on weekends or to report to the shower room. Kids were groped or fondled in hallways, in confession, in church. One of the first reports came in 1886, after Indian Affairs translator and student recruiter Jean L'Heureux, who worked for the Roman Catholic schools in Alberta, was accused, many times, of sexually abusing the boys in his care. No criminal investigation took place.[33] From early on, the pattern was set. Schools and churches covered up the abuse. Principals often did nothing about complaints. Neither did the police. And schools never told the parents what was going on.

Again, the numbers of kids who were sexually and physically abused will never be truly known. Only now are survivors coming forward. As of the end of January

2015, the Independent Assessment Process, created under the Indian Residential Schools Settlement Agreement, received 37,951 abuse complaints. By the end of 2014, 30,939 cases had been settled and $2.69 billion paid out in compensation.[34]

What the statistics don't tell you is how some of the older children would form their own abusive circles, preying on the younger, more vulnerable kids. The abuse suffered at the hands of adult supervisors took its toll on the students. They became further disengaged from the classroom, angry, and in need of someone to take their rage out on. For some of these kids, the younger children were easy victims.

This is the life Chanie ran from.

IT WAS ON A Sunday, October 16, 1966, that Chanie decided enough was enough. He discussed the idea of running away from Cecilia Jeffrey with his buddies Ralph and Jackie MacDonald. Ralph was thirteen and Jackie eleven.[35] The brothers were orphans. Ralph was an experienced runaway. He'd bolted three times. Each time, he was caught and brought back to the school.

Chanie had never tried, not until that day.

Something must have been going on within the school. On that particular Sunday, nine students tried to escape. Maybe they knew the weather would soon turn and if they were going to make a break for it, it would be now or never.

It was a warm day. Chanie and the MacDonald brothers wore light jackets, plaid shirts, jeans, and leather ankle boots. They slipped through the opening in the fence at the back of the school and headed for the surrounding forest.

The three boys ran through the bush, around the Kenora airfield and toward a secret path they knew of. Their destination was Redditt, a small community along the MacFarlane River, twenty-seven kilometres north of Kenora. The MacDonalds' uncle, Charles Kelly, lived there, just a few kilometres outside town.

The boys moved through the bush like lightning. Within eight hours they made it to Redditt, but they had to stay a night in town. A local man took the boys in, fed them, and let them sleep on the floor. Early the next day, they made their way to the Kellys' place. To their astonishment, so did Chanie's best friend, Eddie Cameron, who was also related to the Kelly family. Eddie, who was Chanie's age, had made the entire thirty-two-kilometre route north of Kenora to the cabin all by himself.[36]

Kelly, a trapper, was overjoyed to see the boys, but now he had too many mouths to feed. The Kellys started to call Chanie "the stranger." Eddie remembers Chanie pulling out his map and telling him that home was really far away, near a big body of water.[37] They had no idea where it was or how to help him get there.

Soon Chanie didn't feel welcome; he was the only boy who was not related to the Kellys. One morning, Charles said he was taking his nephews out to the trapline, but there wasn't any room for Chanie in the canoe. He had to stay behind. To everyone's surprise, Chanie showed up at the trapline at Mud Lake. He had walked almost five kilometres to get there.

After they all spent the night in the bush, Charles told Chanie he would have to make his way back on his own. This is when Chanie made his move. He told the others he would head home, first six hundred kilometres east to Nakina and the last rail stop, and then on to Marten Falls. All he had with him was his map of the railway, which he had found after he escaped with the MacDonald brothers, and Clara Kelly had given him seven matches, which she placed in a glass jar with a tight lid. If he was to survive in the bush, he had to be able to light a fire.[38]

Charles told Chanie to follow the railway tracks and to stop and ask for food and directions at the stations.

That was the last time anyone saw the twelve-year-old boy alive.

CHANIE'S DEATH CERTIFICATE SAYS he died twenty kilometres east of Redditt.

On October 23, 1966, Canadian National Railway workers of train No. 821 found him lying beside the tracks. His body was cold and his clothes were wet.

He had died the day before from exposure to cold and wet. The autopsy showed he had pulmonary congestion, minor cuts, bruises on his legs, abrasions on his forehead, and a cut on his lips. There was gravel in his mouth and lips. He must have stumbled along the tracks and fallen on the rocks.

Dr. Glen Davidson, coroner for the District of Kenora, called for an inquest to be held on November 15, 1966.

He gave two reasons for the inquest. First, there was a

"great deal of truancy" at Cecilia Jeffrey. And second, to ascertain whether or not the Kellys had sent Chanie out on his own, with no food or supervision.

"The deceased was not strong and was very quiet and likely timid, as many young Indian children are who have little to do with town life," Davidson said.[39]

It was the only written comment he made on Chanie's death.

DAISY WAS IN RED LAKE when she heard that her brother was dead.

She had been kicked out of school because the administration thought she was pregnant. She wasn't, but she took the opportunity to head up to Red Lake to stay with her good friend Sarah.

It was Sarah who told Daisy that she heard on the news that Chanie's body had been found. Later that night, a minister and a police officer came to Sarah's door, looking for Daisy to tell her the news. They offered to drive her the 240 kilometres south to Kenora be with her younger siblings and to take Chanie's body home to Ogoki. She accepted the offer.

From Kenora, Daisy, along with her two younger sisters Annie and Lizzie, who were students at Cecilia Jeffrey, travelled with Chanie's casket by train. The train went east to Sioux Lookout, northwest of Thunder Bay. In Sioux Lookout, they picked up their mother from the hospital and their older sister Margaret, who was living and working in the small community.

"Mom kept saying, 'Your father doesn't know,'" Daisy recalls.[40]

Daisy is nearly the spitting image of her sister Pearl. They have the exact same tiny build and height, and the same dark eyes that stare intently at you when you speak. She's also sharp as a tack and doesn't waste her words. When she speaks, she always has something relevant to say.

She remembers the dismal plane ride into Ogoki, everyone stoic and grey with sadness as they flew over the trees. There was Pearl, ecstatic and running out to meet them, a look of sheer joy on her face. Daisy remembers how the joyful look on Pearl's face fell instantly away when she told her that Chanie was dead.

Daisy was also given the task of finding her father's closest friends, John and Louis. They knew James was out checking traplines. She asked them to go find him and tell him to come back, which they did. Hours later they returned.

As soon as he walked in the front door of their house, he saw all his children and his wife, who was supposed to be at the hospital. James looked at Agnes and said, "Is it true?"

When she said yes, he fell to the floor. For the longest time he did not move. Hours and hours passed. At some point, he was able to get up, but Daisy doesn't remember when that was. She does remember him refusing to eat or talk for days. When he did leave the house, it was because he had something to do. He needed to dig his son's grave.

When he was finished, he officiated the funeral and gave the service.

"And then my father buried my brother," says Daisy.

THE WENJACKS WERE NEVER told an inquest would be held to determine the circumstances leading to their son's death. They were given no opportunity to attend and they were offered no legal counsel.

An inquest is an investigation run by medical professionals with the sole intention of learning lessons from the dead in order to protect the living. Coroners' investigations cannot lay blame or make accusations. They cannot lay charges of murder or assault. A coroner's court can only listen and make suggestions for future change.

In the family's absence four recommendations were decided upon by four members of the jury. The names of those who served on the jury have been redacted.

The first two recommendations say the exact same thing: When Chanie and the boys showed up at the first two residences, the authorities should have been called right away. The children should have been handed over to police and returned to school.

The third recommendation called for more teachers to be hired at Cecilia Jeffrey so that the students could be properly watched and cared for at all times. Clearly, there was a problem with discipline if they couldn't contain the kids.

"The Cecilia Jeffrey school needs more supervisory staff to adequately control the number of students involved," the findings read.[41]

The fourth admits the "Indian residential school system causes tremendous emotional and adjustment problems. It behooves we, who are responsible for this organization, to do everything possible to mitigate their problems."

The jury suggested a study be made of the Indian residential school system and its philosophy.

"Is it right?" the jurors asked.[42]

Enrollment in the residential school caused a disruption in the basic family unit. Enrollment, they suggested, should be on a "smaller geographic scale" that would allow for family liaison, and brothers and sisters should never be separated.

The jurors even called for schools to be built on reserves where there are "sufficient numbers."

They also called for children to be boarded in private homes instead of residences and for the schools to be smaller in size so that the administrators could get to know their pupils.

The findings of the jury were not immediately shared with the Wenjack family. They read about all that had happened to Chanie in a *Maclean's* magazine article by the journalist Ian Adams when it was published in February 1967, nearly three months after the inquiry.[43]

MORE THAN TWO DECADES after Chanie's death, a copy of the inquest findings was slipped to Daisy in a secret envelope. She'll only say that a sympathetic lawyer gave them to her. She read the papers and kept them. She never told Pearl or anyone else in her family about them.

When Daisy got the envelope, she was dealing with her own agony. Her husband, Henry, had recently disclosed that he had been sexually abused as a child at the Pelican Indian Residential School in Sioux Lookout. All his life, and throughout their life together, raising three children, Henry drank and he had never told her why. Then one day he told her about his abuser, Leonard Hands, an Anglican priest who was later sentenced to four years in prison after he pleaded guilty to nineteen counts of sexual assault against boys at Pelican between 1966 and 1971.[44]

Henry told her he didn't want to deal with the sexual abuse he had suffered. He didn't want to think about it or tell anyone else. He wanted her to know and deal with it as she chose, but not now, only after he had died.

It was around this time that Daisy found out that Chanie had been sexually abused at school. One of Chanie's friends, who has never publicly come forward with allegations, wanted Chanie's sisters to know what really happened at Cecilia Jeffrey and why Chanie ran.

Out of the blue, this friend called Daisy. He told her the older boys at the school used to abuse them in the dormitories at night. On that Sunday when Chanie took off, so did the friend. Nine other kids had run for their lives that day.[45] A critical mass of kids, all running, could not have been a coincidence. They must have been running from something.

This boy, the confessor, did not run to Redditt with Chanie and the MacDonald brothers. He escaped to a farm, where he was given food and a warm place to stay, until the farmer called the police and turned him in.

CLOSE TO A HALF century after Chanie's death, Pearl received a phone call from one of his best friends. He and Chanie were virtually inseparable when they were young boys. It had been fifty years since Pearl had last spoken to him. He had not recovered from his days in residential school. His life was a toxic mix of addictions and pain.

He reached out to Pearl, asking to meet because there was something he desperately had to tell her.

Pearl made her way down to Thunder Bay and met the man at his home. He told her that at Cecilia Jeffrey, he was sexually abused. The abuse was non-stop and vicious. And he said that Chanie was abused as well.

Their abuser wasn't the principal or a teacher, but it was the same person. He was unable to tell her when the abuse had started, just that it happened and that his life was ruined because of it.

Pearl began to sink inside and a sense of knowing, of understanding, began to take shape. She knew what had gone on at the school. She recalled one particular day, after lunch, when she had accidentally walked in on one of the female teachers sexually assaulting a young girl. That teacher later cornered Pearl in the change room and beat her senseless with a four-foot-long stick.

When Pearl heard there would be a joint inquest held into the deaths of seven Indigenous students in Thunder Bay, a deep unrest filled her soul. *So little has changed*, she thought. There is still a lack of schools on reserves. Children are still being separated from their families and sent hundreds of kilometres away to get an education, and once they get there, they are years behind the other pupils because their elementary schools are substandard. Once the students arrive in Thunder Bay, they are isolated, alone, and alienated. They are placed in boarding homes where people are paid to take care of them. For the most part they are not living in nurturing, loving environments.

Pearl called Dr. David Eden, the Northwestern Ontario regional coroner, to discuss what had happened to her brother. She wanted another inquest. This time, she wanted a proper one where Chanie's family could participate.

She also wanted the police to investigate the allegations of the sexual assault and abuse that had happened to her brother and his friends. Eden advised her there was nothing he could do about a police investigation. She would have to go to the police if she was looking for a criminal probe. But, Pearl argued, the crime had taken place a half-century ago, and the man who'd told her what had happened was in absolutely no shape to speak to the police. Pearl had no evidence other than what the man had said and the feeling she had deep inside that told her this was why Chanie ran.

"I asked the coroner when I met with him, 'Why didn't anyone follow the recommendations made after my brother's death?'"

She knew there were only four recommendations but they were something.

The most important one for her was the establishment of proper schools on every single reserve. This way kids would never have to leave their community.

"When I heard about the kids in Thunder Bay, I could feel them running, of being scared," Pearl says.

She understood their anguish. Their deep loneliness for home. Their confusion living in a big city so unlike where they were from and communicating in a language that was not their own.

"When I am alone at home, I think about my brother. The drive to go home was so strong. I don't want his death to be in vain," she says. "As a residential school survivor, you can feel it all over again, what these students felt. Yes, you can feel it."

- 3 -

WHEN THE WOLF COMES

IN 1996, THE LAST RESIDENTIAL SCHOOL WAS FINALLY shut down. About 150,000 children had been sent to these schools, passing down the horror and trauma of the experience to their children, grandchildren, nieces, and nephews. By the mid-twentieth century, the Department of Indian Affairs began the long process of slowly dismantling what they had been building for the past seventy years. But it would take decades of bureaucratic meetings and conferences where policy papers containing new ideas were presented and debated before the officials could actually achieve closure of all the schools. The powerful Roman Catholic Church believed they should be in charge of schooling Indigenous people, and plans to wrest control away from the Church were met with opposition. In 1973 the Anglican Church's Pelican Lake Indian Residential School in Sioux Lookout was shut down, and the notorious Cecilia Jeffrey closed in 1974. The last residential schools to shut in Ontario were three run by Mennonites: the Cristal Lake School for Girls closed in 1986, Poplar Hill Development School closed in 1989, and the Wahbon Bay Academy shut in 1991.[1]

As the department started to choke off funding to the church-run residential schools, a great gulf emerged in the northwest.[2] Suddenly, if families wanted to send their children to school, they had to go to provincially run schools in urban areas. First Nations kids — some from as far north as Hudson Bay — were being sent to provincial high schools in Sioux Lookout and were boarded in private homes. Some students stayed in the old dorms at the closed Pelican Falls Indian Residential School and were bused into Sioux Lookout every day for class. Pelican Falls sat on a picturesque 172 acres of Lac Seul First Nation's traditional lands and it was only twenty minutes outside of Sioux Lookout.

Tribal councils started to come together to help fill the void and have a say in how their children were to be educated. In the northwest, the Northern Nishnawbe Education Council (NNEC) was established in 1978 with the belief that Indigenous people should exercise self-governance over the education of their young. The chiefs and Elders organized NNEC to run the boarding programs that watched over the children who were going to high school in Sioux Lookout, and in 1979, the NNEC became an education authority, directed by the Sioux Lookout area's twenty-four chiefs. The first executive director was Richard Morris, from Kitchenuhmaykoosib Inninuwug First Nation.

Soon after the students began living in Sioux Lookout, NNEC workers noticed that they were falling behind in the provincial high schools. Kids weren't happy and dropout rates were high. The kids boarding at Pelican Falls weren't doing any better. Using the old school as a dorm did not sit well with some of the chiefs — there were too many ghosts. This was the school where Daisy's husband was sexually abused by the notorious convicted pedophile Leonard Hands. Pelican Falls operated from 1926 to 1973, and many of the former students were now the parents of the kids living in the dormitories.

The NNEC leadership at the time thought there had to be something better for their students — a way to offer them an education while they were still living at home with their parents. By 1989, a robust, ingenious, remote-education plan was hatched. NNEC educators Margaret Fiddler, Darby Harper, and Brian Beaton started a distance education system, which included North America's first radio school, the Wahsa Distance Education Centre, which opened in 1991. Run from 10:00 a.m. to 10:00 p.m. — or 11:00 p.m. in Fort Severn and Fort Hope — Wahsa is a regular high school with classes that are fifty-five minutes long. The classes are broadcast from a radio station in Sioux Lookout, where the teachers open up thirteen telephone lines and students call in. It's like a high school radio talk show.

One of the first people on board was Norma Kejick, a young mom from Lac Seul First Nation. Norma, a quiet go-getter, married into the family of former Lac Seul Chief Sam Kejick who, eighty years earlier, had questioned the treatment of students at Cecilia Jeffrey. She loved her husband, John, and their traditional way of life, hunting and living on the land at Lac Seul and in the small cabin the two of them built. Norma is one of those people who manages to pack everything she can into life: she got both a university education and had three young boys. This was the life she was living when she was recruited to become Wahsa's receptionist. It was important to NNEC that everyone on staff be from the community they served and Norma fit the bill. It was quickly noticed that Norma is one of those women who rises to the occasion — if you throw problems or obstacles at her, she'll quietly work it out while making supper. She charmed everyone she worked with, and in no time she became the distance education co-ordinator. The staff at NNEC had great plans for Norma. They wanted her to one day be principal. Norma knew she couldn't go any further in her career with her educational background, so she went back to university, doing distance education at the University of Ottawa.

She had done all this — she studied, got her principal's qualifications, was promoted to principal, and raised her boys — when she agreed to take on one more job: being an adoptive mom to an abandoned baby girl. On January 27, 1995, exactly thirteen days after she was promoted to principal of Wahsa, she received a call from the Ojibway Family Tribal Services in Kenora, asking her if she wanted a baby. The mom was from Lac Seul. She had had the baby in Winnipeg and left her in the hospital. Winnipeg authorities told Ojibway Family Tribal Services that they had until February 17 to find the baby a home in Lac Seul or they would make her a ward of the city. Tribal Services called Norma because her sister-in-law Doreen had told them Norma had always wanted a girl. Norma, true to form, took the baby in.

While the students performed well at Wahsa — the school was provincially inspected and was steadily graduating more students every year — NNEC educators, again, wanted something more for their kids. They wanted a real high school. Respected educator Margaret Fiddler and Kitchenuhmaykoosib Inninuwug chief James Cutfeet's dream began as a pilot project in 1992, with classes housed in portables on Pelican's grounds. Again, many community leaders did not approve of opening a school at the site, given the history of trauma there. But some Elders, including former NAN grand chief Frank Beardy, argued that they needed to put the past behind them and turn negative history into a positive future. He insisted that the school should be seen as a place of reconciliation. The community relented. Eventually, NNEC was given government funding to open up a brand-new school at the site. Construction soon started and the school would be ready to open its doors by September 2000.

Educators were stunned when more than three hundred students applied to attend Pelican Falls High School — the school could accommodate only two-thirds of those students. There were thirteen houses on-site and fourteen beds in a house — a total of 182 beds. Some students were bused in daily from Lac Seul, but the majority lived in residence.

Armed with the demand from their communities, educators decided to look for another school building. They got lucky in Thunder Bay. The old vocational Northwood High School was sitting empty after having been shuttered in the mid-1990s for budgetary reasons. NNEC put a bid on the property and the sale went through fast.

Norma remembers it was a frenzy trying to outfit both schools by the fall. Both needed desks, chairs, blackboards, and school supplies. Staff needed to be hired and trained, and boarding homes needed to be sorted out quickly. They decided to delay the opening of the school in Thunder Bay, which they christened Dennis Franklin Cromarty High School, until October. The school was named after the former beloved Nishnawbe Aski Nation grand chief, who was first elected in 1979 and served numerous terms before he had a heart attack and passed away suddenly in 1993.

It soon became apparent to the NNEC that the 1960s-era school, which looked more like a factory than a centre of learning, needed a lot of work. Not only did it need to be fully furnished and equipped, the school was full of asbestos, a cancer-causing insulation popular in the 1950s and 1960s. The asbestos was in the walls and ceilings of the main floor. But with time marching on, only one wing of the school could be cleaned out before school started. Another issue was the heat, which came from an anti-quated boiler system. The boiler needed to be repaired and none of the parts were sold in North America — they came from a factory in Ukraine.

Another complication was arranging boarding for the close to 150 students who might enroll in the school every year. Each pupil was from a remote, northern First Nation around five hundred kilometres away. With no student residence at DFC, each child would be placed in a boarding home. Boarding families had to be screened quickly and students placed in the houses. Informational pamphlets with a list of guidelines were printed up to give to new, prospective boarding parents.

It is NNEC policy to thoroughly investigate prospective boarding parents by conducting criminal background checks, in-person interviews to see why someone wants to be a boarding parent, and home inspections to see if there is enough room for the students. Before the students arrive, boarding parents also go through an NNEC orientation and training program.[3] Boarding parents are expected to follow certain rules. They need to "be responsible for the welfare and conduct of students while he or she is in your care." They need to discuss and set up "reasonable patterns of conduct and discipline with the students regarding meal times, curfews, access to the kitchen, telephone," and they are instructed to "treat the students as your own children and include them in as many family and social activities as possible."[4]

Some boarding homes were better than others. Some had more than one boarder; some were in apartments and others in houses. Some kids got bounced around from home to home until they could find a proper fit.

Since the students would be so far away from home, it was imperative that both the right school staff and proper boarding homes be chosen. Students between the ages of fourteen and twenty-one were coming down to Thunder Bay, and for many of them, it would be the first time they'd lived in a city or were far from their parents. The culture shock would be startling. Some of the kids had never seen traffic lights, a movie theatre, or a shopping mall before. In fact, the change was so immense, each DFC student was given a guidebook called *What Every Student Needs to*

Know, which offered advice on everything from road and bus safety to the effects of alcohol. On street safety, the guidebook points out to students that they must always follow these rules:

· Learn what traffic signs mean.

· Before crossing a street, stop at the curb or the edge of the road and never run into the street.

· Look and listen for cars and trucks to the left, then to the right, and then to the left again.

· Look confident, walk with your head up as if you know where you are going. The appearance of being lost or being anxious may render you vulnerable to unwanted attention.

The guidebook even tells students how to ride the bus: "Find a seat, sit down and look forward. Keep the aisle clear."[5]

Parents sent their children to DFC by choice. It is not a residential school. It is not run by the church, nor is it strictly regulated by Indigenous and Northern Affairs. It is an Indigenous-run private school. But the only other choice parents had was to abandon their children's high school education or pick up and move to a city.

In most communities in Canada and the Western world, there are well-built, local high schools with libraries, science labs, well-equipped gymnasiums, qualified teachers, and a clean, sanitary environment. In northern fly-in communities, high schools like that simply don't exist. And the elementary school system is woefully underfunded and neglected by INAC.

Perhaps one of the most egregious examples of government neglect is the elementary school in Attawapiskat, a fly-in Cree community on the James Bay coast. In 1979, a diesel spill leaked one hundred and thirteen thousand litres of fuel into the earth directly underneath the elementary school. Five different species of mould were growing in the walls, and the students and teachers were getting sick from the smell of carcinogen-laden fumes. The people of Attawapiskat were desperate. They could no longer send their kids to a toxic dump to learn, so they shut the school permanently in May 2000. As a stopgap measure, INAC set up fourteen temporary classrooms that were placed on a plot of land between the Attawapiskat airstrip and the contaminated soil. The portables became the school for the foreseeable future after three successive Indigenous Affairs ministers handling the file — Robert Nault, Jim Prentice, and Andy Scott — all promised to build a new school but never made good on their promise.[6]

The federal government should never have been in the education business in the first place, but the Indian Act put them there. The Indian Act does not call for, or impose, education standards. There is no legislated core curriculum. There is no stipulation that elementary school teachers meet the provincial standard. So elementary schools varied from First Nation to First Nation. Some schools were well staffed and well run while others were not. A lack of basic standards meant that many kids found the transition to high school completely overwhelming — especially in a brand-new city, far away from everything they knew.

On top of all that, the schools were underfunded due a 2 percent funding cap established by Prime Minister Jean Chrétien's government in 1996. In 2015, Prime Minister Justin Trudeau promised to eliminate the funding cap, which had left First Nations communities struggling as it did not address the 29 percent growth in the Indigenous population during that same period. (As of June 2017, NAN says the cap remains.) The Indigenous birth rate far outpaced non-Indigenous Canada's, but that fact wasn't taken into account when money was handed out to schools.[7] Incredibly, the provincial school systems were not under the same funding pressures. Between 1996 and 2006, funding to provincial school systems increased annually by 3.8 percent, almost double the Indigenous cap.[8]

Not surprisingly, sending Indigenous kids to poorly funded reserve schools with subpar equipment and teachers who haven't been properly trained has not led to student success. A study conducted in 2010 found that the high school completion rate for former residential school students living off reserves is only 28 percent, and it is 36 percent for those who did not attend residential school. Further, only 7 percent of parents who attended residential school have a university degree, compared to 10 percent of Indigenous parents who did not go to a residential school.[9]

The education system for the Indigenous population differs across the country. The federal government funds the schools and then hands over "control" to local

First Nations without offering any statutory authority or adequate financial means for the communities to make changes. Thus the curriculum resembles what is being taught in the provinces. It is not culturally appropriate and it doesn't take into account language differences.[10]

In April 2000, INAC was blasted by Canada's office of the Auditor General, the watchdog that conducts audits of federal departments. Auditor General Denis Desautels reported that INAC had no idea if the money it was spending was helping to close the woefully large education gap between Indigenous and non-Indigenous children. He called INAC's work "unacceptably slow" and said that "immediate action" was needed.[11] INAC needed to clearly state its role in education, work to resolve outstanding problems, and develop measures to grade performance.

So when Dennis Franklin Cromarty High School opened up its rust-coloured metal front doors in October 2000, it was a place of hope for many. It was Indigenous run and directed, and staffed with Indigenous teachers; a nurse and an Elder were on-site every single day. Each student was assigned a guidance counsellor, a contact person who acted almost as a surrogate parent. Everyone on staff—from the teachers to the office workers to the Elders and the custodial staff—pitched in to look after the kids.

The one problem the educators couldn't foresee was that every single one of those children brought the ghosts of the past with them. Some of the kids were leaving an idyllic family life, but most were not. Many came from homes touched by the horrific trauma of residential school—abuse, addictions, extreme poverty, and confused minds.

There was one more thing that almost all the students shared: they came from homes of little means. There was often no extra money for new clothes like a warm coat or another pair of shoes. There was no money to pay for extracurricular activities, and if there was, the students' parents weren't there to drive them to and from practice. If they wanted to call home, they needed phone cards because the boarding parents weren't expected to pay the long-distance bills. At the time, not everyone carried a cell phone and few had computers. And no extra cash meant airline tickets to fly home for a weekend were few and far between.

Many of the teens were not used to living essentially on their own, especially those who were only fourteen and starting grade nine. They were strangers in a strange land. The mall was a new experience. Some of the kids didn't have friends. The kids were on their own and homesickness plagued them. For some, the change was just too hard to handle. There was so much going on around them — the lights, the excitement of the city, and the inevitable loneliness, the boredom. So they did what a lot of kids do when their parents aren't around — they got together and relied on each other for comfort and support. They goofed around. Some of them partied.

The staff at Dennis Franklin knew what their kids were facing so they went above and beyond what regular high schools offered. They looked after their own and they did so with pride. No one on staff worked from only 9:00 a.m. to 4:00 p.m. No one was on a clock. They were all on call twenty-four hours a day, acting as surrogate parents for every new crop of students that walked through the door.[12]

With the bright expectations and the positive buzz surrounding the opening of the new Indigenous-run high school, no one could have anticipated what would happen that October. Within the first month of Dennis Franklin Cromarty's grand opening, every single one of the DFC and NNEC staffers would be faced with their greatest challenge: the disappearance and death of one of their students.

SHAWON WAVY BOUNDED his lanky self up the concrete steps of the front doors of Dennis Franklin Cromarty on the first day of school. He was in grade nine, finally in high school, fourteen years old and living away from his home reserve of Mishkeegogamang First Nation. Mish is an Ojibwe reserve and one of the only DFC communities that is accessible by road, a six-hour drive north of Thunder Bay.

A wafer-thin string bean of a kid, Shawon weaved and bobbed through the halls, nodding to some of his new buddies. He saw Jethro Anderson in the halls, another niner.

Shawon and Jethro became friends. They were both from small northern communities, Jethro from Kasabonika Lake First Nation, near the Hudson Bay coast, where the First Nations people are a mix of Cree and Northern Ojibwe.

The two were friendly in the way teenage boys are friends, sharing jokes about stuff only fifteen-year-old boys find funny. Talk was never too deep, usually about sports or school, but they got on well. They had just met at the beginning of October, the start of the new school year.

Shawon remembers the last time he saw Jethro. It was on October 28, the last night Jethro was seen alive. They were at a party down by the docks on the Kam River waterfront. There are two entrances to get to the fifty-five-metre-long scenic walkway along the fast-moving Kam. One is at the south end of Syndicate Avenue and the other is at the base of Donald Street, just down from City Hall. The city has taken pains to spruce up the riverbanks. Benches are arranged by the river's edge and docked on the north side is the red-and-white *James Whelan*, a hundred-year-old decommissioned tugboat.

For kids new to the city, this was a good place to party, far from the prying eyes of adults or the police. The underpass and the trees gave students lots of cover if they wanted to drink and socialize.

Shawon remembers it was cold and dark. Kids from school were partying there. He saw Jethro stumble and sway as he tried to talk to a couple of girls who seemed kind of familiar to him.

Shawon, who was with other friends, watched Jethro as he got into it with the girls. It appeared as if they were fighting over him. The more he watched, the more he recognized the girls. They were from Mish — Chantelle Skunk and Roberta Skunk.

One of them looked like she was kissing Jethro and the other immediately became pissed off. Jethro was laughing. He thought it was funny. The girls clearly didn't think so. They began getting into a loud argument.

The boys Shawon was with were impatient and wanted to go.

"C'mon, man," they said to him. "Let's leave them."

Shawon watched Jethro and the girls argue for a minute longer.

Oh man, Shawon thought. *Yeah. Time to go.*

IT WAS SATURDAY, OCTOBER 28. Frost caked the ground outside of Stella Anderson's home in Kasabonika.

There was a wolf staring at her.

Stella drew in a sharp breath. A wolf always brings a message.

"LEAVE!" she said, trying to shoo away the animal before her.[13]

The wolf gave her a final look and then it was gone.

Two days later, Stella found out that her son Jethro was missing.

Her baby. Her eldest boy. Her first-born son.

JETHRO ANDERSON DID NOT go home on Saturday night.

Jethro, who had just turned fifteen on October 1, never missed his curfew.

The last time Dora Morris saw Jethro, he was with her son Nathan, who was two years older than her nephew. Dora, a tiny woman with a mighty heart, was not only Jethro's aunt, sister to his father, Sam; she was also Jethro's guardian, his boarding parent, his second mom. Dora was a mother figure to all the kids in the neighbourhood, who often congregated at the happy, two-storey home she shared with her husband, Tom Morris, in the Fort William end of the city. Dora was from Kasabonika Lake First Nation and Tom from Kitchenuhmaykoosib Inninuwug (Big Trout Lake) First Nation. Their descendants followed the animals and travelled when the seasons changed, settling high up in the northernmost region of Ontario. Human bones found on the shores of Big Trout Lake date back nearly seven thousand years, proving people had occupied this harsh and remote part of the world far earlier than the time of first contact with Europeans.[14]

When Jethro was young, his father, Sam, and his mother, Stella, were having marital problems. To make things easier, Jethro lived with Dora and his cousins up in Big Trout. Jethro had two sisters, Lawrencia and Sarah, and eventually a younger brother, Clinton. Jethro loved his extended family and being with Dora and the kids.

Jethro was a kind soul, always finding new animals to befriend and bring home. From a very young age, he had an uncanny ability to calm other living things. When he was six years old, he had a pet owl he'd found in the bush. The white-and-brown barn owl had intense yellow eyes and a small, curved yellow beak. It would perch on his arm as he carried it around the rez with his pet dog scampering at his heels. Dora remembers it was a remarkable sight.

Dora, a slight yet physically strong woman with loose, curly hair, was a source of comfort and stability for Jethro. She was always there for him, and over the course of his short life, she gave him the family life and the stability he needed to thrive. She provided for him; she fed and cared for him. She treated him like he was one of her own.

Dora's mind was spinning in circles on that first, awful, long night. She felt every tick of the clock as she waited for her nephew to walk through the door. As soon as the sun began to rise, Dora couldn't wait any longer. She picked up the phone to try to get a hold of Stella. [15]

She choked out the words. Speaking them made it harder — it made them true: "Jethro didn't come home last night."

THE LAST TIME DORA saw Jethro, it was a Saturday afternoon. The boys were at home, anxious to go to the mall.

Nathan and Jethro had always been close. They had spent countless hours in the bush, climbing trees and using their slingshots to snag partridges for supper. Both spoke Oji-Cree until they were adolescents and moved to Thunder Bay where they shared a room, played video games, and hung out in comfortable silence on the couch.

Before Dora left for work at the Wequedong Lodge, a housing service for people travelling from remote First Nations into Thunder Bay for medical care, she gave the boys $2.50 each to buy a pop or a snack and told them to be home later for dinner. She told Nathan that he was in charge while she and Tom were out. Tom was an executive at Wasaya Airways, an Indigenous-run airline that services the remote communities in the north. When he went on a business trip, it usually involved an eight-hundred-kilometre round trip on a puddle jumper plane.

Seventeen-year-old Nathan often looked after his younger siblings — Adrienne, who was twelve, and David, who was fifteen. Dora knew he was responsible, and that he and Jethro wouldn't blow their 10:00 p.m. curfew.

When the boys left she went upstairs to get ready for work. Dora had been hired by the lodge to help the many elderly patients who didn't speak English well or had lost the ability to communicate in the settlers' language to time and dementia. She spent her days translating from Oji-Cree to English, so the caregivers could understand what the patients needed. Even at work, Dora was always busy caring for someone.

When she went on break at 9:00 p.m., she called home to see how the kids were doing. Nathan, David, and Adrienne were at home with their friends, but Nathan told her that he had separated from Jethro hours earlier and that Jethro hadn't made it home yet. She thought this was strange and she began to worry.

When Dora got home from work at 11:00 p.m., she met Tom, who was just returning from another business trip, in the driveway. When they walked through the door, their kids were hanging out in the family room with their friends.

Dora instantly saw that Jethro wasn't there. She looked at Nathan and he told her Jethro still wasn't home.

A few years back, they had gone through a similar experience when Jethro was twelve years old and staying with them in Thunder Bay. He had disappeared for a couple of days, though everyone in the small community knew he was staying at his girlfriend's house. When Dora found Jethro walking along the road with his girlfriend, she had hauled him into the car and taken him home. But three years on, it was completely out of character for Jethro not to come home when he was expected, especially if he was out with his older cousin.

Nathan confessed to Dora that they hadn't gone to the mall like he had told her. Instead, they went to their cousin Leeanne's house to drink. Earlier that morning, Nathan had dropped off some beer, which he had gotten from a runner. In Thunder Bay, a "runner" is an adult over the drinking age of nineteen who buys alcohol for underage kids in exchange for a tip or some booze.

Nathan and Jethro had hung out that afternoon with Leeanne, her boyfriend Chris, her sister Debbie, and Starlight Frogg. Nathan didn't stay long. He had promised a girl he was seeing that he would go visit her at the Intercity mall where she worked. He left Jethro at the house and headed for the bus stop.

Nathan would see Jethro once more that day, through the window of the bus. His cousin was walking down the street. He could have been headed to the corner store. He could have been going to the mall or to another friend's house. Nathan didn't know. All he knew was that Jethro looked happy.

Dora hid her rising fear from her kids. She and Tom told them not to worry; they were sure Jethro would be home soon. Just in case, she asked Nathan to go out and check with his friends at their usual haunts, to see if anyone knew where Jethro was.

While Nathan was out, Dora and Tom got into their van and drove up and down the residential streets — Victoria Avenue, Vickers Street, Balmoral, and Red River Road. Dora scanned all the doorways and the driveways, and looked down the sidewalks. They also cruised the Arthur Street strip.

After four hours, they went back home; it was 3:00 a.m. Nathan was there and reported that none of his friends had seen Jethro. Fitful, exhausted panic came creeping in. Dora spent the next few hours waiting, but to no avail. She decided to call the police.

"My nephew hasn't come home," she said.

"He's just out there partying like every other Native kid," the officer said. Then he hung up.

Shocked, Dora put down the phone. His comment felt like a slap in the face.

Dora began to make more calls.

The first was to Stella, who was more calm and measured. She believed her son would be home soon.

Next, Dora tried to find Sam, Jethro's dad, in Kasabonika. He didn't have a phone, so she called other relatives, looking for him. She thought about calling her own father and then stopped herself. She didn't want to alarm him in case Jethro suddenly walked through the door. She called the police again, who said it was too early to file a missing persons report. Jethro had to have been gone for at least twenty-four hours.

When the sun came up, Dora and her husband went back out. Daylight was a blessing. One of Adrienne's friends had told her the night before that a lot of the kids hung out at the Kam waterfront by the underpass and the tugboat, where they could drink. It was the first that Dora had heard that going to the river to drink was a popular thing to do among the teens.

Dora and Tom picked up Adrienne's friend and drove down to the river. After the girl showed them the underpass, they drove her home and went back to search the area. There was no one there at that early hour. Clearing away the long grass and brush, they poked through litter and twigs, looking for any sign of Jethro.

They got to a wire fence near the underpass with a sign that read *Private Property*. Dora had her husband hold up the fencing so she could crawl underneath to see if her nephew was on the other side.

Nathan also went back out, canvassing the kids he met on the street. He got lucky. Somebody told him that Jethro was seen at the Brodie Street bus terminal, but that he stayed for only a short time before heading down to the river. The bus terminal was another popular meeting place for many of the students who didn't have cars and travelled everywhere by bus.

When Dora got back to the house, Nathan told her what he had learned. She called the police again, asking if there were any leads. Her queries were met with silence. She was told again that maybe he'd be home later. When the party was over.

At 8:20 p.m., on Sunday, October 29, Dora walked through the doors of the Thunder Bay Police station and filed a missing persons report.

FROM THAT FIRST NIGHT ON, Dora and Tom never stopped searching for Jethro.

"I just drove and drove, day and night," she said. She

felt like Jethro was her responsibility, and what was worse was that he was someone else's son.

The first Monday after he went missing, she went to the school in a state of agitation. She walked to the office and told someone, she can't remember who, that Jethro was gone.

"They just told me that he would be back. That he was out there with his friends," she said. They told her not to worry. But she could feel something was horribly wrong.

She asked for his list of classes and then went to every single classroom on his timetable. She hoped against hope that he had stayed out partying all weekend but would turn up in one of his classes. She peered through the windows of the classroom doors, searching each desk for Jethro.

On the Tuesday after Jethro went missing, Dora was walking the school hallways when she was approached by an older man. She doesn't recall who the man was and she never got his name, but she thinks he was an Elder or a teacher.

"I can't believe what I am hearing, what they are saying to you," he said. "They should be out there looking for him, helping you." He told her that he thought Jethro was probably hurting and in need of help.

His comments pierced her. She ran out of the school, got in her car, and started to drive, scouring the streets once more, looking for Jethro.

A FEW DAYS AFTER her son went missing, Stella arrived from Kasabonika along with her family and other members of the community. Volunteers in Thunder Bay were also recruited to help search for Jethro. Among those who answered the call were Alvin Fiddler and his wife Tesa. They joined the teams of searchers — practically all were Indigenous — as they combed the Kam's banks, looking for any signs of the boy. The Fiddlers had just moved to Thunder Bay and Alvin had taken a job as the health coordinator for Nishnawbe Aski Nation. Tesa insisted on searching even though she had their newborn adoptive daughter, Lynette, with her. Everyone hoped that Jethro would be found safe, but as time passed the reality of the boy's disappearance from the brand-new high school was setting in. It seemed everyone was out looking for Jethro — everyone but the police.

"They didn't even put up a notice in the media until a week after. It was November 5. I still have the news clipping," Dora said.

Police did not start a missing persons investigation until six days after Jethro's disappearance.

Dora continued to call the police to check on any leads, and each time she was treated like a nuisance. "Right away, every time I called there, I got used to somebody answered the phone and hearing, 'There are no leads,' or other comments like, 'He is just out there partying.'"

By that time, Dora was an emotional wreck. "I wasn't eating. I was puking out all food. I was physically sick."

Dora's experience with the Thunder Bay Police was not unusual. Decades before Jethro's disappearance and even a decade after, Indigenous people have complained that the Thunder Bay Police did not take their calls seriously. Family members felt they were not given regular updates, and there was little communication with the officers conducting searches or investigating cases of missing persons or victims of murder.

This was particularly felt by the families of the Missing and Murdered Indigenous Women and Girls (MMIWG), whose disappearances and deaths some say are far greater than the RCMP's statistic of 1,181 from 1980 to 2012.[16] The deaths and disappearances of Indigenous women is Canada's hidden shame. For the longest time, it seemed as though the only group raising alarms about generations of women disappearing was the Native Women's Association of Canada — a national organization created to fight for the betterment of the lives of Indigenous women. It wasn't until the discovery of the gruesome horror of Robert Pickton's pig farm and his subsequent arrest for the torturous slaying of dozens of women from Vancouver's Downtown Eastside — he disposed of his victims' bodies using a meat grinder — did Canadian society begin to pay attention to the stark reality that Indigenous women are being murdered and maimed at a rate several times higher than non-Indigenous women. Then the beaten, bludgeoned, and sexually assaulted body of fifteen-year-old Tina Fontaine was found floating in Winnipeg's Red River in the summer of 2013, and the issue exploded when national media woke up to what Indigenous communities had known for years: someone was stealing our women.

In 2014, the RCMP released its first report strictly focused on Indigenous women and girls, culled from officers' notes and solve rates from across the country. The

RCMP claimed that about 90 percent of the murder cases were solved and that, in most cases, Indigenous women knew their killers. But those numbers never sat well with the Indigenous community, who for decades had been fighting to get some police attention to the national tragedy. The number of MMIWG seemed too low and the solve rate absurdly high. Many Indigenous families say the killers of their family members remain unknown and they are probably right — the RCMP got their 90 percent solve rate by asking their officers if an arrest had been made, or was intended to be made, which is what accounted for the number. The RCMP report did not look at convictions or the outcomes of the court cases. They didn't have the capacity or infrastructure to follow each and every murder case through the court system and record the outcome.

The 1,181 MMIWG number is also in question since not every murdered or missing Indigenous woman was identified as Indigenous by the police. Not every Indigenous person holds a status card. Families also felt some disappearances were not recorded properly and were classified as runaways instead, and that in many cases the possibility of murder was overlooked by police who assumed death was accidental and not a homicide.

In 2015, the *Toronto Star* took a closer look at the national RCMP numbers and asked the force for all their analyses and sources. The RCMP refused, so the *Star* — five reporters, Jim Rankin, David Bruser, Joanna Smith, Jennifer Wells, and I; librarians Astrid Lang and Rick Snjzdar; and data analyst Andy Bailey — spent a year and a half making its own list from news reports and court documents. The *Star*'s numbers differed from the RCMP's findings. The *Star* found 1,126 cases of MMIWG, with 936 of those from 1980 to 2015. However, the *Star* could not gain access to official RCMP data so case counts differed. Overall, the newspaper found 766 murder cases, of which twenty were identified as murder suicides. Of the murders, 224 were unsolved. The *Star* found 170 missing Indigenous women and girls, which was comparable to the RCMP number of 164.

The *Star*'s solve rate numbers, however, were significantly different from the RCMP's. Between 1980 and 2012, the solve rate compiled by the *Star* was 70 percent, lower than the 88 percent solve rate the RCMP reported in 2014 for the same time frame. Another difference was the unsolved cases. The *Star* analysis found 180 unsolved cases between 1980 and 2012, while the RCMP cited 120 cases for the same period.

Looking specifically at the Thunder Bay area, the *Star* found that of all the MMIWG cases from the 1960s to 2014, fifty-four Indigenous women had been murdered or gone missing in the area. Of those, police had solved twenty-three cases.[17]

On February 13, 1992, Sandra Johnson, eighteen, was found brutally murdered on top of the frozen Neebing-McIntyre Floodway, a thin riverbed that bleeds into the Kam. Her naked body was lying on the ice underneath a busy overpass. Her death remains unsolved. On February 28, 2003, Rena Fox's body was discovered curled up in a fetal position, her long black hair fanned out around her, on an infrequently travelled road in

Kakabeka Falls just outside Thunder Bay. The Ontario Provincial Police have not officially classified her death as a murder, but her family says on the night of her death she called a friend from a bar, asking her to come pick her up because it was nearly closing time and she felt uneasy. But her friend was late. By the time she got to the bar, Rena was gone. Rena's daughter, Bryanne Machimity, was only thirteen years old when her mom died. As an adult, she said she repeatedly called police to see if there was any new information in her mother's case. She said her calls were never returned.[18]

The communication issues with police have existed for years in Thunder Bay and throughout Northwestern Ontario. The uneasy relationship goes back decades, back to when the police helped to scoop up kids to send them to residential school, and continues to this very day.

ONE WEEK AFTER JETHRO'S disappearance, Dora got a call asking her to come down to Dennis Franklin. Police had set up a command post in the school parking lot. They had found a pair of black lace-up boots by the shoreline and wanted Dora to see if they were Jethro's. She left her house immediately.

When she arrived at the command post, her heart was racing. Police showed her the boots. They weren't Jethro's. They asked if she was sure: the boots were found, tied together, down by the river. She said she was certain and then left, thinking that maybe her nephew was still out there.

About a week later, someone from DFC phoned Dora and asked her to come down to the school again. Once again, she steeled her nerves. She remembered walking into a room full of people. There was one, maybe two officers. She had no idea who the others in the room were, but figured they were with the school. She made a beeline for the brown paper bag the police had. Inside was a black cap with the brand FUBU written across it in giant letters.

She knew right away it was Jethro's.

Police asked her if she was certain. They told her that this type of cap was sold in lots of sports stores around town. Everybody had one.

She told them again, without a doubt, that the hat was Jethro's.

She closed the paper bag and pushed it away.

Then she ran out the door.

DORA WAS A MESS when she got in her van. Her mind was racing. She was hysterical and spilling tears of anger.

She started to drive. But this time, she wasn't combing the streets looking for Jethro. This time, she drove to the highway, put her foot on the gas, and headed straight out of town.

She went north, toward Gull Bay, and was gone for three hours, maybe more, crying her heart out. When she arrived back in the city, she went straight to see Ron Kanutski, her son's counsellor.

When she got to his office, she saw he was on the phone. He looked up, startled. He was trying to phone her.

He asked Dora if it was her nephew Jethro that was

missing. He had just read about it in the newspaper, which was open on his desk.

Dora cried. She told Ron everything. She told him what had happened, how she had been looking for Jethro, how his hat had been found. She said no one had believed her when he first went missing. She begged Ron to help. She wanted him to get the police to start dragging the river.

She had a feeling. She knew that Jethro was in the water.

EVER SINCE ADRIENNE'S FRIEND told Dora about the spot by the river where the kids went to drink, she had been drawn to the water. She would drive to that particular place every day, scanning, searching, and wondering. One day, about a week after he was gone, a feeling washed over her while she was driving around. She just knew Jethro was in the river.

She remembered how Jethro hated having a bath when he was a young boy. At the time they were living at Big Trout, near Kasabonika, and Jethro had come to stay with her and Tom and the kids. He was just eight years old.

Her house was full of her little ones, all under the age of ten. She remembered being in the bathroom with Jethro. She drew the warm water and spoke to him while helping him remove the clothes from his spindly little body. She remembered he stood there, shaking uncontrollably. He was afraid of the water.

She drove home in a fury and blew in like a storm, telling the kids that it was time to go fishing. She went running through the house, getting their rods, jackets, and boots.

Startled, the kids asked why they were going fishing. She told them she thought Jethro was in the river.

The kids got upset. She stopped, realized what she was doing, what she was saying, then put the rods away.

But every day after, she would go down to the river, sometimes twice a day. She would park her car and scan the rushing water. Maybe he had dropped something, a clue, something only she would recognize.

But every day, nothing.

IT IS NOT EASY to drag a river. And the Kam is a cold, swift snake. Boats with large poles attached to hooks motor oh so slowly on the water, fighting its force.

On Friday, November 10, a team from Kasabonika was organized to search the river and police came with their boats.

Dora went down to the Kam the next morning, Saturday, November 11, Remembrance Day. She spoke to some of the Indigenous searchers, who told her they were coming up empty. The river was cold and unforgiving, and they were thinking about stopping for the day.

She begged them not to. She had a feeling. She asked them to persevere and finish out the day.

As the police and the search team continued to scour the water, Dora went home and waited. In the early evening, someone from DFC asked her to come down to the auditorium for an emergency meeting.

She told her children she was going down to the school, that there was a break in the case. Elation broke out among the children. They thought Jethro had been found. Their cousin was coming home. But Dora knew better. She told them to stay home and wait. She muted their excitement, told them not to get their hopes up.

Dora remembers heading to the DFC auditorium and walking through the big steel doors. The gym was packed. Students, searchers, community members, family, everyone was there.

Dora can't remember who broke the news. She just remembers the gym erupting into chaos. The crying, the moaning, the screaming swirled around her.

Jethro's body had been recovered from the river.

IT IS IMPORTANT TO know this: Dora never received a call from the Thunder Bay Police informing her that Jethro's body had been found.

Dora had filed the missing persons report. She had called the force multiple times, asking to speak to someone, wondering if they had any leads. She had begged them to get in the fishing boat, get out the long hooks, and drag the bottom of the river.

She was never given the common courtesy of a phone call. Not from Thunder Bay Police or the Thunder Bay coroner's office, who retrieved the body from the funeral home and performed the autopsy.

Instead, this is what Dora saw — a press release from the Thunder Bay Police that went out on Saturday, November 11:

Thunder Bay Police detectives are investigating the discovery of a body in the Kaministiquia River late this afternoon.

The body was discovered by a group of searchers, who were dragging the river looking for a missing Kasibonka [*sic*] Lake First Nation's youth. Jethro Anderson was reported missing on October 29th by relatives. The searchers discovered the body around 5:15 p.m. Although a positive identification of the body has not been completed, the physical description and clothing are similar to that of the missing 15-year-old.

Members of the Thunder Bay Police Criminal Investigation Branch, Scenes of Crime Unit and Uniform Patrol Branch were at the scene. Thunder Bay Fire Service helped in the retrieval of the body from the river. Searchers found the body about 250 metres south of the restored James Whalen Tug near the Kaministiquia River Heritage Park. They were dragging the river in about 20 feet of water 4 feet from the riverside walkway.

At this point foul play is not suspected but a postmortem will be conducted tomorrow morning to try to determine a cause of death.[19]

Police immediately came to the conclusion that foul play was not a factor, that Jethro went into the river of his own accord, in late October, when the warmth of the northern sun slips into below-zero blackness at night.

Dora was livid. There was no way her Jethro went into the water voluntarily or tripped and fell in.

She called the police afterwards. She spoke to the chief,

demanding to see the autopsy report. She was refused and was told only the parents could get access to that information. She would have to ask her brother or Stella.

When Jethro's body was released to the funeral home, she drove there with Jethro's other aunt, Seloma Anderson, and demanded that the funeral director show them Jethro's body. They wanted to see him for themselves.

The funeral director refused, telling them the body was not something any relative should see, that it was going to be a closed-casket service. Bodies change after they have been in the water. They would not recognize Jethro.

Dora was defiant. "I told him I wasn't leaving."

The funeral director relented.

She took a few minutes to compose herself before he brought them inside and opened the casket.

Dora remembers looking at Jethro and thinking that he didn't look as bad as the director had made out. But when she looked more closely, she saw a three-inch-wide gash, starting from the top of his forehead and ending at the middle of his head. There were round contusions on his cheek. She immediately thought it looked like someone had extinguished their burning cigarette butts on his face.

She checked his tummy. It wasn't bloated. She looked at his hands, which weren't purple or blown up with water.

Dora took in a sharp breath. She knew she was right: This was no accident.

TWO YEARS LATER, NATHAN MORRIS was at a bar called Sunny's in Thunder Bay.

He was having a drink when a woman named Melissa approached him. She told Nathan that a guy at the bar kept talking about Jethro and how sorry he was about what he had done.

Nathan asked Melissa to take him to the man. They walked outside the bar, where they found the man crying. Nathan asked him what he had said to Melissa.

He said, "I am sorry I kill—I am sorry what I did to your cousin."

Nathan was stunned.

Two men walked toward them. One had a goatee and all three were Indigenous. They told the man it was time to go and they took him away.

Nathan did not tell Thunder Bay Police what had happened until nearly ten years later, when the Ontario Provincial Police questioned him before the start of the inquest into the seven students' deaths.

At the inquest, Nathan told Thunder Bay Police lawyer Brian Gover why he hadn't told the police what the man had said: "No, I didn't tell them, 'cause I don't trust the Thunder Bay Police."

NONE OF THE TEACHERS at DFC or the educators at NNEC could ever have foreseen that a student would go missing and die within the first month of operation at the school. Norma Kejick remembers the confusion the teachers felt when Jethro was first reported missing.

"We never had missing students at Sioux Lookout or Pelican. When Jethro went missing, that was a first. We never thought he wouldn't come home. We always thought we would find him," she says.

In hindsight, she realizes how naive they all were.

In January 2001, the NNEC board of directors asked for an operational report of the two high schools. Educator Bob Pearce, who had thirty-three years of experience as a teacher and guidance counsellor and then later as a Ministry of Education supervisory officer, was put in charge of the task. He conducted one hundred interviews and sent out 190 questionnaires. He submitted his report in May 2001, saying he realized the report had been done quickly, under time constraints, so his recommendations should not be taken as absolutes, more as suggestions worthy of consideration. Chief among his findings: It was advisable to turn Pelican into a school strictly for grades nine and ten. Once the students matured and were able to gain fourteen credits and pass a literacy test, they should be sent to Dennis Franklin, which should operate as a school for grades eleven and twelve only.

"It is extremely difficult for students who come from a northern reserve to go immediately into an urban environment. Students often come with a number of social and academic problems and are soon overwhelmed. Appropriate specialized counselling should be provided to address drugs, alcohol, suicide prevention and a host of other social issues," he wrote.[20]

Also in 2001, another report, this time by Garnet Angeconeb, was commissioned to perform an organizational review of the NNEC operation for the NNEC leadership and for NAN. Alvin Fiddler had called Angeconeb, telling him they were concerned about the all-around health and well-being of the students. Angeconeb, who submitted his report in July 2001, had come to similar conclusions as Pearce, echoing his warnings: "It is with a strong sense of hope that the issues facing the students will be 'nipped in the bud' before more damage is done. If haphazard effects are made to heal the situation it is likely these young people will live with long lasting effects into adulthood. Such negative scenarios of the future must be averted at all costs."[21]

Over the course of the next decade, Bob Pearce and Garnet Angeconeb's words would prove to be prophetic.

HURTING FROM THE BEFORE

IN NOVEMBER 2004, CANADA'S AUDITOR GENERAL SHEILA Fraser blasted INAC again for wasting money while producing no results. She concluded that INAC "made limited progress" in addressing any of their concerns: "The Department does not know whether funding to First Nations is sufficient to meet the education standards it has set and whether the results achieved are in line with the resources provided."

Fraser also pointed out that INAC was spending about $1 billion a year with few tangible results. In fact, it seemed like the department had set back progress in education in First Nations communities: "We remain concerned that a significant education gap exists between First Nations people living on reserves and the Canadian population as a whole and that the time estimated to close this gap has increased slightly, from about 27 to 28 years."[1]

That same month, a 176-page report written by Jerry

Paquette, entitled "Support, Safety and Responsibility: A Review of the Secondary Student Support Program of the NNEC," landed with a thud on the desks of the leadership at NNEC. A former teacher and principal turned educational consultant with the province of Ontario, and professor emeritus at the University of Western Ontario, Paquette was the third consultant brought in to do a review of the school program since 2000. Paquette studied the system for nearly a year, interviewing NNEC students, teachers, and board members. In the end, his conclusions were both damning and passionate, and he made eighty-one sweeping recommendations. He told the education directors that he could have written a more tepid report, but it wouldn't have been honest and wouldn't have let him "sleep well given the profound problems with the (program) that I have come to know with great intimacy."[2] He decried the community's lack of participation — he had travelled to First Nations north of Sioux Lookout to hold community consultations but hardly anyone had come. In Sandy Lake, no one showed up. In other places, some parents told him the NNEC never communicated with them — staff didn't return phone calls and it was unclear to them who was responsible for what and whom. When the parents did have something to say, they felt ignored, and in some cases, parents weren't notified when their kids went missing.

Paquette knew his findings would spark controversy, but he felt he had to write what he had seen and that fundamental change was needed in the way the NNEC "supports" its students. Right now, he said, all they were doing was mirroring the worst practices of "total institutions," and while some good was happening, the support given to students was completely at odds with the fundamental principles of Indigenous approaches to justice and social and communal welfare.[3]

In many respects, Paquette's report echoed the report filed in 2001 by Bob Pearce. Both strongly urged that Pelican turn into a school for grades nine and ten, and that when the kids proved they were ready, they should move on to DFC in Thunder Bay for the senior grades and post-secondary prep courses. Paquette wanted to see a residence built for the senior students at DFC within two years, and he demanded that the rules around boarding parents be tightened and beefed up. He wanted boarding homes categorized into a three-level graduated system. Level one homes would be hands-on, stricter with set rules and aimed at younger students who needed more support. Level two homes would be a bridge between level one and the more relaxed level three category that would be ideal for more independent, older students who could handle more freedom.

Paquette believed wholeheartedly in the need for First Nations to be in control of their own education, but he wanted to see a "joint arbitration style board" put in place until the NNEC implemented the eighty-one recommended changes and could turn things around. To his critics, he denied he was a "sell out" to his beliefs and said it didn't matter if it was INAC or a First Nations body funding or controlling the system — these recommendations would still stand.

"More of the same is just not good enough," he wrote.[4]

He warned that if change didn't come, it would be at the students' peril.

BY THE EARLY 2000S, First Nations in Northern Ontario were in deep crisis. Waves of suicide were sweeping across the communities. The epidemic caught like wildfire, starting in one community then spreading with vicious ferocity to a neighbouring First Nation, then to another, and another. Children as young as ten years old were killing themselves, along with teenagers and young adults. Parents were coming home to find their sons or daughters hanging in their rooms or from the trees outside their homes. In almost every case, youth took their life with a noose. Everyone was profoundly disturbed by these acts of sheer desperation. Hope seeped out of the communities, along with the young spirits that chose to leave this life.

Northern Ontario Indigenous communities had battled the plague of suicide since the end of the residential school era in the 1990s. Indigenous leaders did not know what to make of it. It was almost unheard of. In traditional Indigenous culture, it was rare for people to take their own lives — and it was especially rare for children to do so.

From 1986 to 2016, there have been more than five hundred suicides in the Nishnawbe Aski Nation territory alone. A staggering seventy of those suicides were of children between the ages of ten and fourteen and more than two hundred were youth between the ages of fifteen and twenty.[5]

In the early 1990s, NAN chiefs called a state of emergency. No one knew what to do but they knew something had to change. A huge part of the problem is that there are scarcely any mental health and medical services available in the northern communities and the services in northern hub cities, such as Sioux Lookout, Timmins, and Thunder Bay, are overloaded — not to mention hundreds of kilometres away. Indigenous communities have little control of how health dollars are spent and on what programs. Funding health care is the job of the federal government. Indigenous leaders worked with them and the province of Ontario (provinces deliver health care) to provide emergency measures, which included flying in mental health care workers. But these experts would leave once the immediate crisis was over. Similarly, mental health care programs would be started only to soon end due to lack of funding or a change in programs.

In 1996, a report on suicide by the Royal Commission on Aboriginal Peoples found that there were four key contributors to suicide among Indigenous populations: mental illness, anxiety, schizophrenia, and unresolved grief.[6]

The reports and studies on youth suicide seem endless. But it is important to remember that behind every statistic is a child. From November 29 to December 9, 1999, a coroner's inquest was held to look into the death of Selena Sakanee, fifteen, from Neskantaga First Nation. When she was six months old, Selena's father died in a house fire. She had a turbulent life fuelled by alcohol addiction and solvent sniffing. She was found hanging on November 23, 1997. The inquest resulted in forty-one recommendations to stem the crisis. The last recommendation was particularly poignant: "The governments of Canada and Ontario should recognize that the Nishnawbe Aski Nation suicide epidemic is a social crisis of immense proportions. This sad and tragic phenomenon has affected every family and community in NAN and should be addressed."[7] Few of the recommendations were acted on.

Since Pelican Falls High School first opened in 2000, it has lost seven students to suicide — eerily, the same number of students to have died in Thunder Bay from 2000 to 2011. Norma Kejick, who was principal at Wahsa until 2010 before becoming NNEC's education director then executive director, says that suicide has become so normal it is almost seen as part of everyday life.

"You expect it to happen now," she says. "It seems to hit every community. Every week you hear of another suicide. It is now just like another day."

All the staff have been to conferences and have received training on how to deal with suicide, but she feels that most of them probably have post-traumatic stress disorder.

She says trying to get the teachers or anyone to talk about the seven deaths at Pelican is not easy. Pelican, she says, is like a small reserve. There are nearly 180 kids enrolled in a school with few resources and living in a community with little for them to do. The students arrive broken, grappling with sexual abuse and drug addictions.

"They don't come to us and then all of a sudden get traumatized here. They bring that baggage with them. Then it comes out here because now they have a place to talk," she says.

Norma remembers being at the funeral parlour in Sioux Lookout one weekend. The funeral director said that when he was in training, he was told that the average person will lose seven people in their lifetime.

"He said to me, 'Norma, I see you every week in this

funeral home. You are either related to half of them or the other half are your kids,'" she says with a sigh. "He is right."

Then, one night, the phone rang. Her middle son, Jonathan, was calling from his boarding home in Thunder Bay. He was a student at DFC. He was wildly upset and said he was having suicidal thoughts. Norma was at home in Lac Seul, a five-hour drive away from him. Alarmed, she called her son's counsellor at DFC to tell her that her son was in crisis and that the counsellor needed to get over to Jonathan's residence right away to check on him. The counsellor told Norma off. "I have a life too, you know," she remembers her saying. She was stunned and didn't sleep at all that night. The next morning, she drove to Thunder Bay and pulled her son out of Dennis Franklin. She brought him home to Lac Seul, where he could live at home and go to Pelican Falls.

Norma and her son survived that crisis and he is now doing well. But it was the suicide of her nephew Eric, on March 27, 2005, that left a mark on her. Eric was twenty-two and a student at Dennis Franklin. A star athlete, he hung himself wearing his DFC Most Valuable Player volleyball jacket.

"He was so proud of that jacket. That was not the jacket that he was wearing when he left my house [that day], but he went home and he put it on and that is what he was wearing when his mom found him," she says.

It had been Easter. Eric's mother Doreen, Norma's sister-in-law, was peeling potatoes in the kitchen for their holiday dinner. Eric kept bugging her. He wanted to talk.

He had just had an argument with his sister. Doreen kept peeling potatoes and told him to go outside to the shed, calm down, and have a cigarette. She would be outside in five minutes. Five minutes later, Doreen walked out to the shed and found her son hanging.

Norma had breastfed Eric. Her son Clinton and Eric were only two months apart. Norma would nurse Eric when Doreen headed to Sioux Lookout to grab groceries.

"She would do the same for me," says Norma.

At high school, Clinton and Eric were always together. They were like brothers and Eric was always at his aunt's house. Eric's suicide was a blow to Norma and to Clinton.

"I never dreamed he had problems. He seemed very happy and popular. At DFC he was so proud of his volleyball. His name is up on a banner for winning the championship two years in a row. He loved to sing, play guitar, write music," she says. "My sister-in-law blamed herself for wanting to peel her damn potatoes. She blamed herself for a long time. For me, I'm the educator of the family. I am a principal. I have had so much suicide training. Why didn't I see the signs? I blamed myself. I should have, I should have..."

IN 2004, THE OFFICE of the Chief Coroner for Ontario began tracking suicide epidemics in First Nations communities. Their statistics showed that 23.5 percent of Ontario's Indigenous suicides occurred in Pikangikum First Nation, a devout Christian, Ojibwe, and NAN community with one of the world's highest suicide rates. And for reasons still largely unknown to health professionals, the youth suicides happened in clusters. Groups of three to five kids living in the same community would take their own lives within weeks or months of each other, thus driving up the rates. Pik has lost at least 100 of its 2,100 members over a twenty-year period.[8] The yards at Pik are full of white crosses. It is an old Pik tradition to bury your dead in your front yard. The practice was started after the Elders said the children could not be buried in the cemetery because they had taken their own lives, which was seen as an act against God. Some houses have full graveyards in the front yard, so families have had to start burying their dead in the back.

In the early 2000s, Pik was reeling. Its children were sniffing gas, glue, and a host of other inhalants, causing irreparable brain damage. There was no clean water and no work. The extreme hopelessness and poverty had brought on a suicide epidemic that was devastating this small, isolated community.

At the time, it seemed Ottawa was more interested in offering aid to other countries in crisis. In the final days of 2004, the Earth's crust broke apart and shifted deep inside the Indian Ocean off the coast of Sumatra, Indonesia. The shock was violent: an undersea megathrust, in geological terms, of sheer force caused the Indian tectonic plate to be subducted, or pushed and pulled, by the Burma plate. Cascades of salty water from the Indian Ocean rose up, creating tsunami after tsunami with massive waves that relentlessly hammered the shores of 14 countries killing more than 230,000 people.[9]

As the new year turned, the might of water would leave

its soak on 2005, dominating the year. On the second day of January, Canada's sitting prime minister, Paul Martin Jr., a lawyer and shipping tycoon and the owner of the prosperous Canada Steamship Lines, sent Canada's Disaster Assistance Response Team (DART) to Sri Lanka to provide fresh water to displaced survivors. They brought food and sent doctors to perform emergency health care. DART is internationally known for sending rapid, mobile response to disaster areas all over the world. Up to two hundred Canadian Forces can be deployed at a moment's notice. The team is able to produce up to fifty thousand litres of clean water a day and repair any infrastructure.[10]

The people of Pikangikum had something in common with those in Sri Lanka. Both did not have access to clean drinking water. But Sri Lanka was getting relief from the Government of Canada. Pik was not. Over the course of its time stationed in an old Sri Lankan sugar factory, DART would treat 7,620 patients and supply 3.5 million litres of clean drinking water.[11]

Pikangikum First Nation sits on about 4,470 acres in the far northwestern reaches of Ontario, near the Manitoba border, about 300 kilometres northeast of Winnipeg. The name Pikangikum comes from the Ojibwe word *biikanjikamiing*, which describes the movement of the Berens River as it flows into Pikangikum Lake and out the other side. The Berens River is named after the first chief of Pikangikum.[12]

The First Nation is surrounded by some of the most pristine boreal forest in the world. Towering black spruce trees, Jack pines, and trembling aspens border the reserve.[13]

Pikangikum's soaring fir and cedar trees are part of a forest known as "the lungs of the Earth," trapping all the southern urban centres' carbon emissions. Without the actions of the boreal forest, which covers 50 million hectares in Ontario, it is estimated the temperature of the Earth would increase dramatically.

Pikangikum is one of the largest settlements of Ojibwe people in the north and everyone clings to the old way of life while desperately trying to navigate their way in the southern world. The traditional language retention rate among the population is remarkable at nearly 100 percent. In their first year of school, children arrive speaking Ojibwe. English is a second language.

Yet Pik lacks the basic necessities of life.

In 2005, there were roughly 450 homes; of those homes, 340 did not have running water or proper sewage systems. The tap water was contaminated and most kitchens were built without sinks. People collected water from a communal standpipe, hauling it back to their homes in buckets. They drank bottled water, showered and bathed in contaminated water, and most used outhouses — a small wooden shack with a deep hole in the ground. Once the hole was full, you just picked up and moved your shack to another location.[14]

Only the schools and band office had plumbing, and just forty homes were connected to a sewage lagoon. In 2005, the reserve was not connected to the power grid but was powered by a diesel generator that would often die due to overcapacity, most often in the winter, when temperatures plummeted to minus forty degrees Celsius.

Inadequate power supplies meant water couldn't be puri-
fied; pumps couldn't run.

Most of the houses are old and crumbling or they are
trucked-in, prefabricated buildings that are ill-equipped
for such a harsh climate. The dwellings are small and families are crammed in, often sharing one bedroom with
their extended family and grandparents.

Intergenerational trauma from the residential school
experience is entrenched in Pikangikum. One hundred
years of social exclusion, racism, and colonialism has
manifested as addiction, physical abuse, sexual abuse, and
lack of knowledge on how to parent a child. Few of the
kids discuss the sexual abuse they've suffered, yet more
than 80 percent of the children and youth in Indigenous
residential treatment centres come from homes where they
were sexually abused.[15]

The list of horrors some of Pik's kids face at home is
endless. And in 2005 there was nowhere for them to go to
escape the onslaught. There was no well-equipped community centre. No gymnasium, library, or movie theatre.
There was no McDonald's or local shopping mall and there
still isn't.

To cope with the abuse and the despair, the kids began
sniffing gasoline to get high, to self-medicate and escape
the stress and violence at home. A remarkable 27 percent
of grade three and four girls in Pik said they sniffed gasoline.[16] Many had parents who were addicts themselves,
either sniffers or alcoholics.

But the solvents leave lasting brain damage on young
users. A former principal of the Eenchokay Birchstick

School in Pikangikum told the *Canadian Medical Association Journal* that there were fifth-grade children who were "extremely intellectually challenged because they have done so much damage to their brains. It doesn't go away when you stop."[17]

Chemicals found in solvents, aerosol sprays, and gases can produce a variety of effects. Sniffing can give a rapid high that resembles alcohol intoxication. It produces serious excitation followed by drowsiness, disinhibition, light-headedness, and agitation. If you sniff enough of it, it can produce an anaesthetizing effect. You no longer feel anything and eventually you pass out, unconscious.[18]

The after-effects are just as daunting. They can make you belligerent, apathetic, and can impair functioning at school or in social situations. Vomiting is a common side effect, along with slurred speech, dizziness, and muscle weakness. Sniffing also produces long-term side effects — besides brain damage, it can kill your organs.

PIK SENDS ALL ITS high-school-age youth to DFC, and in early September 2005, eighteen-year-old Curran Strang travelled the five hundred kilometres to Thunder Bay to attend Dennis Franklin Cromarty. He had been a student there since 2003 and he had not had an easy time. He was struggling to finish courses for grades nine and ten, and so he was older than most of the other students who were starting their secondary school education, an age difference so vast during those teenage years. But he fit in well with the younger students due to his youthful smile and friendly demeanour.

He had not had the best elementary school education. The school he had attended back home was overcrowded and teachers would come and go, in and out of the community, burned out by stress, poverty, and the out-of-control children who sniffed gasoline. A high volume of teachers left, not knowing how to cope with the despair. The kids suffered the consequences, their lives a constant cycle of trauma and interruption. As a result, on average, Pik students arrived at DFC about three years behind other students.

The kids from Pikangikum stuck together. They were a quiet group, separate from the rest, partly because many spoke Ojibwe and struggled to learn English. Often, the kids from Pik would ask student James Benson and his friends for help translating when they went out shopping or at the convenience store.

An outgoing and thoughtful kid, James was from Weagamow First Nation, another remote, isolated community, high in the hinterland north of Sioux Lookout. He was on the student council and was a practicing Christian. He didn't drink or party and was actively involved at school.

James could see that Curran didn't speak much and figured it was because his grasp of English was not very strong. But when Curran did speak, he made you feel important. Curran was about five foot seven. He liked wearing baggy pants that hung low in the crotch and he had blond streaks in his dark brown hair. He was social, liked to talk to the girls and joke around, and stood out in the crowd with his wide smile.

The two boys eventually became friends. James and Curran, whose family was devout, bonded over their common religion. James, who was part of a Christian youth group, often took Curran to an all-gospel church on Sundays. Curran loved to sing soulful gospel songs in Ojibwe and everyone would gather around to listen to him.

"'My Jesus, I Love Thee,'" says James. "That one song in particular, he sang it so beautifully."

James knew Curran had never been to the city before and how hard it was for him, and many other students, to adjust to the culture shock, especially the racism. All the students at DFC experienced some form of racism every day. They were often treated by non-Indigenous people like outcasts and with great suspicion.

"We would get egged by white kids," James says. "People would yell out of passing cars, 'Go back home! Go back to your land!'" he recalls. "Meanwhile, this is our land."

An undercurrent of racism runs through Thunder Bay society. It can be subtle and insidious but it can also be in your face. Ask any Indigenous high school students in Thunder Bay if they have experienced racism and they'll undoubtedly tell you about racial slurs and garbage or rotten eggs being thrown at them from passing cars. Others have been hit on the back of the head with beer bottles by unknown groups of assailants, who leave them bleeding on the side of the road. One racial slur they often hear is "bogans," a term used by the whites on Indigenous people in Thunder Bay.

Indigenous people have learned to silently put up with the abuse. When they complain to police, they are often not taken seriously or their claims are ignored. At the time of the writing of this book, the entire Thunder Bay Police Service's handling of all Indigenous murder and disappearance cases was under investigation by the Office of the Independent Police Review Director (OIPRD), a provincial civilian watchdog body that operates at arm's length from the Attorney General's office. Also under investigation is the Thunder Bay Police Services Board, by the Ontario Civilian Police Commission, for its failure to effectively supervise the police.

BY 2005, DFC WAS well aware of challenges students faced. Since it first opened its doors in 2000, the high school had been teaching students who came to them well behind provincial standards. Dennis Franklin was prepared for this challenge, offering extra teaching support, smaller classes, and courses tailored to each student's needs as much as possible. The teachers knew they were also acting as pseudo-parents, so they always tried to reach out and get to know the kids.

But the resources DFC students needed inside the classroom were dwarfed by the resources they needed outside the classroom. Many of the students found themselves alone, dealing with whatever trauma they brought with them when they arrived. They could head out into the city and let off steam or medicate their grief without anyone really watching. The school lost twenty to thirty students a year due to severe homesickness or risky behaviour.[19] Some of the kids just couldn't cope. They would beg to go home or refuse to abide by school rules in order to get sent back.

Sending kids back was never an easy option. DFC teacher, and later principal, Jonathan Kakegamic worried about what he was sending troubled kids back to and whether they'd have the support they would need to survive whatever it was their home community was going through, be it addictions, self-harm, or psychological trauma.

Five years after Jethro Anderson's death, the school was well versed in dangerous behaviour — blowing curfew, drinking in the streets or in parking lots, partying down by the river. The guidance counsellors were charged with filling out an occurrence report if a student was caught breaking the rules. The more occurrences that piled up in a student's file, the more likely that student was to be kicked out of school and sent home.

The school, along with NNEC, set up a system of night watchers, employees who were on call twenty-four hours a day. At night, the watchers would head out in vans, slowly driving the streets, looking for their wayward kids.

Jonathan Kakegamic routinely slept with his pager beside his bed. Despite how tall some of the students were or tough they looked, he knew he was dealing with teenagers and he was the head parent. The kids were vulnerable, far away from their parents, their siblings, their extended families, and living alone in the big city for the very first time in their lives. And even though he had kids of his own, Jonathan had students boarding at his house. One of those students was Paul Panacheese, about whom we'll learn more later.

Many of the kids lived in boarding houses with people who were paid to look after them. Some of the

DFC kids — like Jethro who'd lived with his aunt Dora, his uncle Tom, and his three cousins — were extremely lucky. But most kids had no family in Thunder Bay, so they had to live with people they did not know and they had to get used to new family rules. Many students shared rooms with other kids, kids they were meeting for the first time.

Curran Strang felt the loneliness of living in a boarding house with boarding parents more than most. Soon he was struggling at school and he began hanging out with two wildly different crowds. He had his friends from Pik who he partied with, and then there was James and his friends. Eventually, one group gave way to the other. James could see that Curran was in trouble. He had a constant need to party, to get drunk, to get high. He may not have vocalized his pain to his teachers or counsellors, but you could see it in the pages and pages of police reports and school occurrence reports.

The first occurrence report was filed in 2003, when he was sixteen. Just two weeks after school started, he had been picked up by police for public intoxication and underage drinking. Police kept him in a holding cell overnight and let him out the next day with a $70 fine. Once a counsellor at NNEC filled out an occurrence report, the parents were notified.

Curran was also made to sign a "behaviour contract," in which he said he understood he had been given his first warning and that he realized he would be subject to disciplinary actions if he disobeyed his boarding house rules. He was grounded for one week and had to be home by 6:00 p.m. every night. In addition, he had to report to a school counsellor weekly, he couldn't use alcohol or drugs, and he had to attend all his classes that semester. He was also assigned a 250-word essay on the consequences of the over-consumption of alcohol.

Curran signed the contract on September 22. His penmanship was extraordinary, his letters round and strong with a hint of a flourish.

In exactly one month, Curran found himself in trouble again. He was drunk at school and his boarding parent, Patsy Cote, had to pick him up and bring him home where he could sober up. But shortly after they got home, he took off for the Intercity mall. Within a few hours, Curran called his boarding parent, apologized, and asked for a drive home.

He had to sign another behaviour contract. This time he was grounded for two weeks and again he had to abide by the 6:00 p.m. curfew. He was also given a 500-word essay and referred to an Elders program, a place where he could spend time with an older Indigenous community member. Elders were a key part of DFC. Administrators believed their presence could provide a solid foundation for kids who were struggling to adjust.

Both Curran and his father, Robert Strang, signed the behaviour contract.

Over the next two years, his file grew to contain nearly sixty pages of occurrence reports and behaviour contracts, each signed by Curran, by board counsellors, and by his father.

Each incident involved missing curfew and drinking. Students later said that Curran had a favourite spot to drink, down by the riverbank near the mall. It was a popular place for kids to hang out. They were often seen walking in gangs, by the water. Curran was often picked up by school officials on their nightly rounds looking for kids who were out past their curfew. They searched all the hotspots — the McDonald's, liquor store parking lots, the Brodie Street bus terminal.

Every time Curran was picked up, the routine was the same. He had to sign another behaviour contract and agree to go to class daily, abide by curfew, and avoid drinking.

The essay topics were particularly poignant, a foreshadowing of what would soon be lost:

· "Why my life and my future is important!"
· "My life."
· "The importance of an education."
· "My future."

BY OCTOBER 2004, A full year before Curran would be found dead, his education counsellor from NNEC, Tamara Day, made a notation in the file that Curran wanted to see someone about his problems. The counsellor wanted to send him for a suicide assessment.

On Friday, October 14, Day wrote: *Spoke to Curran today, feeling down, says he feels a little depressed, did not elaborate in what "a little depressed" means. He seemed very unusual today. "Cranky." Made sure he has my cell number and on-call.* The note also indicates that one of the teachers had come to the office to talk about Curran.

This teacher said some things to Day that concerned her.

Three days later, on Monday, October 17, Day spoke to Curran again. *He seems okay,* she wrote. *Says he is a little sad, asked to go home. Told him he must speak to his parents, get them to call me. Spoke to Curran's father today. Informed him of Curran's up and down times, informed him that Curran is seeing Lydia Big George. Made sure again that Curran has my cell phone number and on-call.*

Tamara then spoke to administrator Lydia Big George at NNEC's head office. Tamara told her that she would try to get Curran a suicide assessment test and see him the very next day.

Tamara talked to Curran a second time that Monday. He told her that he wanted to move. He was unhappy with his boarding roommate but he liked the boarding home. Tamara wrote: *He states that he feels bad for roommate because he sleeps downstairs, wants to have roommate move upstairs, I told him to voice his concerns to his B.P. [boarding parent].*

There is no further mention in Curran's education file of a suicide assessment.

In fact, the next issue in his file is an occurrence report dated November 10. Oddly, the occurrence report was about asking his father for money. Curran wanted a $100 cheque deposited into his account.

By the end of February, Curran was asking for help again. He told Tamara that he needed to talk to someone about some personal issues, but he felt uncomfortable talking to anyone on school property. Tamara filled out the forms so Curran could see someone associated with the Anishnawbe Mushkiki Aboriginal Health Access Centre. On the bottom of the February 25, 2005, referral form, Tamara wrote under the column for additional information or comments: *Best friend committed suicide approximately 1.5 years ago.* This was the first and only mention of Curran's best friend's suicide in any of the files brought forward during the inquest into his death.

For the next several months, Curran continued his downward spiral. On the last day of March, at 2:22 a.m., he was charged with two offences by Thunder Bay Police. The first was for consuming alcohol under the age of nineteen, for which he was given a $260 fine. The second was for being intoxicated in a public place. When Curran was arrested he was lying on the sidewalk of a residential street in Fort William. Both charges were under the Ontario Liquor Licence Act.

On April 7, 2005, Curran filed a court motion requesting to pay the fine at a later date, "due to being unemployed student with no income," his motion stated.

Curran filled out the forms himself. What is interesting is his signature. Gone were the happy, loopy, firm letters from two years ago. His handwriting slanted severely to the right and was barely legible.

Around the same time, Tamara Day organized a teleconference at NNEC with Curran's parents. It is unclear what the outcome of that teleconference was. There is no public record of notes on the meeting. There is also no mention of whether he followed up with counselling about his personal problems. But what is clear is that the occurrence reports continued to pile up.

At the end of April, he was found intoxicated, walking down Arthur Street alone at 1:50 a.m. The school tried to call his boarding parent but there was no answer. Then, at the beginning of May, Curran was picked up at the Brodie bus terminal, where he was found with a girl who was drinking. A note in Curran's file states that his boarding parent confirmed he was not drunk when he returned home at 12:45 a.m.

Also in May, he called the school because he thought someone was following him and his friend Chrissy. He was told to go to the Prince Arthur Hotel, where a Dennis Franklin staffer would pick him up.

He said there were three people/cannot describe them/ he said he felt scared because they were following him and the girls. He stated that they did not actually touch him/ just scared him so he called O.C. [on-call worker] *and O.C. called police as a precaution,* Tamara's note in the file states. *I reminded Curran that it was good for calling. But if he had followed curfew at 10:00 p.m. this would not have happened.*

Another occurrence report from the Dennis Franklin team dated May 13 noted they'd picked Curran up at the shoreline but they were unsure if he had been drinking.

At the end of July, Curran was picked up by police once again, this time near midnight, for public intoxication. He was held overnight.

Curran was clearly free-falling. The support system that was put in place to help guide him in Thunder Bay was powerless. It simply couldn't catch him. At this time — his seemingly most vulnerable time — Curran and a group of Pikangikum students were called home.

There had been two more suicides. This time it was his cousin and a friend.

AFTER THE FUNERALS CURRAN returned to Thunder Bay with the other students on Monday, September 19, and then, almost immediately, his behaviour went south. On Tuesday night, Curran was spotted by NNEC staff at 10:00 p.m. out drinking with other students in the Limbrick neighbourhood. Limbrick is a street full of small homes and a social housing complex. It is an area of the city that struggles with violence and often has an increased police presence.

On Wednesday morning, Donna Fraser, a NNEC student support worker, spoke to Curran at school about his drinking from the night before. She told him he was grounded for one week and she gave him a warning. She also asked him if he was doing okay, and according to her notes he told her he was fine. She then said she thought he should see someone, a counsellor, at Wiichiiwewin Wellness Services about what had just happened in Pikangikum. Curran went back to class and Donna tried to contact someone at Wiichiiwewin about Curran but everyone was busy. Her notes indicated she tried contacting Wiichiiwewin all day but was unsuccessful. She also tried to get hold of Curran's parents, Robert and Inez, in Pikangikum but she was told they were out of the community. Curran came back to see Donna later that day, asking if she had seen his friend Max King, that Max had a package for him. She didn't know where Max was so Curran left to find him.

The last time James Benson saw Curran was at the Intercity mall on Thursday, September 22. Curran asked him for money. James knew Curran was looking to buy some alcohol. He was with four or five girls, all from Pik. James refused to help. He could see Curran was having a hard time, but he did not want to enable his friend.

When Curran walked away from him, an ominous feeling washed over James. He knew in his heart that he would never see his friend alive again.

On Friday morning, Donna Fraser arrived at work to find an occurrence report on Curran. His boarding parent, Patsy Cote, had called in the night before at 10:30 p.m. to say that Curran had skipped curfew again. But this time, he never came home.

At 11:00 a.m., Patsy called Donna's cell phone to say she still had no idea where Curran was. She called the school and he wasn't in class. Donna drove to the school at lunchtime and assembled all the Pikangikum and Cat Lake kids in the boardroom to ask if anyone knew what had happened to Curran or where he was. Nobody answered. She told DFC principal Irene Linklater that Curran had not come home the night before. They called his name out over the school intercom. There was no response. Donna left the school, got in her car, and began to drive around the city, looking for Curran. If he wasn't found by 9:00 p.m., they would file a missing persons report with the police.

AS WITH JETHRO ANDERSON, no one really knows what happened to Curran before his body washed up in the

McIntyre River, near the underpass where he often drank.

Clarissa Fox, a boarding parent to one of Curran's friends, Adam Peters, testified at the inquest into the seven students' deaths that Adam came home late that Thursday night when Curran disappeared.

He was "very drunk and very dirty," Fox said. "I could tell something happened."

Adam had been with Curran and another student, Starla Strang. Adam told Fox that he and Curran got into an argument and that he and Starla left Curran, passed out, by a tree near the river. Then he went home.

Before school on Friday morning, Adam left his boarding home and raced down to the river where he and Starla had last seen Curran. Adam found his sweater and hat and Starla's purse, but there was no sign of Curran.

On Friday evening, Traci Lyons, an NNEC staff member, filed a missing persons report. Lyons was an intake worker and she was also the sister of Tamara Day, Curran's counsellor.

There were three errors on the missing persons report.[20]

The first was the date. The report said that Curran was last seen on Friday, September 23, at 5:30 p.m., but his boarding parent, Patsy Cote, last saw him at supper the day before — on Thursday, September 22. Time is of the essence in a missing persons case. If the date on the report is wrong, precious hours slip away.

The report also said the probable reason for Curran's disappearance was that he was a "runaway" and that he lived in a "foster home." Both of these statements were incorrect.

On the night of September 24, at 8:45 p.m., two days after Curran went missing, Thunder Bay Police started to work on his case. His friends had already been out looking for him. Norma Kejick had hopped in her truck and driven down from Sioux Lookout the moment she heard Curran was gone. James and some of the other students at DFC went searching for Curran. Adam Peters was calling the NNEC intake workers, asking if anyone had seen him. Starla Strang called Donna Fraser's cell phone at 10:15 p.m. to say she had been drinking with Curran and Adam the evening of the 22nd at the underpass, near the SilverCity movie theatre. She said Curran was "really intoxicated" and that they'd had to "cut him off the alcohol" and that he could barely stand. They got into an argument and Curran refused to leave their drinking spot. So she and Adam had left him there.[21]

Curran Strang's body was found in the McIntyre River on September 26, 2005. The Ontario Coroner's Office officially listed his death as accidental, having determined the cause of death was by drowning. Authorities believe he decided to head into the water, alone, on a cold September night. Just like Jethro Anderson, who was afraid of the water.

There is absolutely no evidence that either Jethro or Curran ended up in the river of their own accord.[22]

Did Curran and/or Jethro accidentally fall into the water and drown? Provincial drowning statistics indicate boys like Jethro and Curran are among the lowest age group to drown by accident. In 2005, the death rate by accidental drowning among this age group was 1.3 percent of 100,000, or 164 people. According to the Ontario Drowning Report, the vast majority of victims were men over the age of sixty-five. Those between the ages of fifteen and nineteen have one of the lowest water-related death rates, lower than those between the ages of twenty and twenty-four, twenty-five and twenty-nine, and even lower than children under four years old. The fact that Curran and Jethro were eighteen and fifteen respectively calls into question the theory that they both accidentally drowned.[23]

THE YEAR AFTER CURRAN died, Pikangikum spiralled into an unprecedented suicide epidemic. Between 2006 and 2008, sixteen children and teens between the ages of ten and nineteen took their own lives. On June 8, 2007, Pikangikum's only school — a refuge for kids that was described as cheery and bright with cutting-edge computers — burned to the ground. The school went from kindergarten to grade twelve and it was a community hub, hosting feasts and local gatherings. Losing the school threw the community into further despair.[24] Most of the youth who died were under the age of fifteen and almost all of them were gas sniffers. More than half of the kids had a parent or a brother or sister who had committed suicide.[25] In the month before each of their deaths, none of them got help from a doctor or another trained professional. All of them took their lives by hanging.[26]

- 5 -

THE HOLLOWNESS OF NOT
KNOWING

A LONG, GREY CLAY-AND-GRAVEL ROAD LEADS UP TO
Maryanne Panacheese's house on the Mishkeegogamang
First Nation. Maryanne's neighbourhood is made up of
scattered roads that are dotted with grey-and-cream-
coloured one-storey houses sitting on wide lots with muddy
driveways full of all-terrain vehicles and F-150 Ford trucks.
Mish is actually the joining of two reserves — the
bureaucratically named 63A and 63B. Founded in 1785 by
John Best, a Hudson's Bay Company employee, Mish was
originally a settlement that the colonials called Osnaburgh
after the local trading post at the base of the Albany River.
Best had been sent to establish a post deep in the heart of
First Nations territory. At the head of the Albany River, he
found a low, sandy point and decided to "stop here until
I see if any Indians come this way or not that can inform
me if this is the right place or not."[1]

The new settlement attracted many Indigenous families, who soon complained the goods they traded for were second-rate. Blankets had holes in them and the guns didn't work properly. Those traditional families are still here. They are the Panacheeses, the Loons, the Skunks, and the Masakeyashes. They still get the same $4 in annual treaty payouts that their ancestors did when they signed Treaty No. 9 back in 1905.[2]

In 1993, the Ojibwe First Nation changed the name back to Mishkeegogamang. Those who live here often refer to Mish as Oz, a poetic name for a place that is near the end of Highway 599, directly north of Ignace, a truck stop of a town located on the Trans-Canada Highway. The 599, a two-lane road with no shoulders, cell service, or gas stations, is the northernmost highway that is still maintained by provincial authorities. A three-hundred-kilometre-long weave through the Eastern and Central Time zones, the 599 flips in and out of the Thunder Bay and Kenora regions, with nothing but the occasional bald eagle flying overhead.

The land of Oz is not a very merry place and the streets are not paved with gold. Close to one thousand people live on the rez and many of them are young and unemployed. Mish residents have to leave if they want to find work, go to high school, seek medical attention, or shop at a grocery store. The poverty rate is high, with the unemployment rate at about 97 percent.[3] Those who don't own trucks travel everywhere by foot. Mish is actually a smattering of communities, spread out over the two reserves, connected by Highway 599. The main communities are Poplar

Hill, Bottle Heights, and Sandy Road. There is a smaller community about twenty-four kilometres south called Ten Houses, which now has more than ten houses. People walk long stretches of the highway to get from one community to the other. It is not uncommon to see a solitary figure or a gang of kids walking for miles down the road.

Water is everywhere in Mish and it is nowhere. The reserve is surrounded by large freshwater lakes and hundreds of streams, but on most days you can't drink a drop. The water smells like iron and magnesium. People have allergic reactions to it and their laundry turns yellow. Some houses are not built with sinks and tubs because the pipes can freeze and burst in the winter. As a result, there are homes with no indoor plumbing or running water. Some people use plastic slop pails as toilets.

On Maryanne's front lawn, there is a beat-up concrete stairway leading to nowhere. Broken plates, the motherboard of an old computer, and nails are among the debris that has settled into the gravel driveway. An old truck is parked out front. To the right of the front door is a small wooden deck with two wooden chairs. Inside the house, Maryanne is perched at the kitchen table. She likes to sit on her wooden chair, sipping coffee while gazing out the picture window. Black letters that say *Merry Christmas* are stuck on the window all year round, along with a few black stick-on jack-o'-lanterns. Maryanne watches the stray husky puppies jump at the pickup trucks cruising down the road.

This is a relatively new home for Maryanne. She moved back to Mish after her divorce from her abusive ex-husband, Joe, and after Paul died. In 2005, the year before Paul's death, Joe had removed all the mattresses from the house, put them on the front lawn, then set the house on fire. At the time, Joe was starting to lose his mind. He was removed from the community and hospitalized. Joe was diagnosed with Parkinson's disease and put into a long-term care facility in Thunder Bay. He never came back to Mish.

Poverty and overcrowded, substandard housing means fire is a constant threat in Mish. People rely on wood-burning stoves fashioned out of empty oil barrels and rigged up to chimneys to heat their houses during the punishingly long winter months. In the last thirty years, thirty people have died in house fires at Mish, a traumatizing number in a community this small.[4] The tragedy touched Maryanne on February 13, 2014, when her daughter-in-law Maxine lost her sister, Joyce Wassakeeysic; her two nieces, Serenity and Kiralynn; and her nephew, Nathan, in a horrific house fire. Maryanne said Joyce's home, which was heated by an old wood stove and a rusty chimney, often felt like an "ice box" in the winter. Mish's lone community fire fighter responded to the call within thirty minutes. But the truck was useless. It had been used the night before, responding to another house fire, and was later stored in an unheated garage.[5] The next day, the water inside the truck had frozen solid. Temperatures in Mish during the winter often hover in the minus-twenty-five-degree Celsius range.[6]

Paul's presence is still everywhere in Maryanne's home. It is full of pictures of Paul, the walls cataloguing his life from when he was a toddler to his teenage years. In one black-framed photograph with *Love...* painted on the glass, Paul is pictured sketching, a lead pencil in his right hand. He is looking intently at the camera over his black wire-framed glasses. There are other photos of him — as a giggling baby in a white ExerSaucer, as a pouting toddler sitting on a brown-and-white-plaid chair. Maryanne has framed his last DFC student card from 2006–2007 with his last school photograph — Paul handsome in a black long-sleeved T-shirt, his hair trimmed close to his skull, highlighting his delicate cheekbones and his long, fine nose.

Paul's art also hangs on the wall. Maryanne's favourite piece is a pencil drawing that resembles the famous scene from Michelangelo's *The Creation of Adam*, where the hand of God reaches for the hand of Adam. Beside Paul's drawing is the Lord's Prayer. There is also a framed blessing for this house.

If anyone knows grief it is Maryanne. Her sixty years on this planet have been full of hard living, untold sadness, and trauma that would wither lesser people. She has a quiet grace that wraps her in a shell of solitude. She laughs in an almost singsong, melodic whisper, her dark eyes showing sparks of light sprinkled over pools of sorrow.

When she was eight years old, Maryanne and her younger brother Georgie and their little sister Ruth were sent more than two thousand kilometres away to residential school in Brantford, Ontario. That children from an Anishinaabe background were sent south across the province to a residential school that was predominantly

Akwesasne — a Mohawk Nation and a completely different cultural group — shows the government's complete lack of regard for the diversity of Indigenous cultures. Maryanne remembers vividly the nearly one-week-long train ride from the north to southern Ontario, Georgie and Ruth crying the entire way. What made it harder was that the three of them were the only ones in the family of eleven siblings who were sent away, and all of them spoke Ojibwe. She remembers the first time the train pulled into Toronto's Union Station and seeing the tall buildings and the stately Royal York Hotel. She felt daunted and filled with fear. When they got off the train, the younger ones started to run around on the platform. It felt like they were waiting forever when a tall man in a dark suit approached them, introduced himself as Mr. Helen, and said he would be taking them to school.

Maryanne spent the next four years at the Mohawk Institute Indian Residential School, an Anglican-run school that opened in 1850 and closed more than a century later in 1969. Those long months at Mohawk were incredibly lonely and isolating. The children had no contact with anyone from home until the school year was over. There were no letters or packages from their family, and over the course of those four years Maryanne received only one phone call from her mother. Maryanne and her siblings felt alone and abandoned.

Once June rolled around, she knew she and her siblings would be going back home to Mish for the summer break. She had yearned for summer all year long. But on one of her visits home, after her first two years at Mohawk, something happened that would stay with her forever. Maryanne was ten years old when police officers came to the house looking for her older sister, Sarah. She remembers crying as they took her away. They said she was part of a gang of kids responsible for break-ins, so she was being taken away to "truancy" school in the south. The family had no idea what "truancy" school was — they were given no name or details as to where exactly she was going — but after she left, Sarah never really came home again and none of her eleven brothers or sisters knew what became of her. The details of Sarah's life are sketchy. After she finished school she led a nomadic life, completely disengaged from all those she had loved. She became a fleeting presence in their lives, travelling between Northern Ontario and the Vancouver Eastside by car, by train, or by hitchhiking along the Trans-Canada Corridor.

The loss of Sarah wounded Maryanne deeply. She has never let her sister's spirit go; she keeps her close and has spent much of her adult life wondering what happened to her. She has been searching since 1995, when Sarah was last seen by one of her friends in Thunder Bay. Sarah was forty-three then, and she is now one of the 1,181 Murdered and Missing Indigenous Women and Girls.

Maryanne is plagued by a recurring dream of her sister. In it, there is a white two-storey house with a porch out front. Maryanne doesn't know, but she thinks the house is outside Vancouver. Maryanne dreams she is walking toward the house and Sarah comes out the front door to meet her. But Sarah can never walk more than half-way down the path. Something stops her from going any further. Maryanne tells her sister that they have to go and that she needs to come with her, but Sarah says she can't leave the house, then turns around and goes back inside.

Maryanne has a secret fear that Sarah was a victim of notorious serial killer Robert Pickton, who is serving a life sentence in a British Columbia maximum-security prison after being convicted of second-degree murder in the cases of six Vancouver Downtown Eastside women: Sereena Abotsway, Mona Wilson, Andrea Joesbury, Georgina Papin, Marnie Frey, and Brenda Wolfe.[7] Another twenty murder charges were stayed to spare the families the stress and horror of a lengthy trial. Partial human remains, DNA, clumps of hair, clothes, and blood from thirty-three women were found by authorities on Pickton's pig farm. Pickton confessed to murdering forty-nine women.[8]

In 2015, Maryanne and her sister Vicky travelled to Pickton's farm after it had been demolished. She had to be there to see if she got a feeling that this was her sister's final resting place. They stood on the grounds and watched black crows flying overhead. Neither could really sense Sarah's spirit — it was hard to know whose death they were feeling among so much sorrow. The sisters also travelled to Vancouver's Downtown Eastside, a notorious strip rife with drugs and prostitution. Maryanne wasn't sure what she was looking for, but the closure she craved still eluded her.

"It's hard wondering where she is. Is she still alive out there or is she gone?" says Maryanne. "I just want to find my sister."

The Nishnawbe-Aski Police Service began searching for Sarah after the Ontario Provincial Police failed to pick up any leads. In 1996, a body was found in Oregon that was a near match to Sarah's physical description — right down to the scar on her forehead just below her hairline. The unknown woman's description and genetic information was stored in police computers. Eight years later, NAPS sergeant Jackie George unearthed information on the unknown woman, and in 2014 she went out west to investigate. Police also took a DNA sample from Maryanne and Sarah's ninety-one-year-old mother. But there was no match.

The tragedy in Mish sometimes knows no bounds. The pain of the murdered and missing isn't just Maryanne's — so many families in this community feel the same grief. There are eleven cases of murdered and missing people from Mish. Gone are Rena Fox, Sarah Skunk, Viola Panacheese, Paul Panacheese, Lena Lawson, Evelyn and Sophie Wasaykeesic, Jemima Mulholland, Thomas Lyons, Mariah Wesley, and Charnelle Masakeyash, whose body parts were found in a Mish doghouse and also spread out in a clearing off a forest path in spring 2016.

The families left behind feel helpless and voiceless, just like Maryanne. Most feel as if the investigations into the disappearances and deaths have been put on a shelf by investigators with no explanation whatsoever as to what has happened to their loved ones. But Maryanne is the only one plagued by living with the hollowness of not knowing what happened to her sister or to her beloved son.

AT THE START OF the 2006 school year, Maryanne left her two other children with relatives and rented a home in Thunder Bay so she could take care of Paul while he was at Dennis Franklin Cromarty High School. He had spent two years at Northern Eagle High School in Ear Falls, Ontario, but the school only went up to grade ten so he had to transfer to DFC. Northern Eagle, which had a residence program and took about fifty Indigenous students each year, was about to close down. The foundation was crumbling and by the end of the 2007 school year it would close permanently.

The decrepit state of Northern Eagle is not unlike other First Nations schools across Canada. Not every community has a school — Dr. Cindy Blackstock, Executive Director of the First Nations Child and Family Caring Society of Canada, a national non-profit agency that provides policy and professional development support to Indigenous kids, says fifty new schools are required across Canada — and those that do exist are often old, in desperate need of repair, and have a host of problems, including mouldy walls, mice, and even snake infestations. At one school in Manitoba, baby snakes were coming out of taps.[9] Besides the physical problems, most schools are without modern libraries, science or computer labs, music rooms, or gymnasiums. Each First Nations student has been consistently underfunded by the Government of Canada — receiving about $2,000 to $3,000 less than non-Indigenous kids — and statistics show that three out of every four Indigenous students drop out of high school.[10] There are no financial resources provided by INAC for basics such as teacher training, school principals, libraries, computer software, or the development of culturally appropriate curricula, Blackstock says in *Our Dreams Matter Too: First Nations Children's Rights, Lives and Education*, a report she wrote on behalf of the Shannen's Dream campaign. Shannen's Dream was one of the biggest youth-led children's rights campaigns in Canadian history, aimed at providing safe and comfortable schools for all First Nations kids, and presented to the United Nations Committee on the Rights of the Child on the occasion of Canada's third and fourth periodic review.

The situation is so bad that in 2009 the Parliamentary Budget Officer conducted a review of INAC's funding practices and policies at all First Nations schools across Canada and discovered that 49 percent of schools on reserves are in poor condition and that 803 schools will need to be replaced by 2030.[11]

This was the education system Paul Panacheese came from when, at seventeen years old, he first enrolled at Dennis Franklin Cromarty to begin courses in grade ten. Due to the substandard education system he came out of, he was years behind from the start. Besides the academic issues he faced, he had also been sent to a big city — one he was completely unfamiliar with — and he had been sent on his own without any family support. Over the course of the next three years, he lived in ten different boarding houses, with ten different sets of parents and ten different sets of rules. One home was above the Jade Express, a Chinese restaurant in Port Arthur. Half a dozen boys were crammed into the small apartment. The owners put padlocks on the fridge and cupboards. If the boys weren't home when meals were served, they went hungry. For teenage boys, growing kids with insatiable appetites, locking the food away was a particular type of cruelty.

Maryanne could hear the loneliness in Paul's voice when they spoke on the phone. A gentle soul from birth, Paul was extremely attached to his mom. He told Maryanne that he missed her cooking, her bannock, fresh fish, and moose meat. He would also complain about the racist episodes he experienced every day in the city. People often threw eggs at him from moving cars or would holler Hollywood-style Indian war cries or racist insults like "dirty Indian." Paul couldn't understand why someone would do that to someone they didn't know.

How, thought Maryanne, *do you explain racism to your child?*

"Ignore them," Maryanne would whisper into the phone. "This is their problem, it is not yours. Just don't retaliate. Ever. Let it be." Then she gave him the only defence a mother could give her son: she told him to turn the other cheek. "Just don't become racist yourself. Those racist attitudes will always be there. Don't be like them."

She told him she'd head to Thunder Bay that weekend so they could hang out. She'd rent a hotel room and they could go to the movies or go shopping. She missed her youngest son.

Paul was thrilled when Maryanne moved to Thunder Bay to be with him when he started school in September 2006. He told her he wanted to do well at school and eventually become a police officer, and that one day soon, she wouldn't have to take care of him anymore because he hoped to be graduating high school soon. In the months before he died, Paul was opening up to her even more. He confessed that sometimes he experimented with drugs — Percocet, ecstasy. He said he wasn't proud of it, but he did it sometimes to fit in with the other kids.

"You know sometimes when you don't want to do that?" Paul said to her. "I'm called goody two-shoes. Polite Paul Panacheese. The 'Three Ps.'"

He also told her how difficult it was for him after she and his father divorced. Maryanne and Joe had a lengthy, abusive marriage, and in the early 1990s, Maryanne fled to Sioux Lookout with their youngest children, Paul and his brother Gabriel. The other three kids, Mike, Jody, and Elijah, were all teenagers and stayed in Mish with family. Joe and Maryanne kept in contact. She went to counselling but he refused, saying there was nothing wrong with him. One weekend, he came to pick up his sons for a visit. He took them home to Mish but refused to bring them back. Maryanne was filled with despair and she began drinking. She felt like everyone in the community supported Joe and that she was out in the cold. She didn't return to Mish until 1995, when Paul was ten and Gabriel was twelve. Maryanne was clean and sober; she had gotten herself back together, but Joe had not. He was drinking, and the boys weren't being looked after — they were dirty, they didn't have proper clothes, and they were hungry. She decided to get a lawyer and sue Joe for custody. Joe didn't even try to resist.

"I got them back and they never left my side," she says.

Paul told Maryanne that he wanted her to take him to see his father, who was now living in a long-term-care hospital in Thunder Bay. Joe was only sixty-four but his Parkinson's had left him incapacitated and in need of hospitalization.

"I don't know what it was he wanted to talk to his dad about. All he said was, 'I need to talk to my dad about something'," she says.

She promised to take him but they never made it there. Instead, Paul called his father and the two spoke on the phone. Maryanne doesn't know what they spoke about, but it comforts her to know they had one last conversation before her son died a week later.

ON FRIDAY, NOVEMBER 10, 2006, Shawon Wavy went to Paul's house with a big group of guys to play poker, just like they always did on a Friday. Shawon was just back in Thunder Bay, where he was enrolled at Confederation College. He rented a room in a house directly across from Maryanne and Paul's house. It was the first time Shawon had been living in Thunder Bay since 2001. He had left the city less than a year after he lost his friend Jethro Anderson, who was the first DFC student to have died. Shawon had transferred to Pelican Falls in Sioux Lookout after his mother received a call from the hospital, where he had been admitted for broken ribs and intense bruising after being beaten by a group of about a dozen "white guys." He was kicked and shoved, and one of the men struck him across the back with a thick wooden stick. Shawon managed to get himself to a friend's house and the friend called the police. Instead of taking him to the hospital, the police took him to the station and he was put in a cell and held for questioning. After he told the police everything he could remember about the assault, they let him go. Shawon got himself to the hospital, where nurses contacted his mother. She immediately drove down from Mish to be by his side. A few days later, when he was released, she packed up her son and drove him home.

Paul and Shawon had been best friends in Mish. They used to race around in the bush together with their sling-shots, hunting for wild partridges. Paul was dependable and he had a gentle, easy manner. He never said a bad word about anyone.

Shawon remembers Paul was happy that night at the poker game. He was on a winning streak. When Shawon got tossed out of the game, he decided to split and catch up with Paul later. Paul and some of the guys talked about going to a party on James Street. Paul walked over to Shawon and shook his hand as he left. Then he gave Shawon a warm, wide smile. There were no hard feelings on the poker loss. They were brothers.

LATER THAT NIGHT, Paul went out briefly to visit some friends. Little is known about what he did and exactly who he encountered.

Maryanne was asleep when she heard Paul at the front door. She got out of bed and went downstairs to see if he was okay.

"I'm home now, Mom. I'm home," he said.

She turned around and went back upstairs to bed.

She heard him turn on the TV and rummage around the kitchen. He was hungry so he opened up a package of Mr. Noodles and put a pot of water on the stove. Then he ran upstairs, used the washroom, and headed back down.

She could hear him talking to someone on the phone as he moved around the kitchen stirring his soup with the TV on.

Then she heard a loud thud.

Maryanne hurried downstairs to find Paul face down on the kitchen floor. He was lying on his stomach and his arms were at his sides, his palms turned up. His head was between the sink and the stove. She knelt beside him and tried to wake him. She leaned down and said to him, "Paul, get up. Go to your bed or the couch to sleep."[12] She picked up his glasses, which had fallen to the floor, and tried to straighten his bent arms.

She remembers there was just a slight scent of alcohol on him.

"He was not drunk," she said.

She tried to find a pulse but couldn't. *No, it can't be*, she kept saying over and over again in her mind.

Maryanne ran upstairs to wake up sixteen-year-old Richer Keesickquayash, the other high school student living at their house. Richer was also family — he was her cousin's son.

When Maryanne told Richer that Paul was on the floor and she couldn't wake him, he quickly ran downstairs.

"Call 911," Richer said.

Maryanne called the ambulance and told the operator, "There is something wrong with my son." She tried to explain that she could not get him to wake up and get off the floor. Then she ran upstairs to get a pillow.

"I thought he was sleeping," she said.

She came downstairs and placed the pillow gently underneath his head, then Maryanne sat on the floor beside her beautiful boy and waited for him to wake up.

AROUND 2:00 A.M. THAT night, Shawon's cell phone started ringing while he was at a party downtown. It was his girl-friend, Yolanda Skunk. She told him something serious was going on at Paul's house and that he may be dead.

He didn't believe her. He got angry and demanded to know why she would say such a thing. He hung up on her, paused for a moment to think, then asked a girl at the party to drive him to Paul's house. He said it was an emergency.

When they got to Maryanne's, he saw the emergency vehicles around the house. He saw the commotion, the red and blue police lights and the fire trucks at the scene. At that moment he knew that his girlfriend was right. Paul was gone.

ON NOVEMBER 11, 2006, an autopsy was performed on Paul Panacheese.

On the first page of the autopsy, a pre-examination summary stated, "The 21-year-old male returned home apparently intoxicated. His mother saw him on his return home. The deceased was home for 15-20 minutes then he suddenly collapsed. Ambulance was called vsa — lung resuscitation unable to return circulation. No history of trauma. There is no specific suggestion of homicide. Police are investigating the events of the evening and list of possible intoxicants."

The post-mortem listed Paul's height as 180 centimetres and his weight as 78 kilograms. He was "well nourished and well developed." He had dark hair and dark eyes, and at the time of his death he was wearing blue jeans and a black T-shirt with pink writing. He wore blue underwear and a black leather belt.

The pathologist, Dr. Ahmed Arwini, ran drug and alcohol tests but could find nothing in Paul's tox screen: "This is to certify that I have examined this body, have opened and noted cavities and organs as indicated below, and that in my opinion the cause of death was: No anatomical and no toxicological cause of death."[13]

The case was closed. The file was shut and there was no follow-up.

No one called Maryanne to let her know how her son had died.

NEWS OF PAUL'S DEATH quickly made the rounds at DFC. All the teachers were alerted by email and calls were made to community leaders and DFC officials. Jonathan Kakegamic, then a teacher at the school and Paul's former boarding parent, felt as if someone had punched him in the gut. Kakegamic spent the weekend in disbelief, unsure of what to make of the news. The same thought kept running through his mind: "Paul was a sweetheart. A good boy. What happened?"

The news also left Alvin and Tesa Fiddler completely stunned. It was the third death in six years. Alvin and Tesa decided that they would go, right then and there, to Maryanne's house to offer their condolences and try to help in any way they could. Alvin was still in charge of health issues for NAN. He knew Maryanne was from Mish, a six-hour drive away, and that she was a single mom. They got ready, arranged for someone to watch the girls, and went to Maryanne's.

When they got to the front door, people were buzzing in and out of the house. Maryanne was in shock. Alvin and Tesa sat down on the couch in the small living room. Maryanne was rocking back and forth, trying to come to terms with the fact that her youngest son was gone and she had been given no answer as to why.

IT WAS NOT UNTIL late 2015 — nine years after Paul's death — that Maryanne discovered what officials knew about the circumstances of her son's death: they had no idea.

She listened to medical experts announce on the stand that there was "No anatomical or toxicological cause of death." Paul's death was a complete mystery. He wasn't drunk. He wasn't high. He didn't commit suicide. He just collapsed and perished.

"Thus, this is essentially a negative autopsy in a young man," wrote Dr. Toby Rose, the deputy chief forensic pathologist in Ontario who was tasked with reviewing the autopsies of the seven students before the inquest, which would be held nine years later and was one of the largest joint inquests in Ontario. In May 2015, Dr. Rose submitted her review to the inquest.[14]

Dr. Rose never attended the scene of Paul's death. She never examined his body or interviewed anyone in Paul's family. She testified at the inquest that she had examined the coroner's warrant, the original pathologist's report, the police investigation materials and photographs, and then wrote her report, in "which I gave my opinion as to the cause of death for all the cases and I had my knowledge and experience about the manner of death and so that is what I reviewed."[15]

Forensic pathologists now understand that young people can die suddenly with a structurally normal heart, Rose said. She went on to say that in some extremely rare cases a person can die of heart failure with no anatomical trace. Those who die this way often have a genetic condition that predisposes them to sudden cardiac arrhythmia, and some of these conditions are inherited and may affect close relatives such as parents or children. Rose testified that "this could be a type of genetic heart disease that doesn't make changes in the heart that [are] visible either to the naked eye or under the microscope."[16]

In these sudden death cases, the 2014 *Ontario Forensic Pathology Service Practice Manual* recommends sampling tissue for DNA isolation and genetic analysis. Paul's DNA was no longer available for testing, so Dr. Rose recommended Paul's "first degree relatives" — parents and siblings — be tested to rule out such a condition.

After the inquest, Maryanne and everyone in her family was tested and nobody was found to carry any genetic heart abnormality.

The pathologist who had examined Paul's body in December 2006 detected a small presence of alcohol in the system, and there was a slight detection of the cannabis compounds found in marijuana or hash. But the traces were minuscule and were not linked to the cause of death. As for other drugs, none were found.

The contents of Paul's stomach were also reviewed by the toxicologist but they were not examined, the report said. The pathologist clearly states in block, bold, and italicized letters: "Selected items will be stored frozen for five years and then destroyed. Any other items may be destroyed six months from the date of this report."

Dr. Rose testified that she deliberated on whether or not to label Paul's death as "undetermined" or "no anatomical or toxicological cause of death." She told the inquest jury:

> So thinking about the manner of death, there is no evidence of any act either that he performed or another performed to cause his death. So that excludes accident, suicide, or homicide. The scene and circumstances support natural because we know that there are some diseases that cause people to die suddenly and they don't have any findings but there's no specific disease. So I can't give the name between two competing manners of death and I think it will be logical to say he died of a natural disease even though we don't know the name of it and so it could be, the manner could be natural or

you can go to the strict definition of undetermined and say we would have to call it undetermined. So I'm going to leave that to you.[17]

Maryanne had waited nine years to find out what she already knew: not one single medical professional had a clue as to why her son had died. And because the forensic pathologist ordered that items be destroyed in six months and in five years, there is no physical or DNA evidence that can be re-examined.

Maryanne is left wondering what happened to Paul, just like she has been left wondering what happened to Sarah. Maryanne has had to live with the crushing emptiness of having two of the most important people in her life taken from her without any explanation why. Living in this state makes it nearly impossible for Maryanne to find peace; she is constantly looking for answers. And after she has exhausted all possibilities, she is left hollow.

WE SPEAK FOR THE DEAD TO PROTECT THE LIVING

WHEN THE SNOW FALLS IN BIG, SOFT, CASCADING FLAKES, it muffles all sounds of the city. The streetlights blur. So do headlights.

The snow is telling everyone to be quiet. To hush. A reminder to take it a bit slower.

Each step gets more slippery as the puffy, frozen orbs fall gently on the ground. The line of teens are trying to keep up with one another, laughing and sliding as they make their way from the bus stop into the park. Their backpacks are heavy. The glass bottles clink loudly against the tin cans.

Most everybody drinks. It's the great equalizer. You don't have to worry if you're skinny or fat or what you look like. Chug a bit of alcohol and everything feels all right. You get the confidence to open up and talk. Shit don't matter.

The teens walk in a tight-knit group. They keep glancing behind them, wondering if anyone in the passing cars sees where they are headed. They want to go unnoticed, so they leave the sidewalk and step onto the snowy lawn of International Friendship Gardens, a fifteen-acre park in the south end of the city. As soon as you enter the park off Victoria Avenue, there is a red Chinese pagoda with two lions standing sentry in front. The park, a centennial gift to the City of Thunder Bay from the local Soroptimist Club, is full of paths and wooded trails that feature eighteen monuments and gardens representing eighteen diverse cultures found in the city. It's an ideal spot for the kids to go and drink unnoticed.

Someone at the front yells back to the others to use their feet to swish the snow. Or better yet, snap some tree branches off and use them as brooms to obscure their tracks. No one wants to get busted. Not by the school counsellors, who drive around the city on weekends looking for wayward kids. They know to follow tracks to find the kids in the bushes. No one wants to get caught drinking, not right after Christmas break. Not when everyone has just come back to Thunder Bay. Everybody knows after three warnings you're done, sent back home up north.

One of the girls, the tall one in the dark, puffy coat, is giggling as she trudges through the snow.

Her name is Robyn Harper. She is new to the group, new to the school.

Robyn looks behind her at Skye Kakegamic.

"If I get too drunk, make sure you watch me. Make sure I go home, okay?" she says.

Skye smiles back. "Okay."

"You promise?"

Skye promises.

"You'd better," Robyn responds.[1]

Robyn has just flown in from Keewaywin First Nation for her very first week of school. The grade eleven student was on the small charter plane with Skye when it left the community after the Christmas holiday and made the two-hour flight high up over the boreal forest to Thunder Bay. Robyn had run into her parents, Andrew and Tina, at the small Keewaywin airport. They were just flying back from Wasagamack First Nation in northern Manitoba, six hundred or so kilometres northeast of Winnipeg, after visiting Andrew's recently widowed father. All of them had been in Wasagamack— Tina, Andrew, and their daughters, Divona, Lorna, and Robyn — but Tina had sent the girls back early because Robyn had to get ready for school. She told Divona and Lorna to take their youngest sister home to get her packed for Dennis Franklin, while she and Andrew travelled to Winnipeg for Andrew's medical appointments. In 1969, a work accident had left Andrew paralyzed from the waist down. He has no memory of the accident that stole the use of his legs and took away his livelihood. All he remembers about that day back in 1969 is the sound of someone screaming, "Look out!" He was working in the Canadian National Railway yard, helping to load track on trucks. He never received a dime of compensation but somehow managed to support his wife and his three daughters as a bookkeeper.

As they made their way from the landing strip to the

small house that serves as the Keewaywin airport terminal, Tina pushed Andrew's wheelchair over the gravel and around the potholes slick with ice and snow. They were stunned to see Robyn and all the other Keewaywin high school students waiting outside the airport with their bags. Tina hadn't known that they would be leaving so soon. She'd thought she'd have a few days with Robyn before she left, but Robyn gleefully told her that they had got the call to go early.

Tina had wanted Robyn to go to school closer to home, at Pelican Falls in Sioux Lookout. Robyn had already been away for two years, spending grades nine and ten at Northern Eagle High School in Ear Falls, the same school Paul Panacheese had attended. But in December 2006, the Harpers got a letter from Northern Eagle saying Robyn needed to transfer to Dennis Franklin Cromarty for the next semester in order to take classes in higher grades. Tina tried to get Robyn into Pelican but it was full. Robyn desperately wanted to go to Dennis Franklin because that was where her best friend and cousin, Karla, was going.

Tina was apprehensive. Robyn's sister Lorna had been to DFC briefly, but she was sent home because her diabetes wasn't being managed properly. Tina feared the kids there weren't getting the appropriate care and supervision. She knew that three DFC students — Jethro, Curran, and Paul — had died in just over six years. She spoke to Andrew about her fears.

"I said to my husband, 'Are you just going to let her go there?' and he said, 'Yes. Because she wants to go,'" recalls

Tina quietly. "I stayed out of it because she was Daddy's girl. But me, I didn't want to let her go there."

WHEN THE PLANE LANDS at the Thunder Bay International Airport, the first thing every student from the north does is make a beeline for the Tim Hortons coffee kiosk. The brightly coloured sugary donuts and vast selection of smoothies, iced cappuccinos, and flavoured coffees are a huge treat for the kids. There are no Tim Hortons or any fast food outlets in their home communities.

Skye stood near Robyn as they waited for their bags. She hadn't really known Robyn back home; they didn't have any common friends. They had gone to the same elementary school — there was only one in Keewaywin — but at eighteen, Robyn was a bit older than Skye, who was sixteen. Robyn had always been quiet and bookish, a homebody who preferred to hang out with her parents. Robyn was extremely close to her father, who never strayed far from their house because of his reliance on a wheelchair, and the rough, natural world of Keewayin was not exactly wheelchair friendly. Robyn used to sit by her father's side as he worked. When Robyn was a girl, she would tell her parents her life's ambition was to return after she graduated to take care of her dad. Her mother was convinced that if Robyn had her way, she would eventually do just that.

After the students collected their luggage, they went outside to wait for their ride.

"How come you didn't come here the first year?" Skye asked her.

Robyn said she was at Ear Falls, but because it didn't offer any senior classes she was just coming to Thunder Bay now.

"I've never been to this city before," Robyn confessed.[2]

The kids loaded into vans and headed to Dennis Franklin to register, find out where their boarding houses were, and get settled in. Robyn knew where she was going — to her cousin Bryan Kakegamic's house. Tina had called her eldest sister Maida's son, Bryan, and his wife, Cheyenne Linklater, to see if Robyn could stay with them in Thunder Bay. It made Tina feel better to know that her daughter wasn't going to be living in a stranger's house, but that she was going to be cared for by family.

Later that week, Skye took Robyn on an abridged tour of the city, showing her how to navigate the bus system. She pointed out some of Thunder Bay's highlights: the Brodie bus terminal where all the kids met up, the Intercity mall, the waterfront, and the frozen Sleeping Giant, cold and silent in the bleak winter months.

Before Skye got off the bus to head home for supper, she and Robyn made plans to meet up later at the mall. Robyn wanted to meet some new people and hang out.

This is where they found themselves later in the evening: at the food court in the Intercity mall.

The teens, about seven of them, were excited. Skye had pooled her money together with Kyle Meekis and Robyn. Skye had $15, Robyn had $25, and Kyle $20. They got some liquor from Peter, one of the adults from Keewaywin who they knew would "run" to get them alcohol if they needed it. Runners are always easy to find. They are either adult addicts who don't have enough money to buy their own liquor, or they are just doing it for the money. They linger outside the LCBO or at public places where they know the kids hang out. They hover like ravens, waiting to pounce on their prey.

Liquor wasn't the only thing Peter could get you. He was also the purveyor of any drug you could possibly want. All the students knew about Peter. He had provided drugs and alcohol to Skye's older sister. He took care of everyone's needs. It was a stroke of luck that night when they ran into him at the mall. He got the alcohol and took his share. That's how it works. You always have to pay the man.

Peter got them the bomb: a 60-ounce bottle of Smirnoff vodka, three big cans of Smirnoff Ice coolers, and a half-dozen 40-ouncers of Olde English beer. Their teenage brains might not have known how much alcohol they had in their possession; all they knew was that it was enough to get trashed.

The seven teens left the mall and headed for Friendship Gardens, trudging through the deep snow to a clearing near the giant fir trees that formed a protective wall around them. Robyn was getting on well with everybody. All of Skye's friends seemed to like her. She was fitting in.

Hours passed, but not many. The vodka was nearly gone. They had forgotten to buy pop to go with it, so they used the vodka coolers as their mixers. When those were done, it was time for a nightcap of beer.

Skye watched Robyn trying to chug the beer back, but it was foaming. Robyn told them she didn't know how to drink beer. She was trying to take big gulps, but all she was drinking was foam.[3]

Skye laughed, told her that wasn't how you drank beer. She took the bottle from Robyn, poured out the foam, then gave it back to her.

Someone noticed the time. It was getting late. Through the haze, a clear thought formed: their curfew was getting closer. Skye needed to be home by 10:30.

Everybody started chugging what was left of the alcohol. They couldn't let it go to waste.

Robyn tried to stand up straight, but wobbled and swayed. Others in the group started to bury the evidence in the snow.

Robyn fished through her bag for a pipe. Her silver earrings were dangling and her bracelets clinked as her fingers searched. Her left wrist had a blue ink tattoo that said *K II W*, and on her right wrist was a tattoo of her last name.

When she found the pipe, she took it out and filled it with two grams of weed. The kids passed it around.[4]

Robyn tried again to stand up straight but she kept falling over. She couldn't really walk and she was slurring her words.

Roxanne and Alera, two of the other girls in the group, rolled their eyes. They were getting impatient, their body language saying, *I don't want to babysit tonight.* They left the group. Then Kyle, who had come with a girl, wanted to go and the two of them left.

Vanessa, another friend, stayed with Skye and Robyn. The three of them had to get to the bus stop. Vanessa went ahead first, making tracks in the snow to the road so that Robyn and Skye could find their way out.

When Vanessa got to the road, she decided to take off, leaving Skye in Friendship Gardens with Robyn.

Skye held her new friend. She remembered her promise. She weaved and staggered under Robyn's weight, pulling her through the snow. But Robyn was heavy and listless, so tall and powerfully built, a big, solid girl at close to 250 pounds.

Skye tried to hoist her friend on her back, but she couldn't do it. So she picked up her friend's feet and began dragging her up the path. Robyn's puffy coat moved easily on top of the newly fallen snow, but still Skye pulled and sighed, dragging Robyn up to the road. She stopped for a moment, caught her breath, and then tried lifting Robyn upright.

Just as Skye got Robyn to her feet, her friend puked all over the road.

Skye looked around. She was alone and she was scared. It was just her and Robyn.

Skye heaved and hoed and finally managed to get Robyn upright, holding her up as they stumbled toward the bus stop. As Skye was pulling Robyn along the sidewalk, she saw headlights, a car slowing down. She waved for help but the car didn't stop. Instead, it slowed down and pulled up beside the girls and someone threw leftover McDonald's food and wrappers at them.

Someone from the car yelled, "Go back home... Indians!"[5]

Skye kept walking. She'd been living in Thunder Bay for months now and was used to this kind of treatment.

A few more cars passed them by. At one point, Skye fell on the slippery sidewalk with Robyn who was like a dead weight.

As they stumbled along, Skye saw Vanessa walking toward them.

"Where did you go?" Skye asked, exasperated

"I had to meet up with someone," Vanessa said.[6]

Vanessa grabbed Robyn's other arm and they walked to the bus stop.

When the bus came, they hauled Robyn up the steps and placed her in a seat. The driver didn't offer to help the girls, but continued on toward the Brodie Street bus terminal.

Alera was waiting for the girls there. The bus terminal was cold and clinical, with artificial lighting and plastic chairs. This is where the students come and congregate. This is where they catch their connections back to their boarding houses. It's a meeting place, of sorts. Everybody comes here looking for everyone else.

The camera in the corner of the terminal was running.

At 10:13 p.m. there is an image of Skye in a white-striped jacket. Beside her is Vanessa. Kyle Meekis is back.

Minutes pass. Roxanne from Cat Lake arrives and other friends come too.

Robyn has fallen to the floor.

An older woman who works at the terminal comes over, looking annoyed. She asks, "What is wrong with her?" She begins peppering Skye with questions: "What happened? What is wrong with her? Where did you guys come from? Who are you? What is your name?"[7]

Skye told the woman not to worry, they were looking after her. Skye was going to do what she hadn't wanted to do: she was going to call their counsellors. An occurrence report would be miles better than the police.

Skye was petrified of the police. About a week after she had first moved to Thunder Bay, she'd gone out with her cousin. She was fifteen. She and her cousin met up with a group of kids about a block away from the McDonald's near Water Street.

Skye was drunk and she'd staggered into the restaurant. She had trouble ordering, so they caught a bus and headed to the Intercity mall. Halfway to the mall, her cousin decided she wanted to go home. She handed Skye what was left of the bottle she was holding and took off, leaving Skye alone in the big city.

Skye had barely known where she was. She got off the bus near the mall, then found herself in an alley. Suddenly there were more people drinking in the alley.

She began swaying and thought she was going to pass out. Then she saw the blue and red lights as a Thunder Bay Police car pulled up. The car swerved fast and stopped. Two cops, a man and a woman, got out of the car. The male cop was aggressive. He shouted at them to get against the wall.[8]

Skye was confused. What was this about? They were just hanging out.

The officer told his partner to go back to the car and call the station.

When she left, he began frisking the girls, patting them down.

"What is this about?" Skye asked, confused.

"I'm the cop here," he snapped. "You don't need to ask me questions."[9]

Suddenly he was handcuffing her and yanking her long black hair. He spun her around and slammed her head against the top of the police car. When he pulled her up, she remembers seeing a dent where he'd smashed her head.

He threw her and another girl in the back of the cruiser. Skye was crying; her head was throbbing.

When they got to the station, the police shoved Skye and the girl into a cell. Skye couldn't stop crying. She had never been in jail before.

The cops were laughing, making fun of her. They began to draw exaggerated images of a native and called her a savage.

"They'd colour sad faces saying, 'Boo-hoo.' They wouldn't show me their faces or their badge number and they did that to that other student too, laughing at her like it was a freak show or something and that's about it."[10]

Dealing with the NNEC workers would be much easier than dealing with the cops.

A City of Thunder Bay transit controller walks over to them. Skye looks at him; she's not sure what he's saying. After he leaves, Skye stands against the wall, steadying herself.

Alera is standing beside Robyn. So is Raven, another girl from school.

Then David Fox, one of the NNEC staff, walks in and tries to talk to Robyn. He helps her up and walks her to the waiting van. Alera and Raven go with them.

Skye remembers seeing Cheyenne Linklater drive up in a second NNEC van. She sees Skye and walks over. Cheyenne is Robyn's boarding parent. She also works on call for NNEC, driving around at night, sometimes all night, looking for students.

Skye recalls telling Cheyenne they had been drinking, a lot, so Cheyenne offered Skye a ride home. She accepted it and Roxanne climbed into the van with them.

The vans leave the bus terminal in a convoy. When they get to Cheyenne's house, Skye remembers seeing David and Cheyenne each grab one of Robyn's arms, pull her out of the van, and take her to the house.

They walk in the door with Robyn and they walk right back out again.

David climbs into his van and Cheyenne into hers, and they pull out of the driveway.

In minutes, Skye is at her boarding house.

Cheyenne's recollection of that night differs from Skye's. She denies that she was ever at the bus terminal or at the house with Robyn. Cheyenne says she didn't get home from work until 4:00 a.m. and that that is when she checked on Robyn before she went to bed.

IT WAS 10:30 P.M. when David and Cheyenne got Robyn through the front door of the house and into the narrow entranceway. Slippers and shoes were neatly stacked on a black boot tray on the tan tile floor. The hallway led to a sitting room at the back of the home. They laid Robyn down in the hallway. She was placed on her side, propped up against the wall. Bryan, Cheyenne's husband, and his brother Jamie were home.[11] The Kakegamics were Robyn's cousins, but Bryan didn't know her well. He had seen her only a couple of times before, when she was a toddler.

At 2:00 a.m., Bryan woke up to go to work as a news-paper carrier. He got out of bed, walked down the hall, and found his cousin lying on the hallway floor.

He nudged her foot with his foot. When he saw her foot move, he left her on the floor and went to work.

When he returned at 6:30 a.m., he went upstairs to the bedroom. Just as he was lying down, he heard a knock on the door. It was his brother.

He told Bryan that Robyn was dead.

THE ROAD CONDITIONS WERE poor, icy and snowy, when the ambulance was dispatched on January 12, 2007, at 8:59 a.m. to 366 County Boulevard, Bryan and Cheyenne's home.

It was an urgent call. Possible cardiac, medical arrest.

Sirens and lights blaring, the paramedics arrived at the modest townhome to find the fire crews already there. A five-man pumper had responded to the call. Some of the firefighters were crammed into the hallway. The patient had "no spontaneous respiration" and "no carotid pulse." Her skin was a bluish colour, like a newborn's skin after it has struggled to get out of the birth canal. Ambulance attendants noted rigor mortis was setting into Robyn's arms and legs, something the Thunder Bay Fire crew had noticed when they tried to clear her airway.[12] They had also told the paramedics there was vomit in her hair.

The attendants asked the occupants of the house if Robyn was on any medications, if she had taken anything. They said no.

Both the fire and ambulance crews were at the scene for less than thirty minutes before they left Robyn for the police, who were interviewing the people living in the house.

One of the officers called for the regional coroner, Dr. Paul Dupuis, who was on shift at the local emergency ward. The coroners who work in this part of the province often pull double duty, as both physician and coroner.

Dupuis couldn't leave the hospital and head to the scene. The police would have to gather up all the information he needed for the post-mortem.

Robyn was dead hours before they had arrived.

ROBYN HAD CALLED HER mother every night from her boarding home.

"I just want to come home," she whispered into the phone.

Robyn did not call her mother that Friday night before she went to Friendship Gardens. Tina went to bed instinctively knowing something was wrong.

Tina had heard stories about what went on at DFC, of the kids being largely unsupervised, roaming the city and drinking every night. She didn't want Robyn exposed to that kind of behaviour. Robyn wasn't a drinker and Tina didn't want her to start. Robyn was a good girl. The summer before she left for school, she had been a summer student working at the Keewaywin band council office.

There is a picture of her on the community's website. It was taken when she was helping to run a popcorn and slushie stand. She is standing with her hands on her hips, her head tilted to the left, a closed-mouth grin on her face. Her long black hair is tied back in a black-and-white paisley handkerchief. She's wearing a black T-shirt with the word *Sinful* in silver lettering.[13]

When Tina heard the phone ring early on Saturday morning, she automatically thought it was Robyn, apologizing for forgetting to call. Tina remembers the crisp ringing roused both Andrew and her from their sleep. Andrew groggily muttered, "Who is calling us this early?"

Tina picked up the phone and heard the voice of her nephew David Fiddler, who was also Keewaywin's pastor. He was calling from the band council office.

"We're coming to visit you," he said, adding that the chief was coming with him.

Panic set in when she told Andrew who was on the phone. Andrew cast his eyes down. The weight of the moment was on them. He knew, as did she, that something catastrophic had happened. Tina struggled to get Andrew up and out of bed and to dress him before the pastor came. She managed to get him ready and seated in his wheelchair moments before they heard the knock at the door.

THE DEAD TELL THEIR own story.

Coroners know this. So do pathologists. The motto of the Office of the Chief Coroner is: "We speak for the dead to protect the living."[14]

According to the *Guidelines for Death Investigation*, a manual produced in 2003 by the Office of the Chief Coroner, coroners should attend death scenes whenever possible.[15] Coroners see what others don't — the position of the body, the smell and the colour of the skin, the placement of the injuries, and the bodily secretions. Every single detail helps tell the story of the death.

The guidelines say that coroners should respond to urgent cases within thirty minutes. Urgent cases can include an apparent accident in a public place, a homicide or criminally suspicious death, a suicide, or the death of a child. Once the coroner gets to the location, there is a whole host of guidelines to follow — everything from what to do before they enter to where the body was found to interviewing police, fire, and ambulance workers and eyewitnesses, and meeting the lead investigator. The coroner can also conduct preliminary examinations, such as determining if rigor mortis has set in and collecting any evidence near the body that may help tell the story of how a person has died.

The coroner has ultimate jurisdiction over the body. Removal of the corpse by police should be discussed between the coroner and the senior ranking officer at the scene.

Only when it takes more than sixty minutes to get to a scene should the regional supervising coroner review the circumstances of the death over the phone before releasing the body.

It is also expected that the coroner will contact the family of the deceased as soon as possible: "In most cases, the Coroner will gather information regarding a deceased person from next of kin at a very early stage in the investigation and be prepared to inform the family of the results of the investigation as it progresses and when it is concluded."[16]

No one called Tina Harper. She was never given a coroner's name or number. No one kept her abreast of any investigation into her daughter's death. Instead, Robyn's body was transferred to the morgue and no one from the coroner's office called the next of kin.

"Nobody called," says Tina. "Not the police, not the coroner. The only person who called or came [aside from David Fiddler] was the chief of Keewaywin First Nation. That is it. And when the chief came, all he told me was, 'She choked on her own vomit.' That is it. He didn't say anything else. I didn't believe him, that this was all that happened."

Later, many years later, when the coroner Dr. Paul Dupuis took the stand to answer a litany of questions at the inquest into the seven students' deaths, he was asked if he had called Tina Harper.

Dr. Dupuis could not recall whom he spoke to in Robyn's community. He added that the police usually handled notification calls. Dupuis told the court he was working as an emergency room physician on the night Robyn died and could not attend the scene of her death because he couldn't leave the hospital. He told the jury, it was "one of the realities of the northwest. We do our best to get to the death scenes but sometimes it isn't possible."[17]

Dr. Dupuis was also the investigating coroner presiding

over Curran Strang's death. He testified that he couldn't remember if he spoke to anyone in Curran's family about the boy's death.

This was not Dr. Dupuis's only potential error of omission. The coroner's guidelines also state that if a coroner is unable to attend a death scene, he or she has to document fully the exact reasons why. There is no evidence Dr. Dupuis did this. At the inquest, Dr. Dupuis would admit this was an omission on his part. When Chantelle Bryson, the lawyer for the Provincial Advocate for Children and Youth, asked Dr. Dupuis if he "would agree that your investigation was cursory at best," the presiding coroner at the inquest, Dr. David Eden, halted proceedings and excused the jury. Bryson withdrew her question.

Thunder Bay pathologist Dr. Joseph Wasielewski performed the autopsy on Robyn Rose Harper, twenty-five hours after her death. His post-mortem starts with a summary of everything he was told by the first responders who arrived at the scene: "This was an 18-year-old First Nation's female student going to school in Thunder Bay boarding with a family in the city who had been drinking at the bus terminal area into the early morning of the 13th of January 2007. She was brought to her residence and spent the night supine on the hallway floor where she was found dead at approximately 9:00 a.m. She was observed at 4:00 a.m. and 5:00 a.m. and noted to be alive at that time. No other history is currently available."[18]

Wasielewski then described the state of the body at the time of the external examination. His report noticed rigor mortis was not present in the muscles of the arms and legs but it was moderate in the feet. The body was not yet decomposing.[19]

Robyn's clothing consisted of a grey ski jacket, a grey hooded sweater, two black tank tops, a mauve bra, black pants, a black belt with a silver buckle, black socks, three silver beaded necklaces, two silver bracelets on the left wrist, silver earrings, a pair of grey flannel pants, white panties, and a chain bracelet on her right wrist. She also had a homemade pipe made out of a pencil sharpener.

Robyn was about five foot nine. She weighed approximately two hundred and fifty pounds. Wasielewski noted her hair was long and black with auburn highlights, and that she had a contusion in the middle of her forehead that measured about five by two centimetres and a purplish mark over the left cheek measuring eleven by two centimetres. He noted this mottling and discolouration of the skin was consistent with either an "acute contusion" or the possible settling of the heavy blood cells once the heart has stopped beating and rigor mortis is setting in. The patches become bigger as the hours pass.

He noticed a blue tattoo on the right side of her neck that read WOLV. There were also defibrillator pads over her chest and a contusion measuring ten by three centimetres on the base of her left thumb. Her left forearm showed multiple thin, white, superficial slash-like scars. The fingernails on both hands showed partially chipped black nail polish. Three round scars were on the posterior of her right forearm measuring less than one centimetre. Her right knee had a big contusion, six by seven centimetres, and there were multiple old scars on her knee. The left knee also had a series of old scars.

When he turned her body over, he noticed a faint purplish mark over the posterior right hip area, possibly a recent contusion. He drew blood from her right femoral vessels and the heart and took a urine sample from her bladder. The samples were sent to the Centre of Forensic Sciences in Toronto.

He made a note on his post-mortem report: "There was a strong odour of alcohol during the autopsy."

It took three months for the toxicity report to come back. When it did, the results indicated Robyn Harper had died of acute ethanol toxicity. The tests revealed she had 339 mg/100 mL of alcohol present in her body at the time of her death. In her urine, the ethyl alcohol level was 384 mg/mL. Cannabis was also found in her system.

In his report, Wasielewski noted: "In the absence of significant tolerance to alcohol, the detected blood alcohol concentration could cause death. In 259 cases of fatal alcohol intoxication, the average blood alcohol concentration was 356 mg/100 mL, with 90 per cent of the cases between 220 and 500 mg/mL."

For every death investigated, the coroner's office is expected to answer the following simple questions: What is the identity of the deceased, how did the death occur, when did it occur, where did it happen, and by what means? Was it a natural death, a suicide, an accident, or was it an undetermined cause?

Robyn's death was ruled an accident. Thunder Bay Police never asked the NNEC dispatcher for an incident report. The toxicological evidence shows she did not have the average amount of alcohol in her bloodstream to cause fatal intoxication. Robyn was binge drinking that evening in an effort to make friends but just didn't know when to stop.

High-intensity drinking or consuming an unusual amount of alcohol in a short period of time, bingeing, usually causes alcohol poisoning. The body simply can't process the amount of alcohol being consumed, causing the concentration of alcohol in the blood to build to dangerous levels. Vomiting, decreased judgement and control, slurring speech, the inability to walk or stand, and being in a stupor — a sign of reduced consciousness — are all signs of alcohol poisoning.[20]

The problem is, everyone handles alcohol differently. Everyone who drinks has a different metabolic and functional tolerance. No one in Thunder Bay really knew Robyn. She had been in the city for a week. Everyone assumed that she was an experienced drinker and would just sleep it off.

All of the kids out in the Friendship Gardens drank a lot of alcohol that night — an obscene amount. But none of them reacted to it the way Robyn did.

Neither the NNEC staff on call that night nor Robyn's boarding parents considered taking Robyn to the hospital. David Fox, the NNEC driver who took the call that evening, was unaware that alcohol poisoning could lead to death. At the inquest, Jonathan Rudin, the lawyer for six of the seven families, bluntly stated Robyn's death was no accident — he called it a homicide. He argued that alcohol poisoning doesn't have to be fatal if the person in question is taken to the hospital in time. Homicide, in a coroner's inquest, does not require proof of intention — it is simply the killing of a human being due to the act or omission of another. While blame is not supposed to be assigned in an inquest, Rudin stated categorically: "We hold NNEC responsible for what happened to Robyn. There is no question the NNEC is trying its best, and there's not a lot of money, but they did have services they held out to be capable and competent and they were neither."[21]

IN LATE FEBRUARY 2007, nearly a month after Robyn's death, Dr. Barry McLellan, then chief coroner of Ontario, sent a memo to all coroners in the province, blasting them on the quality assurance of investigation statements.[22]

The memo went on to remind coroners of the rules surrounding the guidelines for death investigations and how to produce proper a statement that is "meticulously prepared and clearly documents and reflects a high quality death investigation."

It reminded coroners of standard procedures such as spelling someone's name correctly, properly documenting attendance at the death scene, and ensuring the report "confirms that the family has been contacted, including documenting attempts to reach the family if they have not been contacted."

Then it warned that a formal audit process had just been developed and would be implemented in the near future.

Two months after the memo was sent, on April 12, 2007, newly revised guidelines were released by the Office of the Chief Coroner to replace the ones from 2003. The chief coroner's office relaxed the guidelines around death scenes. The new guidelines recommend that the coroner should attend "whenever feasible" because of the value added to an investigation. It adds, "Timely arrival at a death scene will, in part, be dependent upon an Investigative Coroner's ability to free him/herself of other activities within a reasonable period of time."[23]

BROTHERS

ON FEBRUARY 23, 2007, JUST ONE MONTH AFTER ROBYN'S
death, Cindy Blackstock launched a human rights com-
plaint against the government of Canada on behalf of the
First Nations Child and Family Caring Society and the
Assembly of First Nations (AFN), which represents 634
First Nations communities across the country.

Blackstock had read all of the Auditor General's reports.
She had been a child social worker and she knew what the
conditions were like in Attawapiskat and every other First
Nation community. A member of the west coast's Gitxsan
First Nation, Blackstock is a persistent, academic thorn
in Ottawa's side. She has a doctorate in social work and
twenty-five years of experience in child protection work.
She is a well-known Indigenous orator who has travelled
the world over, championing children's rights.

Blackstock started the Caring Society because of a
young boy named Jordan River Anderson, a member of

Norway House Cree Nation, which is about 456 kilometres outside of Winnipeg. Jordan was born in 1999 with complex disabilities known as Carey Fineman Ziter Syndrome, which kept him in need of hospital care for the first two years of his life until he was stable enough to go home. His parents wanted to take him back to their Norway House community — a plan doctors agreed with as long as he had home care — but a jurisdictional dispute between the federal and provincial governments over the payment of his medical bills kept Jordan languishing unnecessarily in the hospital until he died at the age of five on February 2, 2005.[1]

In Canada, the provinces receive transfer payments from the federal government to help pay for schools and universities, hospitals and health care, even welfare. Each of Canada's ten provinces and three territories uses the money transferred to it, along with its own respective funding, to pay for its own provincial services. But Indigenous people also have a treaty relationship with the Crown and the federal department of Indigenous and Northern Affairs, which pays for on-reserve education and health services. In Jordan's case, the federal and provincial governments could not agree on who should pay for government services for Status Indian children living on reserves.

In her human rights complaint, Blackstock alleged the Government of Canada was racially discriminating against Indigenous kids by providing inequitable levels of child welfare funding to Indigenous children and their families. The result of the inequities affected all aspects of a child's life. Unequal education funding meant Indigenous kids went to substandard schools. There was a higher dropout rate, which often led to unemployment and higher levels of incarceration. Unequal social and health program funding meant more kids were in state care due to broken-down families. In fact, when Blackstock filed the claim it was estimated that anywhere from 23,000 to 28,000 Indigenous children were in foster care — meaning nearly 40 percent of all Indigenous kids were in state care.[2]

That same year, on September 13, 2007, the United Nations held a special General Assembly, the subject of which was the UN Declaration on the Rights of Indigenous Peoples. The document contained forty-six articles and called on all United Nations member countries to sign the declaration and live up to its meaning. The first article establishes the equality of all people, regardless of race, colour, or creed. It states Indigenous people have the right to full enjoyment of all human rights and fundamental freedoms outlined in international human rights law.[3]

The declaration goes on to state that all Indigenous people are "free and equal to all other peoples" and have the right to live free from discrimination based on their Indigenous identity. The article also states that Indigenous people shall not be subject to genocide, or acts of violence, and their children shall not be forcibly removed from their homes.[4] This last recommendation is particularly biting to Canada: currently forty thousand Indigenous kids are in foster care across the country.[5] And from the 1960s to the 1980s, tens of thousands of Indigenous children were forcibly removed from their homes by child welfare authorities and placed in non-Indigenous foster homes before they were adopted by white families in Canada, the United

Kingdom, the United States, and Australia. This dark chapter in Canadian history is known as the "Sixties Scoop."

Another key part of the declaration asserted that Indigenous people have the right to establish and control their own educational systems and institutions, including providing education in their own languages in a culturally appropriate setting, and that Indigenous children have the right to "all levels and forms of education of the State without discrimination."[6]

The eighteen-page declaration posed a problem for four countries: Canada, Australia, the United States, and New Zealand — countries with strong Indigenous populations that got swept aside by incoming white settlers. Those four countries, out of 144, voted against the declaration, saying they did so to protect rights of self-determination, land and resource rights, and the right of veto over national legislation and the management of resources.[7]

The Canadian government argued the declaration went against the constitutional rights of Indigenous people to self-determine the path of their own nations and that the declaration on land and resources was too broad and could hurt treaty rights.

Then, in early December 2007, something positive appeared to be happening. Jordan's Principle, a guide for how governments should behave when dealing with a child — specifically, to always put the needs of that child ahead of cost considerations or liability — was introduced in the Canadian parliament.[8]

On December 5, 2007, New Democratic Party Member of Parliament Jean Crowder introduced a motion in the

House that read, "In the opinion of the House, the government should immediately adopt a child-first principle, based on Jordan's Principle, to resolve jurisdictional disputes involving the care of First Nations children."

On December 12, 2007, the entire House, every single Member of Parliament in Canada, stood up and supported Jordan's Principle.

But this resolution came after another student at Dennis Franklin Cromarty was found dead in the water.

IT IS LATE OCTOBER. The night is black. He is on his back, bobbing and weaving, his body caught in a crushing vise of cold. He tries to use his arms to steady himself, but the water swirls around him, both holding him down and keeping him afloat. His eyes open. In an instant, Ricki Strang realizes he is in the river. He staggers upright in the water and looks around but he can't see his brother.

"REGGIE?" he yells.

He is answered with silence. Reggie is gone.

Fighting the onset of hypothermia and the haze of alcohol after a night of drinking, Ricki stumbles out of the river toward the muddy shore. His adrenalin rushes. He has no idea how he wound up in the water. He tries to stand up straight but the pain radiates from the base of his back like a loud groan. It takes him a moment to get his bearings. He makes his way up the muddy bank and onto the bike path that runs parallel to the McIntyre River; his eyes focus on the back end of the Shoppers Drug Mart pharmacy.

He turns toward the river and yells his brother's name again as he scans the water. He sees nothing. He waits, paces up and down the bike path, calling for Reggie. Hearing and seeing nothing in the darkness, he figures his brother must have left. Shaking and wet, Ricki heads toward the road.

He begins to walk back to the boarding house. He must have been a sight, soaked to the skin and disoriented as he shuffled down the road late at night the weekend before Halloween.

The other boarders remember seeing one of the brothers staggering to the house but they weren't sure who it was — Ricki or Reggie. The boys were barely one year apart, with the same parents but different last names, and they were often mistaken for each other, even though Reggie was slightly heavier than his willowy younger brother.

Ricki started toward the stairs to his second-floor bedroom, desperately wanting to pass out.

Alma Hastings, the on-call telephone operator at the Northern Nishnawbe Education Council and the main contact for boarding home parents, received a call from Deb Elliot on October 26, 2007, at 9:51 p.m. Elliot was at work but Raymond Albert, one of the adult boarders at the house, had called her multiple times to notify her that the boys had not come home for supper and then they missed their curfew. He told Deb that only one boy had returned home, and he was drunk and wet.

Phil Strang, the boys' cousin and one of the other student boarders, saw Ricki come in through the front door, dirty and wet. Phil followed Ricki, noticing he was sopping and disoriented. He dried him off and tried to help him while Raymond took Ricki's clothes and threw them in the washing machine.[9] After Deb's phone call, when Alma finished her shift later that evening, she decided to swing by the boys' boarding home at 123 McIntosh Street to see what was up.

The 9:51 p.m. call from the boarding parent was documented in an NNEC incident report, along with a note that Alma had gone to the house. It also said that Reggie was home. Raymond had mumbled to Alma that it was Reggie who was home but he had misspoken.[10]

It wasn't Reggie.

It was his sixteen-year-old brother, Ricki.

BY THE TIME REGGIE BUSHIE disappeared in the McIntyre River, a familiar pattern had emerged. Reggie's body was pulled out of the river on November 1, less than a week after he was last seen. It was the first time that DFC had lost two students in one year.

Reggie was the third boy to have been pulled from the waters surrounding Mount McKay and he was the fifth student from Dennis Franklin to die since 2000. In all five cases, there are questions of mishandling by the police. In the eyes of the families and of the Indigenous leaders, the investigations into all five deaths were poorly handled from the start — each case was slow off the mark or not investigated at all due to the assumption that the teens were drunk and disorderly and died by misadventure. In all cases, the families were not properly contacted by any of the officials — from the police to the coroner's office — and were left with nothing but questions about how their children had died. Rhoda King, Reggie Bushie's mother, was told that her son was missing three days after he had disappeared.

Thunder Bay was an unfamiliar city to all five of the students. All five of them were well grounded in their Anishinabek languages and all of them struggled in school; English was their second language. Reggie, raised in Poplar Hill in Northwestern Ontario, about six hundred kilometres away, had never been to a big urban centre before. He had never seen city lights, tall buildings, or strip malls with fast food restaurants. The urban world was also a foreign land for Robyn. She had only been to a big city once before, when she visited Toronto for a few days on a school trip. Back home in Keewaywin, she had a photograph of the CN Tower that she'd taken while on the trip.

Ricki and Reggie had grown up in Poplar Hill, a small northern fly-in and winter-road-access First Nation community of less than five hundred people. Poplar Hill is built in the shadow of Poplar Hill Indian Residential School, which operated for more than a hundred years. Shortly after Reggie was born, their father Rex Bushie died suddenly. Ricki doesn't know what happened to his father other than that he died in the water. He doesn't talk to his mom, Rhoda King, about it because he knows it brings back too many painful memories and he hates seeing her cry.

After Rex passed, Rhoda was consumed by grief and, unable to take care of her four young children, she gave

Reggie to her sister Marie Owen and her husband, Rodney; and she sent Ricki to her parents, John and Jemimah Strang. Their eldest brother, Richie, was sent to Manitoba, to Rex's family in Pauingassi First Nation, north of Little Grand Rapids; and Rhoda kept Dixie, who was three years older.

Reggie, who was just fifteen and starting grade nine, didn't like being by himself in the city. He was placed in a boarding home across town from his brother and he was living with a family he had never met before. A few weeks after the start of school, Reggie asked his brother if there was room in his boarding house for another person. He wanted to move in. As luck would have it, the attic room was free and Ricki's boarding parent, Deb, a hard-working woman who supplemented her income with boarders, didn't mind making room for Reggie. The house was pretty packed — a few other student boarders lived at Deb's along with Raymond — but all the boys were well cared for and Raymond tried to keep an eye on the kids' comings and goings. He even shared cigarettes with Ricki if he asked. There was always food in the fridge or Raymond was cooking up something on the stove. Deb gave Ricki a used blue bicycle so he could ride to DFC on sunny fall days. Ricki loved the freedom of biking around the city, but when Reggie moved in he gave the bike to his little brother. He knew Reggie had learned to ride back home and that he'd loved zipping around the rez on two wheels. Ricki told Reggie he had to be careful in the city: "Make sure you stop when you see a red light."

Cheyenne Linklater, Robyn Harper's boarding parent, was the NNEC driver cruising the streets, looking for DFC students in trouble on Friday, October 26, the night Reggie disappeared. She called Thunder Bay Police at 12:45 a.m. on October 28 to report him missing — two days after Reggie was last seen. The official missing persons report stated Cheyenne reported that "Bushie" was last seen by his "roommate" Ricki Strang near the McIntyre River and that the "complainant" said that they had been drinking and that Ricki Strang had returned home but Bushie did not. Cheyenne told the police that later on that evening, students had been found drinking at the McIntyre River by the police but Bushie was not one of them. She told them that Bushie did not have any family in town that the NNEC was aware of. She also said she didn't know who his friends were or the places he frequented. She added that she had been driving around all night looking for Reggie along the McIntyre River. She described Reggie as being five foot eight, Native, a hundred and forty pounds with scarring on his left hand. He was wearing light blue jeans, a black muscle shirt with white stripes, a black hoodie, a black cap, and white runners.

For each of the three boys found in the water so far — Jethro, Curran, and Reggie — "no foul play" was determined within hours of the recovery of the boys' bodies by Thunder Bay Police. The press release announcing the discovery of Reggie's body was sent twenty-four hours after his remains were found. "No foul play is suspected," read the three-line press release.

Each police statement implies the same thing — the deaths were accidental. The boys were drinking and for some reason all three happened to fall drunk into the water.

There was one glaring oversight to this theory. Both Reggie and Ricki were strong, experienced swimmers. They grew up on the shores of Scout Lake, spending endless summer days fishing or seeking out the deep spots of the big blue lake.

"There is no way my brother fell into the water and drowned," said Ricki. "He was too good a swimmer."

RICKI WOKE UP THE next morning hungover and sore. He walked slowly down the stairs and went into the kitchen. Ray was there, along with Ricki's cousin Phil. His back was in agony. The night before was a total haze.

Ricki started to make something to eat. Phil told him that he'd been really drunk when he came home and needed help getting upstairs.[11] They told him that his brother was not home.

At first, Ricki wasn't alarmed. He thought maybe Reggie was "chilling" at someone else's house and that he'd be home later.[12] The boys were popular and well known, and they both played on the school volleyball team. But they mostly enjoyed each other's company. Reggie loved rap music and heavy metal and was always inflicting it on his older brother. The two liked to goof around and go to the mall to check out the latest video games.

Later that afternoon, when Ricki's hangover had subsided and there was still no sign of his brother, he drove around with Deb and Phil, looking for Reggie. They kept driving until late into the night, going up and down the streets near the Intercity mall, the Shoppers Drug Mart,

and the McIntyre Centre, a strip mall with fast food outlets and an H&R Block. At 11:00 p.m., Deb had to leave
for work. She called Cheyenne Linklater, who had started
her overnight patrol shift. Cheyenne agreed to pick up Phil
and Ricki and search along the McIntyre riverbank from
May to Balmoral Streets.

Cheyenne tried peppering Ricki with questions: Where
does Reggie hang out? Who does he hang out with? Does
he have a girlfriend? Could he be at her house?

Each question was met with silence or "I don't know."

She was getting frustrated, and with every passing
second she knew she was going to have to file a missing
persons report.

Just after midnight, on Sunday, October 28, Cheyenne
drove back to the school to call the police.

AS SOON AS CHEYENNE spoke to the police, they went looking for Ricki. He was the last one to have seen Reggie alive.

Thunder Bay Police brought Ricki down to the station
multiple times before Reggie's body was found. On the
day he was questioned three times, he was not asked if
he wanted an adult with him or if he wanted to call his
parents. His parents weren't notified that their son, who
was a minor, was being questioned repeatedly by police.
In fact, Rhoda King, Reggie and Ricki's mother, did not
know that Reggie was missing until October 29 — three
days after he was last seen.[13]

Sergeant Jim Glena led the investigation into Reggie's
disappearance.

Ricki was out of sorts, upset and in shock, while he was being questioned. His memory from that night was not clear. He told the police that he experienced blackouts when he drank too much.

Ricki feared that he and his brother had been mugged. Both the boys had backpacks that night and both their bags were still missing. He told police he couldn't remember Reggie ever going into the water, but he had a feeling that his brother was in the river. He couldn't explain why he felt this way, he just did. Glena asked Ricki if he would go down to the water with them. Perhaps it would jog his memory. Ricki agreed and he took the police to the Shoppers Drug Mart parking lot on May Street. They got out of the car and walked down to the river's edge by the May Street underpass. This is where he last remembers being with Reggie, there by the water.

The boys had gone there after school, to the river's edge, to walk the bike path and to drink in peace. That afternoon, some of Ricki's friends from Poplar had stopped him in the school hallway and asked if he and his brother wanted to go drinking later. They were all friends, Chester, Aaron, and Terry. The pathway lining the river is a peaceful place even though it backs onto a strip mall parking lot. Fir trees form a single-file line running along the McIntyre's edge.

Reggie and Ricki weren't big drinkers. Ricki says they drank a couple of times at home in Poplar, even though the reserve is dry, but that drinking hard liquor wasn't really their thing — especially not Reggie's. But this night was going to be a good night. The boys had been invited out and they were going to do what the other, older guys did at high school — they were going to drink down by the water. The moving water soothed their senses — from the sight of the river's slippery flow to the smell of the seasons to its sound reminding them of home. The riverbank was also convenient for the teens — it was their own space, away from boarding parents who didn't like big groups of kids hanging out at the house.

One of Ricki's friends knew a runner — the boys just had to kick in some cash. Everyone pooled their money. Ricki remembered contributing $25.

When the runner came back, he had bottles of whisky and Budweiser beers. The boys walked behind Shoppers Drug Mart and along the paved bike path until they found a clearing among a patch of tall birch trees just past Balmoral Street. The boys decided to sit down on some fallen logs and spent the next couple of hours talking about home as they plowed through the beer and whisky. When the booze had almost run out, everyone decided it was time to go home.

Ricki still had half a bottle of whisky hidden in the sleeve of his coat. As they walked along the path back to Shoppers, he nudged his brother and told him they should go home and finish the bottle there. As they were walking, they ran into a group of girls they all knew from Pikangikum, which was not far from Poplar Hill. The girls were looking for alcohol and asked if the boys wanted to buy some more with them and continue to party.

It was a fateful moment. Ricki wanted to go home but Reggie wanted to stay with the group — he was having too much fun. So the two stayed. Someone went to fetch more alcohol, while the others lingered by the water, waiting and goofing around.

This is when Ricki's memory begins to fade in and out. He remembers they began drinking again. He doesn't know when the others decided to leave, but he remembers his friends took off and so did the girls. At this point, Reggie was stumbling, even falling once. Ricki didn't want to leave his brother, so they stayed right there, metres away from the Shoppers parking lot. And that is when his memory of that night completely ends. The next thing he remembers is waking up, immensely sore and floating on his back.

Ricki and the police searched the rocks, looking around for any signs of Reggie or their backpacks, but they couldn't find anything. The police officers hung back as Ricki walked slowly over the stones and the dead yellow grass, toward the water, where pieces of garbage littered the shoreline. When he got to the river's edge, Ricki carefully squatted down, resting on his heels. He spent some time thinking before he slowly stretched his arms out over the water, his palms gently skimming the surface. Then he put his hands in the river, his arms spread out as far as possible. His body began to shudder.

It was as if he were reaching out for his brother.

The police were touched into silence. They backed away, giving the boy the time he needed before taking him back to the station.

ON MONDAY, OCTOBER 29, Norma Kejick was having lunch with her friend and NNEC colleague Lydia Big George at the Sioux Lookout Golf and Curling Club. Just when their lunch came, Lydia's cell phone began to ring and she took the call. Lydia's face quickly darkened. When the call ended, she told Norma that another student was missing.

The two headed back to the office right away. Norma, who was still principal at Wahsa, urged Lydia, who was the supervisor of the NNEC counsellors, to take the next flight out to Thunder Bay. Lydia didn't want to fly, so Norma offered to make the eight-hour drive east on the Trans-Canada Highway. They left immediately. All the while, down the highway, Lydia was taking calls from people at DFC and NNEC giving her updates. As they approached Thunder Bay, another call came in and they were told to head to the Thunder Bay Police station on Balmoral Street because some of the students had been taken in for questioning.

When they arrived, Lydia and Norma saw the NNEC's two white vans parked in the lot. Students and counsellors were milling about outside, waiting for the students to be released so they could take them home. Norma sat in the truck while Lydia went to speak to the others. As head of the distance education school, Norma didn't know any of the DFC students. While she waited, she saw a teenage Indigenous boy walk slowly out of the station. As soon as he was outside, he fell to his knees and his body began to heave with sobs.

Lydia and the others rushed over to him. Norma didn't know who he was. She got out of the car, approached the circle surrounding the student, and quickly discovered the boy was Reggie's brother Ricki.

EARLY THE NEXT MORNING, Norma went directly to the Elders' room at DFC, ready to help in whatever capacity she was needed. She was told that this was where students, teachers, searchers, and community members would gather. Tables were set up, food was going to be brought in, and everyone was encouraged to use the room as a refuge, a place to speak to an Elder who was on hand to offer spiritual guidance. Norma sat down and spent the better part of the morning waiting for students and anyone else to come in. But nobody showed up. The odd student would poke their head in the room and then quickly turn around and leave. Norma couldn't believe it. Where were all the people? As the hours passed, Norma's frustration grew. She was told to wait there for updates but none came. She left the room to hunt down teachers and ask them if they'd heard anything about Reggie. But no one seemed to know whether search parties had been organized and if so, where they were looking and what needed to be done.

Someone at the school told her that searchers were out and there were plans to drag the river. Norma spoke to Lydia and both agreed that they should go down to the water and help. The two of them spent the rest of the afternoon walking the bike path along the length of the river, looking for Reggie. They wondered where everyone else was — the police didn't seem to be around and there were no other search teams.

The next day, the mood at DFC was subdued. It was Halloween and a pumpkin-carving contest had been organized for the students. Norma kept her eye on the Poplar Hill kids, trying to make them feel a bit more at ease. In the Elders' room, a few people had gathered to discuss borrowing boats from Fort William to drag the water. But they were also told to wait for OPP divers to arrive from Orillia, outside of Toronto, where the provincial dive team is based. Ricki and Reggie's parents were still in Poplar Hill; they had repeatedly tried to fly out but freezing rain had delayed them.

As frustration mounted and feelings of helplessness grew, Norma decided to call an Elder she knew, Josias Fiddler, to see if he would hold a ceremony down by the river, with drumming, prayers, and an offering of tobacco. She hoped enough people would come to the ceremony that they could then break up into small groups to search for Reggie. Josias agreed and they told everyone in the room to spread the word: they were going to go down to the river at the end of the school day.

IT WAS NEARLY 4:00 p.m. when Josias set up his drum on the shore of the McIntyre River by the SilverCity movie theatre. About twenty people had gathered to sing and say prayers, then walk the river. Once the ceremony was over, Norma and Lydia saw two boys take off and head toward the back of the movie theatre. Concerned, they followed them. The boys ran over to the large Dumpsters and started to pick through the mountains of garbage left behind by theatre patrons. Norma asked the boys why they were going through the garbage.

"We just want to find him and we don't know what else to do," said one of the boys. They were looking for Reggie. Norma could see the anguish on their faces. She asked them why they were looking in the Dumpsters.

"Because he could be hiding. Maybe he is scared to go home," they replied.

Norma told the boys that she didn't think Reggie was hiding in the bins and she coaxed them to come with her back to the river and talk to Poplar Hill chief Eli Moose. The boys were from Poplar. Norma sensed that they had something more to say and that they might feel more comfortable speaking to the chief instead of to her. She asked the boys if they knew Reggie. They said they did and that they had been with him on the night he went missing.

She asked the boys, whose names were Chester and Messier, if they would like to walk the length of the river with her and Lydia. They said yes. The boys opened up to them about the last night Reggie was seen alive. They described to her and Lydia in detail who was there and where they had gone to do the bulk of their drinking — a clearing in the forest of birch trees, just off the bike path. They had sat on the thick fallen trees, and the brush had given them relative privacy from the road backing onto the forest floor, not more than seven and a half metres away. Norma noticed lots of empty alcohol bottles on the ground and empty cans of Lysol, hairspray, and Listerine. Chester and Messier told her they'd had seven 40-ounce bottles of alcohol with them that night and there were seven of them there. Norma couldn't believe it — that was a 40-ouncer per person. She asked what they were mixing the alcohol with and they told her nothing. They had started drinking at around 5:00 p.m., and by close to 9:00 p.m. they had run out of booze. They'd decided to hit the trail so someone could go to the LCBO before it closed. While they were walking, one of the boys staggered and the others started to mock him and laugh. Around the May Street bridge, they ran into another student who had a bottle in his backpack, so they joined up and drank what he had. The boys said Reggie slipped on the rocks and his shoes got soaked in the river. Once the new bottle was finished, the kids walked over to a blue porta-potty that was set up for the construction crews working on repaving the roads. The girls in their group all used the bathroom. Once they were done, they decided to take off—everyone except Ricki and Reggie. The boys told Ricki that Reggie was too drunk to come with them. They feared he could get them all in trouble if the NNEC picked them up. The boys told Ricki to look after Reggie and then they took off, leaving the brothers behind.

NORMA AND LYDIA TOOK the boys back to the school and had the counsellors drive them home. Then Norma asked Lydia to call Larry House, the supervisor in charge of the student support service program, to see if she could meet Ricki. Larry told Lydia that Ricki had been placed on suicide watch at a boarding house outside of town. But he asked Ricki if he would meet Norma and he said yes. As she waited for him in the staff room at DFC, she began to worry. She feared she was out of her depth and could say the wrong thing, pushing Ricki further into darkness. She called her mother, a counsellor in Sioux Lookout, looking for advice. She told Norma to "always go with your gut" and to listen.

Ricki was sullen; his body language clearly showed he had the weight of the world on his shoulders. He walked quietly into the staff room and sat down at the table, across from Norma. He kept his head down, refusing to meet her eyes. Josias Fiddler was in the room, along with an Elder from Fort William. Norma introduced herself. She told Ricki that she was there to help him find his brother. She told him about the prayer service down by the river and the walk with the other boys. Only then did he lift his head to glance at her, his interest piqued. She told Ricki what the boys had told them about that night. She also told him that the boys had said they hadn't been totally honest with the police because they were frightened. Ricki looked up at her again. This statement also struck a chord with him. Then he asked her if she would take him to the river the next day.

Norma hid her surprise. She looked at Ricki and said, "Ricki, I understand you feel like killing yourself, is that true?" Ricki shrugged, his eyes downcast. "Why do you want to kill yourself?" Ricki shrugged again. "Killing yourself won't bring your brother back, it won't help anyone or solve anything."

She reached into her purse and brought out one of her suicide prevention cards, the cards she has carried around with her since her nephew died. On one side of the card there are instructions on who to call if you are having suicidal thoughts. The idea is to give the card to a trusted adult as a way of asking for help. On the other side, there are instructions for the adult recipient of the card. She made Ricki promise that if he was feeling so low that he wanted to die, he was to call her on her cell phone right away. Josias also gave Ricki his number and said he could call him too. Norma said she would sleep with her phone on beside her bed and she would be there for him if he needed her. Only when Ricki promised that he would call her if he was thinking about taking his life, did she agree to take him to the river.

THE NEXT DAY NORMA arrived at the school to find a packed Elders' room. The Poplar Hill students had been called out of class and asked to gather there. They were told that they should no longer speak to the police alone. Instead, they should go through an adult spokesperson. They all wanted Norma to be that person. She was shocked by the request, but accepted the honour. Then she told them that she was going to the river with Ricki and the students decided to come too. Josias Fiddler accompanied them, along with Thunder Bay Police constable Larry Baxter, an Indigenous officer assigned to DFC — he was also married to one of the DFC staffers.

They headed out in the counsellors' white vans. Norma did exactly what she had done the night before with the other boys. She took the students, including Phil Strang, the boys' cousin, to the clearing in the bush and they told her the exact same story — there were seven of them there that night and they drank a 40-ouncer each. They spoke of meeting the other student on the path and of consuming more alcohol. One of them even mimicked the stagger of one of the drunk boys.

As they made their way back to the path, they noticed the OPP dive team from Orillia had arrived and was searching the water. Police vehicles were parked along the side of the road. As they approach the May Street bridge, Ricki suddenly bolted. He ran up to the road and crossed the street, oblivious to the traffic lights and cars. Two of the boys ran after him, while Norma stayed behind with the others. She watched Ricki collapse on the riverbank across from the SilverCity, his arms wrapped around his knees. Norma rushed over to Ricki and squatted down beside him. As she held him, she apologized for taking him back to the river.

"Why did you take off?" she asked. Ricki shrugged. She looked over at the police divers near the May Street bridge. "Is that where he fell in? Where the divers are?" Ricki shrugged again. "Ricki, is that where you fell in?" Again he shrugged. Then she said, "Ricki, you said to the police three times that is where you think he fell in, by the May Street bridge. And that is where you woke up."

Norma was telling Ricki that the police said he was soaking wet from the waist down when he got home that night, when Phil Strang came up from behind and said that was not true. Ricki had been soaked from head to toe when he got home — even his ball cap was wet. Phil was the one who had cleaned him up and put him to bed.

Norma turned to Ricki and asked him why he had been in the water. She asked if he was looking for his backpack.

Ricki shook his head. Then she asked if he was looking for their booze. He shook his head again. Then she asked Ricki if he was looking for his brother. Ricki nodded. She asked where. Ricki pointed straight ahead, toward the middle of the river.

NORMA TOOK THE BOYS out for lunch. While they were eating, she excused herself and called her staff to say she needed to talk to the police. She told the police that they were looking in the wrong spot — that they needed to search the water across from the SilverCity. The police told her that Ricki had said to look under the bridge. She asked them to humour her.

After lunch, she took the boys back to DFC. They wanted to let off some steam so they headed to the gym to play floor hockey. She went to the Elders' room and was told that Rhoda and Berenson King were on their way from the airport; they had finally got a flight out. While she was walking down the hallway, she ran into Tesa Fiddler and Grace Fox, Larry Baxter's wife. Tesa's phone began to ring. It was Alvin. He was down by the river with Chief Eli Moose. Alvin asked Tesa to tell everyone to go to the Elders' room and wait. He was on his way to the school with the chief.

Norma spent the next several minutes pacing the halls. Rhoda and Berenson King arrived and they went directly to the Elders' room. Norma paced in front of the room until she saw Alvin walking down the hallway with the chief. She stopped him and asked if they had found Reggie.

He said they had. She warned Alvin that the parents had arrived and were in the Elders' room. She told him she was going to find a more private room where he could tell them the news.

They found an empty office and asked Rhoda and Berenson to wait for Alvin and Chief Eli. Norma was turning to go when she ran into Josias. She asked him to sit with the others in the Elders' room. He told her to get Ricki and sit with him when he heard the news. Norma protested, but Josias told her she had to finish what she had started.

Norma went straight to the gym to find Ricki. He was laughing and playing hockey with his friends. When Norma called his name, Ricki walked over to her. When he saw her face he became instantly deflated and then went limp. She put her arm around him and led him to the office where his parents were waiting. Ricki sat down quietly beside his parents. Chief Eli began speaking in Ojibwe. He told Rhoda, Berenson, and Ricki that they had found Reggie's body.

Rhoda let out a loud, guttural, mournful howl. The sound was unlike anything Norma had ever heard: it was the sound of a mother losing her child. Norma instinctively put her arms around Ricki, who put his head down while his mother wailed. After a while, one of the Elders told Rhoda and Berenson that they must comfort their son and pray. Rhoda and Berenson put their arms around Ricki and Norma slipped out of the room.

RHODA CAME DOWN LIKE thunder when Reggie's body was discovered in the river on November 1, 2007, six days after he went missing.

She had not been informed by authorities or the school that her son had disappeared until three days after he was last seen down by the McIntyre River. "Why did they wait so long to tell me?" she demanded, but no one seemed able to give her an answer. She arrived in Thunder Bay just as Reggie's body was being pulled from the water by police dive teams. They had found him exactly where Ricki had pointed — in the middle of the river.

Reggie was the fifth student to have died in seven years. Rhoda wanted to know why so many students had perished and why nothing was being done about it. It was clear to all Indigenous parents and teachers that something was not working at Dennis Franklin and that their kids were not safe in Thunder Bay. Parents were sending their children away to school to watch them die.

On November 2, just one day after Reggie's body was recovered, Thunder Bay Police issued a two-line press release: "The body recovered from the McIntyre River on the 1st of November has been identified as 15 year old Reggie BUSHIE from Poplar Hill, Ontario. Foul play is not suspected."

Alvin couldn't believe how quickly Thunder Bay Police had come to the conclusion that no further investigation was required. His mind began to race. He needed help. Somebody had to protect NAN's students.

RHODA'S FIRST LANGUAGE IS Ojibwe and she prefers to use a translator if she needs to speak to anyone outside of Poplar Hill. She wanted answers, so she spoke to NAN and Chief Moose. In February 2008, she hired Aboriginal Legal Services of Toronto (ALST) to ask the Ontario Office of the Chief Coroner for an inquest into Reggie's death.

Alvin supported the call for an inquest and, with NAN, stood behind Rhoda's demand. But Alvin also wanted the inquest to include all five of the DFC students. Every September, hundreds of NAN kids had to leave their homes to go to high school. If someone didn't do something, others would follow in the five students' footsteps.

"Tragically, many of these students lack an adequate network of social support and simply cannot cope with what can be a challenging and sometimes hostile environment," he said at the time.[14]

Alvin knew he needed help to get the inquest. So Fiddler did what he does best. He began to push — he held press conferences, and reached out to media for print and radio interviews. Then he contacted Toronto lawyer Julian Falconer.

Alvin first met Falconer in 2005 at the Ipperwash Inquiry hearings. Alvin had been called to testify about the importance of land and treaty rights in Indigenous culture. During the Second World War, the Canadian government tried to expropriate land from Stony Point First Nation so they could build a training camp; Ottawa promised the government would give the land back to Stony Point when they were done. Stony Point refused, saying the land the government wanted was an old burial ground.

The government took the land anyway. On September 4, 1995, thirty Stony Point members decided to reclaim their land, setting up tents and occupying the area. But Ontario Premier Mike Harris ordered the protest be shut down immediately. Hours before Ojibwe protester Dudley George was shot by an Ontario Provincial Police sniper, Harris uttered the phrase, "I want the fucking Indians out of the park," in a meeting with political staffers.

Eight years after George's death, an inquiry finally began. It was at that inquiry that Alvin watched Falconer rip apart the former premier on the stand. At the time, Falconer was the lawyer for Aboriginal Legal Services of Toronto. He accused Harris of lying seventeen times in the provincial legislature about the existence of the meeting in which he uttered the famous phrase.

Falconer was a born court orator. He used argument like a surgeon uses a scalpel. Educated at McGill University and the University of Toronto, he cut his teeth representing Toronto's Urban Alliance on Race Relations during the inquest into the death of a Black man named Lester Donaldson. A paranoid schizophrenic, Donaldson was wielding a knife when he was shot dead by a Toronto police officer in 1988. This was one of many high-profile cases in which Toronto Police Services was accused of using excessive force against a Black mental health patient.

That case had set the course for the legal career of the Montreal-born lawyer with a Polish-Jewish mother and a Jamaican father. He represented Maher Arar against the Canadian government after he was wrongfully detained by US officials while he was changing planes in New York, then deported to Syria, where he was nearly tortured to death in one of the country's most notorious prisons. He also represented the family of Sammy Yatim, the eighteen-year-old Toronto teen who was wielding a knife on a TTC streetcar when he was shot dead by Toronto Police officer James Forcillo. The officer shot Yatim eight times. Forcillo was later found guilty of attempted murder.

On March 6, 2008, Falconer fired off a letter on behalf of the Nishnawbe Aski Nation to Dr. David Eden, the regional supervising coroner for the Thunder Bay area:

> It is NAN's understanding that the family of Reggie Bushie has called upon the Office of the Chief Coroner to hold an inquest into the death of their son. NAN joins the family's request for an inquest, and adds to the request by seeking a broader inquest that will examine all of the above noted deaths. We note that the deaths have several factors in common including, the deceased are all First Nations youth, they were all attending high school at DFC, they were all from remote fly-in communities, and they were all residing in Thunder Bay in a "foster care" type situation.
>
> Ultimately, as a result of a lack of access to education in their home communities, all of these youth found themselves uprooted from their communities and placed in environments in Thunder Bay which simply failed to provide for their basic physical, emotional and psycho-logical needs. Homesickness, cultural discontinuity and cognitive dissonance marked their existences. NAN is insisting that their deaths do not suffer this same level of

neglect... It is time that the coroner's office responds to First Nations deaths in the same fashion as "non-native people" in our society.[15]

It took three months for Falconer to receive a response.

ON JUNE 6, 2008, Dr. William Lucas, the associate deputy chief coroner of Ontario, issued a press release stating that an inquest into Reggie Bushie's death would begin on January 19, 2009.[16] The half-page press release said the inquest would "examine the circumstances surrounding the death and will explore issues relating to how First Nations youths are impacted when attending schools that are a considerable distance from their homes."

The release added, "The jury may make recommendations aimed at preventing similar deaths."

But the inquest left out the other four students.

Fiddler was apoplectic. He fired off his own press release, saying that while NAN welcomed the announcement into an inquest into Reggie's death, "It shouldn't stop there, as the deaths of the four other First Nation youth who died under similar circumstances in recent years should also be included. We have to ensure that everything possible is done to understand how these tragedies are occurring and what can be done to prevent them."

Up in Poplar Hill, a grieving Rhoda was somewhat heartened at the news of the inquest, but she didn't understand why the other students had been left out. She also felt uneasy about the inquest process. Who would be acting as judge and jury concerning her son's death? What did they know about their Ojibwe way of life and their experiences of leaving home to go to school in another city and culture?

Rhoda asked her lawyer if white people were once again going to make decisions on how to save Indigenous kids from dying. "Let us decide," Rhoda said. "We need to send a strong answer to the whites." Her lawyers at ALST couldn't agree with her more.

Around the same time Lucas announced the inquest into Reggie's death, six hours west down the highway in Kenora, a court case was triggering the same questions. Clifford Kokopenace, from Grassy Narrows First Nation, was charged with manslaughter in the death Taylor Assin on June 17, 2007. The jury on the case failed to reflect the population of Kenora — about one-third of the population of 65,000 was Indigenous. Out of 699 potential jurors, only 29 were Indigenous people who lived on reserve.[17] Kokopenace launched an appeal, arguing for a new trial with a representative jury.

And in October 2008, Julian Falconer agreed to represent Ricardo Wesley's family in a case that would launch a Supreme Court challenge on representational juries. Wesley, twenty-two, along with Jamie Goodwin, twenty, burned to death in a fire on January 8, 2006, while being held in a Kashechewan First Nation jail for public intoxication. An inquest was called into their deaths.

Lawyers gathered in Toronto to argue over where the inquest should be held. Some wanted it held in Ottawa, in Prime Minister Stephen Harper's backyard, so the issue would garner national press attention. But the men's families wanted it held near home on the shores of James Bay, and they wanted Indigenous people from Kashechewan on the five-member jury.

Falconer was standing outside the downtown Toronto Coroner's Courthouse when he read court supervisor Rolanda Peacock's affidavit claiming that no Kashechewan residents were on the jury roll of the judicial district of Kenora. The provincial Ministry of the Attorney General is supposed to include all Canadians in the justice system.

"I looked at it, a sworn affidavit from the province that said no one is on the Kash jury roll," Falconer said. "I could not believe it. That cannot be legal."

The affidavit showed that court officials had travelled to fourteen of the forty-five First Nations communities in the Kenora district. While 12,111 people lived in the Kenora-area First Nations communities, the court heard that only forty-four people were on the prospective jury list for 2007.

This was just like the Kokopenace case. The Indigenous population was completely cut out of the justice process.

On behalf of ALST and NAN, Falconer sent a letter to then Ontario Attorney General Chris Bentley demanding that the exclusion of Indigenous people be rectified. They demanded that immediate steps be taken to establish a formal inquiry into the legality of the jury selection process across Ontario.

"At stake, of course, from the perspective of the First Nations, is the right to a trial by a jury of one's peers along with the right of First Nations across this province to participate in the justice system," Falconer outlined in his letter.[18]

Chris Bentley, a judicious and measured Attorney General from London, Ontario, who also went on to serve as what was then called the Aboriginal Affairs minister, agreed with Falconer, the ALST, and NAN. Something had to be done. He asked to meet with them at their earliest convenience. Meanwhile, the Kokopenace case would be the beginnings of a Supreme Court challenge that would have repercussions all over the north, grinding the inquest and criminal cases to a complete halt for years.

AS FALCONER AND THE LAWYERS AT ALST challenged the justice system, another student was viciously attacked late one night near the McIntyre River.

On October 28, 2008 — the same day that Jethro Anderson went missing in 2000 — sixteen-year-old Darryl Kakekayash was beaten severely and tossed into the Neebing River.

Like Jethro, Reggie, and Curran, Darryl was living in a boarding home, far away from his home community, his family, his language — away from everything he'd known in Weagamow, or North Caribou, First Nation. And like all the other boys before him, because Darryl wanted to go beyond a grade eight education he had to head south. He first went to high school in Sault Ste. Marie, but the school was too far away from home; so in 2007, he transferred to Dennis Franklin Cromarty High School. And, just like the other boys, Darryl bounced around from boarding house to boarding house.

On October 28, barely two months after the start of school, Darryl met his cousin and his cousin's girlfriend at SilverCity. They were going to catch an evening showing of *Alvin and the Chipmunks*. It was a bit of a blast from the past, but they thought the movie would be a riot.

When the movie ended, Darryl worried he'd be late for his midnight curfew, so he decided to take a shortcut back to his boarding home. He beetled quickly through a golf course down by the Neebing River. As he got near a footbridge, he heard some rustling. Three white men approached and asked him if he had a smoke.

He did and he gave it to them.

Then they asked Darryl if he was in the Native Syndicate because he was wearing their colours, white and black. Darryl was decked out in white track pants, white runners, and a white sweater with a panda on the chest and black stripes on the sleeves. The white pants also had black lines down the side. He had just purchased the sweater at the local mall.

He told them he was not part of a gang.

The men demanded to see his arms. They wanted to see if he had any tattoos indicating gang membership.

Darryl refused and told them that he didn't need to show them anything because he wasn't in a gang. Again, he repeated he wasn't in the Native Syndicate.

The men didn't like his answer. They began to beat him, punching, hitting, and kicking him to the ground. One ran at him with a wooden two-by-four and struck it across his back. Darryl fell to his knees. Another man kicked him in the stomach. He remembers they yelled racial slurs, calling him, "Crazy Native shit, you dirt," and threatening him, "You are going to get your ass kicked now, do you like this now?"

Darryl was screaming for help but no one came. He thought he was going to die right there by the river. Then one of the men gave him a solid punch in the face before all three of them began dragging Darryl toward the river.

They heaved him up and tossed him into the ice-cold water, then hauled him out again, beat him some more, and threw him back in.

Darryl's broken body began to go into shock. He remembers looking at the water and seeing a shiny reflection on the surface: ice was forming. Suddenly he was so, so cold. *This is it*, he thought. *Nobody is hearing me.*

He tried to swim but the pain in his back was too intense. He struggled to stand and was buoyed by the realization that the water was only up to his belly button. But his shoes were sticking to the muddy river floor. The ground was so slimy, his entire foot sank downward when he stood up. It was as if he was walking in quicksand. One shoe came off and then he lost the other.

He made it to the grass and the rocks. His feet were so cold and painful, it felt like he was standing on steel daggers. He started to crawl on the grass on his belly, moving as fast as he could to the road. He tried to flag down a car but no one stopped. Then he saw an out-of-service bus coming toward him. He stood in the middle of the road and waved his arms.

When the bus came to a stop, Darryl begged the driver not to call the police but to take him home. He was petrified that if he told the police what had happened, somehow the three men would come looking for him.

Darryl's pleas worked. Petrified and in shock, he started to cry.

When he got off the bus, he ran to his boarding home.

It wasn't until the next day, when he was back at school, that he told the principal, Jonathan Kakegamic, what had happened. Jonathan told Darryl he needed to tell the police or this would happen again to other students. Darryl relented.

The principal called the police, who came to the school to interview Darryl. They told him that they would get right on the case and keep him informed of any developments.

It would take years for the police to contact Darryl again. The Ontario Provincial Police called to interview him about his experience so it could be included in the inquest regarding the deaths of the seven DFC students.

Soon after Darryl was attacked, his mother flew to Thunder Bay from Weagamow to take her son home. She would not let her son complete his high school education in Thunder Bay.

To date, no one has been charged for Darryl's assault.

ON MAY 29, 2008, the Assembly of First Nations held a "National Day of Action for Indigenous People" in Ottawa. Shannen Koostachin and her class travelled from Attawapiskat on the James Bay coast to attend the rally and to ask the government, one more time, for a new school. The school she and her friends attended, J. R. Nakogee Elementary, was made up entirely of portables. The old school was the one that had been condemned due to a diesel leak in 1979, causing mould to grow in the walls.

Shannen, a bright and inquisitive girl, wanted to go to a school that was in a real building with walls and a gymnasium and a library. So she started writing letters to editors at newspapers and to politicians, demanding a new school be built so she could enjoy what most other Canadian students did — the right to receive a proper education.

On the National Day of Action Shannen and her class met with the Conservative government's Indian Affairs minister, Chuck Strahl. Shannen, along with classmates Solomon Rae and Chris Kataquapit, would plead their case. Mushkegowuk Grand Chief Stan Louttit would also be in attendance.

The kids were led to a plush Parliament Hill office with cornice mouldings. To break the ice, Strahl asked the kids what they thought of his office.

Shannen responded, "I wish I had a classroom that is as nice as your office."[19]

Strahl immediately told the kids that building a school in Attawapiskat wasn't on the Conservative government's list of priorities. The meeting was over. Some of the Elders began to cry.

The minister quickly stood up and said he had another commitment. Before Shannen left the room, she looked Strahl in the eye and said she wouldn't give up. She expected Strahl to respond. The children of Attawapiskat had been promised a new school by at least two Indian Affairs ministers. Nothing ever came of those promises.

Outside, on Parliament Hill, Shannen spoke in front of the crowd gathered for the National Day of Action on Indigenous rights. Children of all ethnicities showed up to lend their support. They wore white T-shirts emblazoned with slogans of support and children's palm prints.

Cindy Blackstock was also there, as was Shawn Atleo, the then national chief of the Assembly of First Nations. There is a picture of Shannen just as she takes to the microphone. She is wearing a black Assembly of First Nations–sponsored anti-poverty T-shirt. Her long black hair is pulled back into a ponytail with a few wind-swept strands framing her face. Atleo is looking with pride and conviction at this thirteen-year-old member of Attawapiskat First Nation.

Shannen blasted Chuck Strahl with logic and kindness on his very own doorstep.

"School should be a time for dreams. Every kid deserves this," Shannen told the crowd surrounding her as the cameras rolled. The national media clamoured for interviews with her afterwards.[20]

Two weeks later, thousands of Indigenous people gathered in Ottawa to hear a historic apology: Prime Minister Stephen Harper had gathered the heads of all the Indigenous nations — the Métis, the First Nations, the Inuit — to make a formal apology to the eighty thousand living survivors of the residential school system.

That day Dennis Franklin opened its doors to local members of the Indigenous community as well as its students, so that everyone could gather together to watch the apology, which was broadcast live. Alvin sat on one of the plastic chairs with the students and local survivors of the cultural genocide.

On the floor of the House of Commons, representatives from all Indigenous communities across Canada sat in full headdress, waiting for the prime minister to begin. In a quiet monotone, Harper said:

Two primary objectives of the Residential Schools system were to remove and isolate children from the influence of their homes, families, traditions and cultures, and to assimilate them into the dominant culture. These objectives were based on the assumption Aboriginal cultures and spiritual beliefs were inferior and unequal. Indeed, some sought, as it was infamously said, "to kill the Indian in the child." Today, we recognize that this policy of assimilation was wrong, has caused great harm, and has no place in our country.

The burden of this experience has been on your shoulders for far too long. The burden is properly ours as a Government, and as a country. There is no place in Canada for the attitudes that inspired the Indian Residential Schools system to ever prevail again. You have been working on recovering from this experience for a long time, and in a very real sense we are now joining you on this journey. The Government of Canada sincerely apologizes and asks the forgiveness of the Aboriginal peoples of this country for failing them so profoundly.[21]

As Alvin listened quietly to Harper's speech, he thought about the children of Nishnawbe Aski Nation and the situation they were in right now. Most of them didn't have any clean water to drink or to bathe in. Many lived in houses without plumbing or proper heating. Fires were constantly claiming the lives of NAN kids because they lived in poorly constructed tinderbox houses that used homemade wood stoves to heat the rooms. Alvin thought about the abject poverty most of his people lived in and the addictions they suffered in the hopes of making all their misery go away.

Alvin thought about their parents, even his own older brothers and sisters, who had gone to residential school before his family moved to Muskrat Dam. And he thought about the forced schooling of more than 150,000 Indigenous kids and what it had done to the psyche of the people and the impact it had had on the next generation and the next.

And then he thought about the five dead students there in Thunder Bay. A direct line of causation could be drawn from the residential school legacy to the failings in the government-run education system his people were left with. Alvin thought about all of this as he stared into Stephen Harper's face living large on the screen in front of him.

ON JANUARY 14, 2009, Rhoda and Berenson King, represented by Aboriginal Legal Services of Toronto, officially asked for standing at the inquest into their son's death. Julian

Falconer did the same on behalf of Nishnawbe Aski Nation. NAN argued that Reggie Bushie belonged to one of the forty-nine First Nations represented by NAN and as such, they had a right to be there.

Also requesting standing was Northern Nishnawbe Education Council, the Indigenous group that ran Dennis Franklin Cromarty; the Office of the Provincial Advocate for Children and Youth; and Indigenous and Northern Affairs Canada (INAC).

Both NAN and Rhoda King had an additional request. They filed motions questioning the validity of the selection process of the five-member jury.

"The jury roll issue must be dealt with. In order for the community and the family to have confidence in the process, there has to be transparency in the jury selection," Fiddler said.

By now, the Thunder Bay Police were fully aware of the deaths of the five students and how three of them — Curran, Jethro, and now Reggie — had, suspiciously, wound up in the water. The police were also well aware of the case of Shawon Wavy, who was beaten by a gang of kids, and of Darryl Kakekayash's near-death experience. There was a clear pattern here.

There was also a clear and apparent crisis of confidence in the justice system in the north. Indigenous people did not participate in the jury system. They did not trust the justice system. So they were being charged by white officers and then they were tried and judged by white people.

Fiddler and NAN steadfastly maintained they would not move forward until the issue of providing representational juries for Indigenous cases was rectified. The Bushie family wasn't the only one to challenge Indigenous participation on juries. Another inquest was making its way through the system: one looking into the death of Jacy Pierre, a twenty-seven-year-old Fort William First Nation man who died of a drug overdose in the Thunder Bay Jail in October 2007. His grandmother, Marlene Pierre, and his mother, Elizabeth Pierre, joined the Bushie family in demanding the inquest jury include Indigenous people. Both families asked for a stay of the inquests — a temporary halt — until a judicial review could take place. Both asked their presiding coroners to issue a summons to the director of court operations so they could find out how the jury roll was put together. In both inquests, Jacy Pierre's and Reggie Bushie's, the presiding coroners refused. They also refused to halt the inquest into Jacy Pierre's death, which was already under way, but granted a stay in Bushie's upcoming case. Pierre's legal counsel appealed the decision.

- 8 -

RIVER, GIVE ME MY SON BACK

WITHIN THE SPAN OF TWO YEARS, THE TINY NORTH-western Ontario community of Keewaywin First Nation lost two teenagers at DFC: Robyn Harper in 2007 and then Kyle Morrisseau in 2009. The deaths of two kids in a community of 350 people is the equivalent of losing seven hundred teenagers in Thunder Bay.

Keewaywin is a tight-knit community with many close relations. DFC teacher and principal Jonathan Kakegamic's cousin was Christian Morrisseau, Kyle's dad. Robyn and Kyle were his students.

Everyone knew Kyle Morrisseau. He was a sociable, kind boy who was known to literally give the shirt off his back to his friends. Kyle was also part of Keewaywin's most famous family, the large Morrisseau clan whose patriarch was the famed Ojibwe painter Norval Morrisseau. Norval was Kyle's grandfather. Like many members of his family, Kyle was an artist and had a particular gift, just like Norval. It was only a matter of time before he would go on to do great things in the art world.

NORVAL MORRISSEAU HAD SEVEN children with his first and only wife, Harriet Kakegamic. He met Harriet in the early 1950s while he was a tuberculosis patient in a sanatorium in Thunder Bay. Back in the day, there was a belief that Indigenous people suffered a more virulent, widespread form of tuberculosis, or consumption. Unsure of what to do with all the desperately sick Indians coughing up blood in the bushes, white doctors and public health professionals corralled the sick into sanatoriums strictly for Indigenous people.

Tuberculosis, a bacterial lung infection, spread like wildfire through the Indigenous population because it was a new infection for them, brought over by the Europeans in the 1700s and never before encountered by Indigenous DNA. The death rate among Indigenous people was 700 to every 100,000. For children who caught the disease in overcrowded residential schools, it was even worse — 8,000 out of 100,000.[1]

While lying in the hospital, Norval met Harriet, a Cree woman from Sandy Lake who also suffered from TB and who had had part of her lung surgically removed. They married in 1957 and led a simple life. They lived in the bush in Beardmore and then later, at Red Lake. She taught Norval how to read Cree syllabics and he began to use them to sign his name to his paintings.

Norval painted to support their growing family. First

came David, then Victoria, Peter, Eugene, Michael, Lisa, and Christian.

Norval taught Christian to paint. Christian would stand at his side at their home in Keewaywin and quietly watch as his father freely brushed the stories of the medicine man and the spirits of the Ojibwe.

Born Jean-Baptiste Norman Henry Morrisseau in 1931 in Thunder Bay, Norval was given the Ojibwe name of Copper Thunderbird by a medicine woman trying to save his life from an unknown illness when he was a teenager. Norval's art followed no traditional school of thought. He made up his own style by listening to the spirit within and putting to canvas Ojibwe oral stories and traditions taught to him by his grandfather.

Morrisseau, the oldest of five children, was raised by his maternal grandparents. His grandfather Moses was a well-respected shaman who instilled the legends of their people in his grandson. Like every other First Nations person born after 1876, Norval was born under the Indian Act and was sent to one of the residential schools that were set up across Canada. The Morrisseau family, like nearly every other Indigenous family, is haunted by the after-effects of residential school.

When Norval was six, he was sent to residential school in Thunder Bay. Illness brought him home in grade three and he never went back. Living in Beardmore, he taught and practised his art. An artist from Thunder Bay, Susan Ross, was amazed by what she saw. She convinced her friend Toronto gallery owner Jack Pollock to come up north.

In 1962, Pollock went to Beardmore and was immediately entranced. He offered to exhibit all of Norval's art in
Toronto. The exhibit was held in September of that year
and it was a smashing success. Every single painting was
sold.

His career began to take off and his life forever changed.
Harriet began having babies just as Morrisseau became
a Canadian and international sensation. He was comis-
sioned to create a mural for the Indians of Canada Pavilion
at Expo 67 in Montreal. He travelled frequently to Toronto.
He was living and drinking large.

It would all catch up to him. In 1972, he was severely
burned in a Vancouver hotel fire. One year later, he was
arrested and incarcerated due to alcohol-related offences.
Christian says the judge threw Norval in jail for his own
good, so he could dry out. The prison he was in was so
cognizant of the famed artist inside their walls that he was
given an adjoining cell to use as a studio.[2]

When he was released from prison, his career was back
on the upswing. Documentaries were being made about
him, and he had shows and exhibitions in Germany and
Norway. The Art Gallery of Ontario promoted his prom-
inence by establishing the Woodland School of painting,
one that focused on sacred images of northern spirits and
animals.

But it all came crashing down again in the late 1980s,
when he hit the bottle hard and burned through his
money. He would drink anything he could get his hands
on. Christian tells a story of his father trading sketches
hastily drawn on napkins or scraps of paper in exchange

for a bottle. The family rarely saw Norval at this time but, as Christian says, they didn't chase after him. They let him be.

In 1994, Norval suffered a debilitating stroke, two years after his grandson Kyle was born and the same year Kyle's brother Josh came into the world. Norval was never the same again.

Christian remembers that when Josh was first born, he and one-and-a-half-year-old Kyle hopped on the bus to go to the hospital. Christian will never forget his son's excitement at the idea of having a younger brother. As soon as the elevator doors opened, Kyle took off like a shot, running through the halls, looking for his new baby brother. Instead, he bumped into a nurse.

She caught him and asked Christian if that was his son. She then led them to his wife's room and opened the door.

"Baby!" Kyle said, the moment he saw Josh.

When Kyle was a boy in Keewaywin, Christian walked him to school every morning.

"From the first day he went to school, he liked it. He liked the interaction, all the grades were in one building. Every morning, he would always get me up, yelling, 'Daddy, it is school time.'"

When the winter came, Christian would load his little bundle up and place him on the back of his skidoo in a box sled made out of old panels of wood.

By the time Kyle was in grade six, he started an odd habit. He gave everything he had away — his new shirt, pencils, paper, whatever he had. If one of the other kids liked what he had, he would give it to them.

Kyle's father was tickled by his son's kindness.

"By grade eight, all the kids loved him. They looked up to him, they learned from his sharing. And they loved to watch him dance," Christian says fondly.

The entire community loved to dance and Keewaywin was huge on square dancing. When Kyle was in grade eight, he volunteered to be a dancer in the holiday show. He showed up to one of the concert practices with Josh in tow and began breakdancing to an electronic beat. He got down on the floor and moved like lightning, twirling and spinning on his back. His cousin Robbie, who was organizing the concert, was so impressed he asked Kyle to end the show with a solo performance. Kyle was thrilled. He brought the house down.

IT WAS IN 2007 that the musical boy with the big heart first seriously picked up a paintbrush. That same year, on December 4, 2007, his grandfather, the great Ojibwe master, died of a heart attack, leaving his own large legacy behind.

Christian put down his paintbrush for a while after his father died. "I had stopped because I used to paint with my dad, I used to see him on the other side of the table. When he died, I just couldn't paint anymore. But then Kyle said to me, 'Dad, aren't you going to teach me how to paint?' I told him I would teach him but that he had to listen to what I was saying."

Christian told Kyle the legends of their people, the shaman's words, while he taught him how to balance colour and paint inside the lines. "I told him to hold the pencil at the ends and let the spirit guide you."

What Kyle sketched and later painted was remarkable. His talent was innate. The learning came easy; the painting flowed.

When Christian got a call from an Ottawa gallery owner to see if he was interested in holding an exhibition, he told them only if they would display some of his son's work.

They agreed.

Fifteen of Kyle's paintings were put into the Ottawa show along with his father's work. On opening night, nine of Kyle's paintings were sold compared to three of Christian's.

"I have a photograph of him holding his first cheque," Christian laughs.

While Kyle loved school and his friends, he also loved the comforts of his home and his family. The thought of moving away to go to high school was not easy for young Kyle. He did not want to leave his brother Josh or his dad — both of whom he was incredibly close to. They were the rocks in his life and the three of them were never separated for long. This must have played in Kyle's adolescent mind when he decided not to leave Keewaywin with all his friends to go to Thunder Bay in September 2006. But once they were gone, Kyle realized he had made a mistake. So Kyle did what any kid his age would do — he asked his dad to go with him to Thunder Bay.

Christian, who often travelled to the city for art shows, gave the request some deep thought. He knew the bond they had was special, and as a father he needed to nurture and cherish it. But he also knew he couldn't leave

Josh behind. Kyle wouldn't leave Keewaywin without Josh anyway. So Christian asked Josh if he wanted to go with them and he agreed: the three of them would move to Thunder Bay.

The Morrisseau men first lived in an apartment with Christian's brother Eugene. Christian assumed he could enroll Kyle in the First Nations high school, Dennis Franklin. But at the time, the school had strict rules about who could attend: only those kids coming from a remote northern community. If a student wanted to go to DFC, they had to live in a boarding home. It was a bizarre Catch-22 — Christian and the boys were being penalized because Christian had decided to move to Thunder Bay with his son.

Christian had no choice but to enroll Kyle with Josh at Sir Winston Churchill Collegiate and Vocational Institute — a school directly beside Dennis Franklin which offered grades seven to twelve — until he could sort out the jurisdictional issues with NNEC.

Just like he did back home in Keewaywin, Christian would rise early and walk the two boys to school. It was a time he enjoyed, watching his lithe, enthusiastic, and spirited sons head off to the classroom. By winter, the boys were feeling pretty confident and a bit too cool to have their dad walk them to school. They told Christian he didn't have to come along anymore. They could make it on their own.

Christian remembers that conversation; it is seared into his mind as a father. He knew it was a turning point in their young lives. He also remembers following them that first day they walked on their own, hiding in the bushes to make sure they made it safely to school.

That year was full of happiness. The three Morrisseau men moved out of Eugene's apartment and got a place of their own on Lark Street across town in Port Arthur. It was a hike to get to school but they had more room and some privacy. The boys had their own bedrooms and Christian slept on the couch. He surrounded the apartment with his paints, brushes, and canvases. The walls were filled with his bright, bold paintings of the Ojibwe spirits. After school, all the kids would come over for snacks and to "game out." The boys were big gamers. The house was always full of kids playing video games, spinning music, and breakdancing.

Soon, the apartment was so packed with Christian's art they had to move to a larger place. Christian found them a three-storey home on Port Arthur. Kyle and Josh had the third floor and Christian was on the main floor, while the second floor was converted into his studio.

June came around and the boys celebrated a successful end of the school year. Both had passed their grades. Christian and Kyle decided to stay for the summer in Thunder Bay, while Josh went home to Keewaywin.

"I told Kyle he could go too but he said, 'No, Dad. You came out here so I could go to school. So I won't leave you.'"

At the time Christian remembers he was having difficulties making ends meet. It was expensive, living in the city and caring for his boys while also sending money back home to Keewaywin.

In the middle of the summer, Kyle said, "Dad, let's go home."

Instead, Christian sent Kyle back to Keewaywin, while he stayed behind to sell some art and give away their furniture. Then he would move back home.

That summer, Kyle's mother again tried to get him enrolled in school for September — Kyle wanted to be with his friends at Pelican Falls in Sioux Lookout or at DFC with the other northern kids. Pelican was at capacity, but Christian's cousin Robbie said that there might be room at DFC. Robbie Kakegamic was in charge of the Keewaytinook Okimakanak Secondary School Support counsellors who looked after all the students from KO nations — Poplar Hill, Keewaywin, North Spirit Lake, McDowell Lake, Deer Lake, and Fort Severn. The KO tribal council had decided to look after their own after Reggie Bushie died.

Because Kyle was at home for the summer and had no address in Thunder Bay, he could be considered by the NNEC as a northern student needing placement. He just had to wait to see if any of the kids decided to not return to school in the fall. If that was the case, there would be a spot for Kyle. He just had to wait for the call. It would come at the last minute, and he would have to pack his bags and head to the airport.

The call came when Kyle was out partridge hunting with Josh.

"When he came back, I asked him and he said yes. I packed him up and he took off on his own," says Christian.

But this time, seventeen-year-old Kyle would have to live in a boarding house, without his father or his brother.

He'd have to take a public bus to high school and take care of himself.

"I told him to listen to the new parents," remembers Christian.

At first, Kyle called home almost every night and he kept in constant contact with his family. But the calls became more sporadic as time passed. On October 6, 2009, less than three weeks before Kyle went missing, Christian's cousin Robbie, who was also the counsellor assigned to watch over Kyle while he was in Thunder Bay, wrote an occurrence report detailing Kyle's drinking and noted he had been picked up twice by the police for being intoxicated and underage. He noted on the report that it might be a good idea for Kyle to learn more about the effects of alcohol and what it does to your body.

In Kyle's school file, there were notes about his failure to return to his boarding home after curfew twice. The notes, written by an official with the Nishnawbe Education Council, said that Kyle's boarding parent, Barb Malcolm, called in on both occasions to say that Kyle had not come home and had missed his 10:00 p.m. curfew.

This was peculiar behaviour for Kyle. Kyle loved school. But his first semester final report card shows a kid struggling. His final mark for visual arts was 2 percent.[3]

The teacher commented, "Kyle demonstrates limited understanding of the concepts, elements, principles and theories in this course. Absenteeism and a lack of assignments submitted have affected his mark."

In his career studies class, the teacher couldn't even assign him a mark because of chronic absenteeism.

The Kyle who loved school was suddenly nowhere to be found.

The one assignment he did complete was a resumé. In it, he notes his full name, *Kyle Peter Morrisseau*, and that he went to Keewaywin Public School until grade eight, then to Churchill for grades nine and ten. He listed his awards by saying, *Won lots of gold medals and trophies for being the best at sports (gym).* This was true. In grade school Kyle had been a remarkable athlete. For his work experience, Kyle noted he was a logger, a labourer, a deliveryman on the rez, and that he babysat. Under hobbies, Kyle said they were *Meeting laydies, playing sports, chilling... Any day, any time.*

When Kyle failed to come home on Monday, October 26, 2009, a school night, it was Robbie who got the call from the boarding parent. Robbie wrote down in his notes that Kyle was out drinking with Michael Fox and Ivan Masakeyash and that he had missed his curfew.

On Tuesday at 2:00 p.m., Robbie called Christian to let him know that Kyle was nowhere to be found. He told Christian that Kyle had blown curfew on three other occasions, but he had always come home. Robbie, along with other teachers from Dennis Franklin, had already been out all night looking for Kyle. He told the KO's education director, acclaimed Woodland artist Goyce Kakegamic, who called Norma Kejick, who was now the NNEC director of education. Even though KO assumed responsibility for all their First Nations children, Norma felt responsible for all the students under her watch. To hear that another boy had gone missing, so soon after Reggie, felt like a punch in the gut. As soon as she hung up the phone with Goyce, Norma called one of her colleagues to let him know of Kyle's disappearance. She will never forget what he said to her — he told her it was the dinner hour and that she could fill him in tomorrow morning.

Norma put the phone down and began to cry. The next day, she went straight to her office and got on the phone with Goyce, Robbie, and DFC principal Jonathan Kakegamic and asked to be kept in the loop with any updates.

On Wednesday, Robbie formally filed a missing persons report with Thunder Bay Police.

KYLE MORRISSEAU WENT MISSING when the inquest into the death of Reggie Bushie had just been announced. Morrisseau's disappearance reaffirmed Alvin's suspicions — the kids were vulnerable, living in a hostile city; they didn't have adequate social support and they were attending a school that was struggling to cope. Kyle was the sixth DFC student lost while attending the school. The DFC teachers were desperately trying to do everything they could to keep their students safe. They knew they weren't just teachers or receptionists or janitors; they were also caring for the nearly 150 kids enrolled at the school, all of whom were several hundred kilometres away from their home communities and living in a strange city. DFC staff did everything they could to be parents to their students — they fed them three meals a day, the Elders' room was always open, with bannock and a fresh pot of tea at the ready for anyone seeking comfort, and they had vans patrolling the streets, 24-7, looking for wayward kids.

"I'm on the clock until all the kids are home," said Kakegamic. "I can say that for all my teachers."

The NNEC was also acutely aware of the problems their kids faced in Thunder Bay. They had commissioned numerous reports and written a myriad of policies and procedures intended to help the kids and keep them safe. But all the policies in the world do not help if the proper funding and infrastructure are not fully in place.

When Christian found out his son was missing, he went to his chief in Keewaywin and told him he needed to fly to Thunder Bay. The same day Robbie filed the missing persons report, Christian left the rez on a small plane to Sioux Lookout, then transferred planes to Thunder Bay.

He remembers looking down at the orange and yellow city lights twinkling on Superior. He remembers filling himself with hope and faith. *I'm going to find him*, he thought, *and I won't come home until I do.*

Thunder Bay Police were already searching for Kyle. From the day he went missing to the day Kyle's body was found, police chased at least eight supposed sightings of the teenager at various downtown spots. Everybody thought they had spotted Kyle. Robbie made a diary of the search, and there was a daily entry about either a sighting of the missing boy or something they needed to follow up on. On multiple occasions, Robbie remembers heading down to the police station or calling to let them know about a new lead.

The official police notes entered into the inquest record

the sightings of Kyle and their efforts to track him down. The notes read like they were chasing their tails. So many leads, nothing panning out. And each time there was a new sighting, Norma, in Sioux Lookout, was called. The frequency of the sightings made her believe that Kyle was out there, but for that some reason he just didn't want to go back to his boarding home or to school.

One sighting was of Kyle walking with a "Native blonde girl." Another had him sad and sober under a bridge with an unidentified female. Another had him at the Brodie Street bus terminal on Halloween night.

"There were several times we thought it was him and then we would rush there," says Robbie. "We searched left and right. We barely slept."

But the clothes he was wearing when his body was pulled from the river are consistent with what he had on the last day he was definitely seen, October 26, at Dennis Franklin Cromarty. Security footage shows him in the hallway at 12:31 p.m., walking toward the cafeteria. Again, his image is picked up, leaving a second-floor classroom at 2:52 p.m., and then leaving the school at 2:56 p.m. and walking toward the intersection of Churchill and Edward Streets.[4] He is wearing the same black hoodie, black T-shirt and pants, and black socks that were found on him when his body was discovered in the river.

Student Miranda Kakekagumick ran into Kyle at around 3:00 p.m., on the walkway on the south side of the school. They spoke briefly. Kyle told her he was going to get some money and then he walked toward Edward Street.[5]

There is conflicting evidence as to whether or not Kyle visited his uncle Eugene Morrisseau, whom he usually spoke to daily on the phone. Eugene called Kyle's boarding house every single day to see if his nephew was all right. Morrisseau told police he couldn't remember if it was the Sunday or the Monday, late afternoon, that he last saw his nephew. If it was that Monday, it would explain the lag in time between Kyle leaving school and going to the mall. Eugene does remember Kyle told him that he was bored.[6]

Kyle shows up again at the Intercity mall, at 7:00 p.m. Robbie tracked down two of the last people to have seen Kyle alive and had them come into his office to give a statement to police. Rhanda Kakekagumick and Aaron Bluecoat said that Kyle and a man named Ivan Masakeyash approached them at the mall and asked them if they wanted to go have some drinks. The two accepted so they walked to the train trestle located at the McIntyre River and spent about half an hour under the bridge.

Kyle got drunk fast. Police notes say he asked Ivan if he knew how to get him a gun. He said he needed it for protection. Rhanda told Kyle not to be foolish, he didn't need a gun. Rhanda said Kyle got mad at her and started pushing her. She said that she pinned him to the ground in an effort to calm him down. She told police Kyle apologized and she "ditched him there and left the area."

She and Aaron walked away from Kyle. She said she saw Kyle trying to get up from the ground, that he said he was sorry and asked her not to go. Kyle had never mentioned anything about gangs. When it came to why he wanted a gun, she said that Kyle's shoes had been stolen in the past, as well as his weed and even some Percocets.

Aaron backed up Rhanda's story, saying that they were at the entrance of the Intercity mall between 7:00 and 8:00 p.m. when Kyle and Masakeyash first approached them. He said he agreed to go with the two boys because he was concerned that Kyle was with Masakeyash, who seemed a bit shady. Aaron said the four of them shared a bottle of whisky near the train tracks behind Shoppers Drug Mart. Then he went to SilverCity to get something to eat. He returned to find Rhanda on top of Kyle, pinning him down. He told police he didn't know what they were arguing about.

When Aaron left with Rhanda, Kyle was still with Ivan. Kyle was drinking from the bottle and starting to stagger. Aaron told police what Kyle and Ivan were wearing. He mentioned Kyle was carrying his backpack.

Kyle's mother, Lorene Morrisseau, told police she spoke with her son at 10:00 that evening.[7] He told her he was at his boarding house and that his boarding parent, Barb Malcolm, was at the hospital with her husband.

Kyle asked his mom for his friend Tyler Neekan's phone number. He told his mom he was going to the Brodie Street bus terminal. She told police he sounded high. Kyle told his mother he had been drinking a little. He asked her to deposit more money into his bank account. (Christian deposited $36 into Kyle's bank account, but the money was never accessed.)[8]

Before he hung up, Kyle told his mother that he loved her.

ROBBIE KAKEGAMIC FULLY ADMITS he is no police officer. He has no background in law enforcement. He is a father and a counsellor. He does not know how to conduct an investigation.

But something gnaws at him.

He does not understand why Thunder Bay Police waited two whole weeks before interviewing Ivan Masakeyash.

On the night that Kyle went missing, Ivan was arrested for another, unrelated matter. A man named Frank Williams had called 911 that night, alleging Ivan tried to break in through his window. There was a party going on inside his home. Police notes indicate Williams was "very intoxicated."

Williams told police he didn't know Ivan well, but on the night of October 26, Ivan knocked on his window and broke it. He told Ivan to "get the fuck out of here," but Ivan wanted to fight him. Ivan took off when Williams called the police.

Five days after Kyle's death, on October 31, Thunder Bay Police Constable John Fennell wrote in his notes that Robbie had requested that the police put out another press release, leaning on the fact that Kyle was the grandson of famed Ojibwe artist Norval Morrisseau. Robbie hoped this would prompt the media to take a more active role in the search for Kyle. Constable Fennell also noted that there were questions surrounding Kyle's acquaintance with Ivan: "Concern that Kyle may be involved with Native Syndicate given association with Ivan Masakeyash."[9]

Robbie wasted no time in tracking down Ivan at the Thunder Bay Jail, where he visited him and asked about

Kyle. Earlier, Robbie had searched Kyle's room and found notes regarding what appeared to be debts that someone owed. Robbie worried Kyle may have gotten mixed up with the Native Syndicate.[10]

When Robbie spoke to Christian about his suspicions about Kyle's possible drug debts, Christian did not believe his son wrote the notes. It wasn't Kyle's handwriting and further, he knew his son well — there was no way Kyle could be part of the Syndicate.

Thunder Bay Police made a note of Ivan's whereabouts in jail on Friday, October 30. Police records indicate Ivan was interviewed on November 11, 2009. Ivan told police he didn't really know Kyle; he'd just met him recently when he'd gone drinking with him on October 23 (Ivan would later testify at the inquest that it was the 26th) and that later that evening he was arrested. Ivan also denied he was associated with the Native Syndicate.[11]

AT THE INQUEST INTO the deaths of the seven students, Ivan testified via videolink from Sioux Lookout that the first time he met Kyle had been that night at the Intercity mall.

Kyle had been looking for a runner, and Ivan agreed to buy alcohol for him, but only if he could have some too.

"I met the boy that night there. Before that, I never met him. After that, I never met him," Ivan told the inquest.

The group drank under the bridge.

"The boy said he was in trouble, he needed something to protect himself," Ivan said.[12]

CHRISTIAN SPENT TEN DAYS looking for his son before giving up.

He gave up on the tenth day because his wife, Lorene, woke up screaming, "Dad, come here!"

Christian asked her what was wrong and she wailed, "No, it hurts."

He thought breakfast would help her but she was unable to eat. She asked her husband if he thought someone was feeding Kyle. Christian told her he did not know.

"That hurt me. As soon as I heard that I went to the LCBO and I grabbed a 60-ouncer and started guzzling. I drank all day."

Robbie came by the hotel. He watched Christian's silent breakdown.

Then he said, "Don't give up. Something has got to change."

CHRISTIAN COULD NOT CONTROL his anger. He walked down to the river to curse Nanabijou, the Sleeping Giant, the formation of volcanic rocks that resembles a man lying down on his back, his arms folded on his chest.

He screamed at the giant, asking him what else he could possibly want.

"I paint everything, I share all your stupid-ass stuff, and this is what you give me? Fuck you. Give me my son back!"

Thunder Bay Police found Christian on the street. He had been drinking. He was overwhelmed with feelings of anxiety and shame. He knew he would be punished for cursing at Nanabijou.

He slept all day and dreamed about his son. Kyle was dressed all in red and he was bopping around, twirling fast like the Tasmanian Devil from the Looney Tunes cartoons. He said, "Dad, I'm hurting too."

Christian woke up at 5:00 p.m. to his son Josh, who had joined his parents in the search for Kyle, telling him they had to go to the high school. The police had found a body in the river. "I went to the school but I knew already. They found him floating. I knew it was my son."

Kyle's body was discovered by a man walking down by the water. He saw something floating in the McIntyre River, southbound along the railway trestle. He called police.

Fire crews retrieved Kyle. Police noted there were burn holes in the upper front of his pants and a tear on the outside of the left thigh.[13] The post-mortem noted he had abrasions on both of his shins. His blood ethanol level was 228 mg/100 ml. Between 300 and 400 is considered fatal.

Coroners believe Kyle died of drowning. They also noted Kyle consumed alcohol before he died and that while it was a contributing factor to his death, it wasn't the cause.[14]

Christian was full of rage. "I was so fucking mad."

That afternoon, Goyce called Norma to tell her police believed they had found Kyle's body in the water. Norma remembers she tried to find her boss, to let him know and to ask for permission to travel to Thunder Bay. Even though she was the education director, all her travel had to be approved by her superior. The problem was, she couldn't find him. She wondered if he was on one of his long coffee breaks. Norma called his secretary, who decided to bypass protocol and went ahead and booked Norma on the next flight to Thunder Bay. When Norma arrived, Goyce called and told her to go directly to the hospital where the family had gathered to view the body.

She remembers waiting in Robin's Donuts, the hospital coffee shop, as she watched Christian go to identify his son. Kyle's mother, Lorene, did not want to go. She stayed in the lobby area, surrounded by family. What Norma heard next stopped her cold. Christian had come back upstairs to speak to Lorene, who let out a loud, hollow wail. Norma had heard the same sound just once before, and that was from Rhoda King. It was the sound of a mother learning her son was dead.

They left the hospital and drove to the school, where they were met by police and members of the community. Christian spoke to Constable Baxter and then he turned to Josh and asked him to go with him for a walk. He wanted to head to the nearest river to pray.

"We took some tobacco and when we laid that tobacco we said, 'Miigwetch. Thank you.' That is it. It was not easy to thank the river for taking my son."

LESS THAN WORTHY VICTIMS

THE COURT OF APPEAL JUDGEMENT IN BOTH THE REGGIE Bushie and Jacy Pierre cases came out on March 10, 2011, and it was damning. The Court said they were concerned with the representation in the coroner jury rolls in Thunder Bay and their concern was fuelled by the unwillingness of either coroner to discuss how the jury rolls were formed. The families had had a reasonable question — How do you form the juries? — and both coroners had denied them an answer. "Instead, they got the run around. A lot of time and money might have been saved had the Ministry and the coroners simply provided this information," the Court of Appeal wrote.[1]

The court also ruled that both families had put forward enough evidence that an inquiry should take place on how the Thunder Bay jury rolls were formed. It also granted a new inquest for the Pierre family.

While everyone was waiting for the Court of Appeal

decision, Falconer started to work the back channels, spreading the word about what was happening in the north. He was meeting with high-placed Toronto justice officials in hallways and at restaurants. Ontario's chief coroner Andrew McCallum and Ontario's deputy Attorney General Murray Segal agreed with Falconer: juries must be representational.

Suddenly, a large portion of the entire justice system in Northern Ontario — from regular trial by jury courts to inquests — was put on hold in order to study the problem. Over the next five years, the legal wrangling would delay any movement on the Bushie inquest and nearly twenty other cases.[2]

WHILE THE BUSHIE CASE was stalled and a judicial review was under way, Nishnawbe Aski Nation lost another student. On May 10, 2011, the body of fifteen-year-old Jordan Wabasse, a student at the Matawa Learning Centre, was found in the Kaministiquia River. He was the seventh student to have perished and the fifth student whose body was recovered in one of the city's rivers. Over the course of the eleven years the seven students died, the Government of Canada attempted to repair the fractured relationship it has with Indigenous people: there was Prime Minister Stephen Harper's historic apology for the horror of the residential school system and the beginning of the Truth and Reconciliation Commission that would move across Canada collecting the stories of six thousand survivors. Members of Parliament would stand up and unanimously pledge their faith to Jordan's Principle and they would do the same one year later on Monday, February 27, 2012, with Shannen's Dream, which declared that all First Nations children have the right to a high-quality education and that the funding of First Nations schools should be on par with non-Indigenous schools. But bureaucratic inertia combined with the trappings of history—the confines of the Indian Act, the disregard of Indigenous treaty rights, and the trauma of the residential school system—failed to turn those promising political words into action.

Indigenous communities continue to lack the basic necessities of life, including clean water, safe housing, working fire trucks, basic health care, and access to education. It took Ottawa until December 2010 to finally build a proper school in Attawapiskat. But Shannen Koostachin never lived to hear the news. On June 1, 2010, the fifteen-year-old, who had moved out of her community to go to high school, died of injuries from a tragic car accident.

And yet still the inequities rage. Northern First Nations families are faced with the horrific choice of either sending their children to high school in a community that cannot guarantee their safety, or keeping them at home and hoping distance education will be enough. Families are still being told—more than twenty years after the last residential school was shut down—that they must surrender their children for them to gain an education. Handing over the reins to Indigenous education authorities such as the NNEC without giving them the proper funding tools is another form of colonial control and racism.

For many Indigenous families, keeping young First Nations students safe from harm means keeping them out of Thunder Bay. As Skye Kakegamic testified at the inquest into the seven's death, "To them they just think we are savages. I always heard that word all the time and maybe they think it is funny to pick on something, like how some people think it is so funny to pick on a dog or something and torture it. To them they probably just see us like that. Something not someone."[3]

In 2013 Statistics Canada crowned Thunder Bay the hate crime capital of Canada. At 20.9 hate crimes per 100,000 of the population, Thunder Bay had more reported hate crimes than any other city in the country.

Chris Adams, executive officer of the Thunder Bay Police, explained away the statistics, turning them around and presenting them as a positive: "I think it reflects the fact that more people are coming forward, as well as our officers are utilizing the training they've been given to recognize and be able to investigate hate-motivated crimes more thoroughly."[4]

That same year, Alvin Fiddler and NAN filed an Ontario human rights complaint against high-ranking police officers after a member of the force accidentally sent out a phony press release following the murder of sixty-five-year-old Adam Yellowhead. The title of the press release read, "Fresh Mouth Killer Captured!!!" Yellowhead had been drinking mouthwash with the man who was later jailed for killing him. The lead investigator on the case wrote the release. When he was later questioned about his actions, he said it was meant to be funny and that he didn't mean anything by it. The chief of police and the mayor accepted his apology.[5]

Thunder Bay was also home to a Facebook page called "Thunder Bay Dirty," which posted pictures of drunk, homeless, or in-distress Indigenous people when they were at their most vulnerable. There were links to Twitter and YouTube posts of more of the same. At one point, "Thunder Bay Dirty" had more four thousand Facebook followers.[6]

The previous year, on December 27, 2012, a thirty-six-year-old mother was brutally raped, beaten, and left for dead on the side of the road. The woman, who does not wish to be named for fear of reprisal, had left her home momentarily to pick up some milk for her kids when a car pulled up beside her and the occupants began throwing garbage at her while calling her a "squaw" and a "dirty Indian."

Then they grabbed her, threw her into the back seat of the car, and took her far out of town. Once in a secluded area, they viciously beat and assaulted her. As they were raping her, they told her she liked it because she was Indigenous. They also warned her to keep her mouth shut, that they had done this before and they would do it again if she said anything.

The woman fled Thunder Bay after she saw one of her attackers in the mall with his family. She now lives in Winnipeg. Police say the case, which has been classified as a hate crime, is still open but no new information has come to light.

ON MAY 11, 2012, Julian Falconer wrote a letter to Chief Coroner McCallum on behalf of Nishnawbe Aski Nation, reminding him that there were now seven dead students — two more since the Reggie Bushie inquest was put on hold. NAN was demanding that all seven students be included in the inquest. Falconer implored the coroner to use his jurisdiction under the provincial Coroner's Act and expand the inquest to include all seven.

"In addition to a serious level of family and community grief over the losses of their children, a general community anxiety has now developed over the safety of their youth going forward," wrote Falconer. "Five of the deaths have occurred from drowning and six of the youth went to the same school, DFC. There are patterns to the deaths that are readily discernible but there are also major questions being raised across NAN territories on the role of intentional acts in these deaths."

After the attack on Darryl Kakekayash, Alvin and Julian saw a clear and disturbing pattern. They could not help but wonder if First Nations kids were being targeted and murdered. It was extremely rare to hear of Indigenous kids drowning on their reserves. Most First Nations people were born and raised on the water. Equally perplexing was how quickly the Thunder Bay Police wrote off investigations into the deaths. For Jethro, Curran, Reggie, and Kyle, police had issued press releases that came to the same conclusion: foul play was not suspected. Each of the deaths was classified as accidental: death by drinking too much and then drowning. To Thunder Bay Police, no one was readily responsible for the deaths of the students.

Falconer also mentioned in his letter to McCallum that he and the lawyers from his firm had travelled through Northern Ontario as part of retired Supreme Court Justice Frank Iacobucci's review of the jury system. In late summer 2011, the Ontario government appointed Iacobucci, a highly respected member of the Law Commission of Ontario, to take on the daunting task of reviewing the jury roll practice, identifying the problems, and making recommendations to fix the system. NAN and Falconer took Iacobucci to the communities where the seven young students were raised so he could meet their families and understand where they came from. Iacobucci travelled to every remote community that each of the seven students had lived in. In total he met with leadership and people from thirty-two First Nations. He called the assignment one of the most important in his distinguished legal career. The more he learned, the more he wanted to keep digging. What he found was a system in crisis: "I am of the view once Canadians see the truth of what is going on, they'll be convinced we need to do something about it."[7]

Falconer wrote that the pain the families felt was immeasurable and there was a palpable fear among the parents of sending their children away to school. The parents were also plagued by questions of the quality of the police investigations into their children's death. Having been given so few facts, they had to fill the void with rumours and half-truths. There was a collective feeling that the kids' deaths were not accidental; that they were homicides. What both Falconer and Iacobucci found most troubling was the strong possibility that the authorities had not taken the necessary steps to address these cases because the students were Indigenous. The only option, Falconer argued, was to hold an inquest into all seven deaths.

After a five-year fight and mounting evidence against the Northern Ontario justice process, the chief coroner granted Nishnawbe Aski Nation the inquest into the deaths of the seven students. It would be one of the largest inquests ever held in the province of Ontario.

Now that the battle for the inquest was over, the next hurdle was ahead. Alvin insisted the scope of the inquest should be expanded to include issues of the racism the students experience in Thunder Bay, along with federal treaty and constitutional obligations, and the quality of the Thunder Bay Police Service's investigations into the deaths of the seven students. The coroner had brought in the Ontario Provincial Police to reinvestigate the cases due to the lack of information in the Thunder Bay Police files. The re-investigation would take years and be called Project Middlesbourgh. It would explore areas not fully examined by the Thunder Bay Police in the initial investigation.

While the families of the seven kids waited for the date, location, and duration of the inquest to be announced, Iacobucci completed his report, *First Nations Representation on Ontario Juries*. His independent probe, released in February 2013, stated there was "systemic racism" throughout the court, justice, and policing systems in the north, including the mistreatment of First Nations inmates, general disrespect by police, and "discriminatory public reaction to First Nation complaints." Iacobucci wrote that Indigenous people told him there was a fundamental conflict between their cultural values, laws, and ideologies of traditional approaches to conflict resolution and the values and laws that underpin the Canadian justice system. Indigenous people wanted to re-attain harmony and balance — they wanted truth rather than retribution or punishment, he said.

There was a long-standing mistrust, an intergenerational mistrust, of all aspects of the judicial system, from the police to the courts, Iacobucci found. "If we continue with status quo we will aggravate what is already a serious situation, and any hope of true reconciliation between First Nations and Ontarians generally will vanish," he wrote. "Doing nothing will be a profound shame."[8]

Iacobucci made seventeen recommendations to fix the courts, prisons, and jury process, including setting up an advisory committee to deal with the probe's finding and establishing a body for Indigenous justice issues that would report directly to him. He appointed Marlene Pierre, the grandmother of Jacy Pierre, to that committee. Iacobucci called for changes to be made on how people are recruited to the jury pool, including using Ontario Health Insurance Premium cards and driver's licence information to obtain more comprehensive lists of residents of Indigenous communities. He also recommended bolstering First Nations policing, reviewing legal aid representation, and creating an Assistant Deputy Attorney General responsible for Indigenous issues.

Alvin was more than pleased with Iacobucci's efforts and called the report a needed "wake-up call" for the rest of Canadian society. "Justice Iacobucci has told the truth,"

Alvin told the *Toronto Star* upon the report's release. "He has not pulled any punches."[9]

Julian Falconer was a bit more blunt and to the point. He praised Iacobucci for shining a light on the total absence of basic civic rights in Northern Ontario.

"The rule of law does not operate in the north," Falconer said.

THE INQUEST DID NOT begin until October 5, 2015. It was held in the brand-new $473 million Thunder Bay court-house and presided over by Dr. David Eden, the coroner who originally was assigned to preside over the Reggie Bushie inquest. Eden rejected the idea of broadening the scope of the inquest to include racism, saying racial issues would naturally be addressed as the facts of the inquest unfolded. He also refused to try the actions of the Thunder Bay Police Service, arguing the technical nature of investigating the actions of police would add months, if not years, onto the inquest and that the inquest needed to be "agency neutral" regarding the roles and responsibilities of who was caring for the students.[10]

Six of the students' families participated in the inquest, and they were represented by Christa Big Canoe and Jonathan Rudin of Aboriginal Legal Services of Toronto. Curran Strang's family declined to participate. The grief was still too raw.

Julian Falconer would be representing NAN along with Meaghan Daniel, who had worked with Falconer since 2011 and who eventually moved to Thunder Bay to handle the firm's expanding human rights violation caseloads in the north. Chantelle Bryson would be acting for the Provincial Advocate for Children and Youth. In total, eleven parties would be granted standing at the inquest or would have the legal right to represent their interests and participate in the process: the Government of Canada, the Province of Ontario, the Northern Nishnawbe Education Council, the City of Thunder Bay, the Ontario First Nations Young Peoples Council, the Thunder Bay Police Service, the Thunder Bay Police Services Board, Matawa Learning Centre, and Ontario Regional Chief Stan Beardy. The inquest would also be live streamed on the Internet, and it was expected to last eight months and to include testimony from nearly two hundred witnesses.

ALVIN ASKED ELDER SAM ACHNEEPINESKUM to attend the inquest to offer the families of the students spiritual guidance. Sam has a long, thin silver-and-grey goatee and a skinny handlebar moustache, giving him the air of an Indigenous Fu Manchu. In fact, he uses Fu Manchu's image as his Facebook avatar.

Sam was a perfect choice. He cut an imposing figure on Thunder Bay's streets and nearly every single Indigenous person in the city knew who he was — an Elder, a man blessed with a good ear and a wise word for those in need. He doled out his quiet kindness from coffee shops, in prisons, on the streets, and at the Thunder Bay courthouse. His wisdom comes from the ten thousand lives he has lived.

He is a survivor of three residential schools, and

suffered sexual abuse at one of them. He travelled the province and bore witness to the stories of hundreds, if not thousands, of residential school survivors as Nishnawbe Aski Nation's program coordinator for the Truth and Reconciliation Commission.

He is also Chanie Wenjack's cousin.

Sam is a product of the residential school system. He first went to McIntosh Indian Residential School in Vermilion Bay, Northwestern Ontario. When it burned down on March 18, 1965, he was sent to Cecilia Jeffrey, where he spent only half a year, from February to June 1965. Since he was a Catholic and Cecilia Jeffrey was a Protestant school, he was moved again, in September 1965, this time to the notorious St. Anne's Residential School at Fort Albany on the James Bay coast. While abuses happened at most of the 140 residential schools across Canada, St. Anne's had a reputation for being one of the worst, with reports of whippings, electrocutions, beatings, and sexual abuse.

Sam remembers Chanie well. He remembers watching him play marbles with the other kids in the yard. The large Wenjack clan all stuck together. Chanie's mother, Agnes, was the sister of Sam's father. Sam remembers Pearl and her sister Daisy often worked in the kitchen at Cecilia Jeffrey during recess, cleaning up and preparing meals. He also remembers they never had warm clothes to wear when it was cold out. And he remembers Chanie's sisters surrounding their little brother at recess as he played with his marbles. They were always telling him that he could do anything he put his mind to.

Sam was one year older than Chanie. Even though they were cousins, they didn't really hang out. When you're twelve, one year's age difference can feel like ten. But he recalls everyone in the schoolyard talking about running away, about where they would go and when they would leave. Sam remembers thinking to his twelve-year-old self, *Where will they run to? We are out here in the middle of nowhere.*

When the inquest began on October 5, Sam Achneepineksum arrived early. He found himself not only providing comfort to members of the community, but also moving furniture into a brand-new glass-and-concrete courthouse.

The court system had assigned one of the largest, most complex inquests in Ontario's history to one of the smallest rooms in the building. The room could accommodate only ten spectators. The room allocation was beyond a serious miscalculation — it was a slap in the face to the parents who had waited years for the formal investigation into their children's deaths to begin.

Outraged and insulted, Achneepineskum, Falconer, and NAN staff began moving chairs from other courtrooms and the lobby and jamming them into the tiny box they were allocated.

To the families, this scheduling gaffe was indicative of how the cases of the seven students were handled by authorities from the very start. Real life became a metaphor for how they had always been treated in Thunder Bay and by the Canadian justice system.

JUST TWO WEEKS AFTER the inquest began, on October 19, 2015, the body of another Indigenous man was pulled from the river. According to police, forty-one-year-old Stacy DeBungee, an auto mechanic, had passed out drunk on the shores of the McIntyre River, then rolled over, slipped into the water, and drowned.

Less than twenty-four hours later, police issued a news release stating DeBungee's death was "non-criminal" and that there would be no further investigation. But hours after his death, someone used his debit card. While this didn't seem to concern the police, Stacy's brother Brad wanted answers.

"They gave me the runaround, like they tried to brush everything off, saying, 'We see it as an accidental drowning,'" DeBungee told a local radio station.

DeBungee and the chief of Rainy River First Nations, Jim Leonard, would file a complaint in March 2016 with the Ontario civilian police oversight body, the Office of the Independent Police Review Director. Leonard would hire Julian Falconer to assist them because no lawyer in Thunder Bay would take the case. He believes that was because of the big blue wall — most lawyers in town, at some point, work either for the police or for the city.

DeBungee and Leonard argued there was a pattern: within hours of a body being discovered, Thunder Bay Police always seemed to declare any First Nations death as "not suspicious." The cases are simply not investigated.

Thunder Bay Police had made two similar decisions after the bodies of two students, Jethro Anderson in 2000 and Reggie Bushie in 2007, were discovered in the river.

Just ten days before Stacy DeBungee's body was discovered, Falconer had taken Thunder Bay staff sergeant Allan Shorrock to task for those decisions during the inquest. He grilled Shorrock, who was the former head of the Criminal Investigations Branch, about the "knee-jerk" decision the force made to close the case on the death of Jethro Anderson. He also wanted to know why it took six days for police to launch a criminal investigation into the fifteen-year-old's disappearance.

Jethro was the first of the seven students to go missing, on October 29, 2000, but the Criminal Investigations Branch didn't get involved in the case until November 4, 2000 — six days later. Every day, Jethro's aunt Dora would call Thunder Bay police, asking if they had any leads on her nephew.

Shorrock admitted Anderson fell through the cracks and that the investigation into his death should have started earlier, at least five days sooner. He could offer no reasonable explanation for the "gap" in time.

Falconer was outraged. Time is of the essence in any missing persons investigation. "If you're with senior officers, you're identifying a gap, it's a serious one, are you quite certain as you're sitting in front of this jury today nobody brought up why it happened?" he asked. "All the officers chatting who are in charge, nobody says this is why it happened?"

"Not to my recollection sir as to why, why it happened," Shorrock told the jury.

On November 11, 2000, the day Jethro's body was recovered from the water, police issued a press release stating "no foul play suspected," and that a post-mortem would be performed the following day.

"What you wouldn't do is declare that no foul play is suspected before, for example, the post-mortem came in, correct?" Falconer asked.

Shorrock replied, "Correct."

"Right. And the reason why you wouldn't do that is it would reflect the closed mind to the possibilities, agreed?"

"Yes sir."

"A kind of tunnel vision, agreed?"

Shorrock admitted this to be true. "Yes sir."[11]

Seven years later, the death of another Indigenous student, Reggie Bushie, received similar treatment by the police. The official police press release announcing the discovery of Bushie's body was two sentences long and again stated, "Foul play is not suspected."

Falconer argued that how the Jethro Anderson case was handled in 2000 showed a bias in police attitudes on the investigation of Indigenous deaths. "It sadly creates a mark in time, the year 2000, on how these deaths are treated." Add Bushie and DeBungee and there was a clear pattern. "I think that this matters. It proves the police don't care. Or they don't have any control over the rank and file. What is going on is not a fluke."[12]

The investigation into Jordan Wabasse, the last student to have died, on February 7, 2011, was concluded after half-hearted interview attempts. "How can the same thing happen, over and over again?" Falconer asked.[13]

In his closing submissions on May 26, 2016, Falconer pointed out to the jury that verdicts of "accident" are really all about exercises in damage control. "This concept of 'no foul play' is deeply linked to the 'accident' verdicts because it reassures the police that the worst did not happen," he said. "And because investigations were bungled, we don't know if the worst happened," Falconer told the jury.

Falconer reminded the jury that even Dr. Toby Rose, the pathologist brought in by the inquest authorities to re-review all the post-mortems, said she could not rule out the possibility of homicide. She told the inquest that nothing in the autopsies suggested that theory but she couldn't completely rule it out. There were cuts and abrasions on all the bodies recovered from the rivers, but it was impossible to tell if the boys had been pushed into the water.[14]

"I've already said that forensic pathology cannot distinguish, based on pathology findings, between drownings that occur by accident, as a result of suicide, or by someone else by homicide," the inquest jury had heard Dr. Rose testify.[15]

Jonathan Rudin, the counsel for the families, had pointed out that the jury never heard any explanation as to how any of the boys ended up into the river. "These young men were all fully clothed, they weren't going for a swim. You don't go for a swim in Thunder Bay in the winter," Rudin told the jury on May 25. "You have heard no evidence as to how any of these young men got into the water."[16]

The heavy cloak of racism, of a sinister motivation behind why the kids ended up in the water, seeped into the inquest proceedings and those questions remain to this day.

"We need to be certain that evil doesn't exist and one way to deny it didn't happen is to declare them accidents," Falconer told the jury. "Racism is an awful, awful, awful thing. There is evil in the world. These parents are entitled to know it didn't happen because good investigators did good work — or they're entitled to the truth that we don't know. The truth is, we don't know. And you can't...make it an accident by calling it an accident. There has to be evidence."

The truth is, none of the kids were safe by the river but it wasn't because they were drinking, Falconer argued. They weren't safe because Canadian society set them up for failure as human beings. "We didn't have space for them in our world and we didn't make space for them in theirs," he said. Without schools they couldn't be educated in their world, so they had to leave to come here, said Falconer. "They died of flat neglect."[17]

EIGHT MONTHS AFTER IT BEGAN, the inquest into the deaths of the seven Indigenous high school students ended. On June 28, 2016, the jury made 145 recommendations. It took more than two hours to read them aloud in court so they could be added to the record.

The families, who had waited years for an explanation for their children's deaths, got none. If anything, they were left with even more questions.

The jury ruled that four of the seven deaths were undetermined. It was deemed unclear how or why Jordan, Kyle, and Jethro were found in the waters surrounding

Thunder Bay. The death of Paul, the only boy to die at home, was also ruled as medically undetermined.

"The issue of the finding of 'undetermined' sends a clear message that what the Thunder Bay Police did in terms of investigations did not even meet a benchmark that permits a conclusion," said Falconer.

The families are still left with no answers and with the impression that Kyle, Jordan, and Jethro were killed deliberately, and that they will never know exactly what happened because the inquest is over. "Now that is a tragedy," Falconer said.[18]

Thunder Bay Police chief Jean-Paul Levesque pointed out that the jury did not recommend that the three boys' deaths should be re-examined.

"That could have been one of the recommendations but it wasn't," he said at the time. "With any inactive investigation, if there is any new evidence that comes forward, we'd make it active again. The Ontario Provincial Police looked into all seven cases on behalf of the coroner and they didn't find anything that the Thunder Bay Police didn't find."[19]

The 145 recommendations echoed what Justice Murray Sinclair and Canada's Truth and Reconciliation Commission had said one year earlier in the release of the commission's long-awaited report. Both the inquest and the commission acknowledged that Jordan's Principle must be followed, in its entirety, for all Indigenous children across Canada. All children in Canada must not be subject to jurisdictional arguments as to who should pay for what service. They must be treated the same as all other non-Indigenous kids and the bill is to be sorted out afterwards.

Canadian prime minister Justin Trudeau wholeheartedly supported all ninety-four TRC recommendations. The price tag for implementing them was close to $1 billion. To date, few recommendations have been carried out.

The inquest into the seven called for schools for every northern First Nation community that wanted one. It called for early education, daycare, and schools that have funding equivalent to that of every other school in Canada. The funding gap between Indigenous and non-Indigenous Canadian children must disappear. Reserve schools should have gymnasiums, music and art classes, and cafeterias that serve three meals a day. It called for clean water and working sewers for all northern communities.

Bernice Jacob, Jordan's mother, was sitting in the courthouse that June 28, surrounded by her family. At the inquest's conclusion, she walked outside the courtroom and straight to a podium set up for a family press conference. She calmly said: "I have three other sons back home. Two of them are in high school. I didn't allow them to come out to the city to further their education. We have a high school in our community of Webequie First Nation but I'm glad the recommendations recognized we need better funding in our own communities so our kids don't have to leave until they are older and ready to be on their own."

Then she broke down and cried. "We want everyone to be treated equally as we are all human."[20]

Yet the inquest heard, time and time again, of how the

students were treated differently because of the colour of their skin. Of how they were beaten up, pelted with eggs and garbage, yelled at by people driving by in cars. Of how the very people in charge, the police, were so hard on them; in some cases, mocking them as they sat in holding cells.

The racism the students felt and experienced had an impact on everyone.

"I don't think there is any doubt at all that racism, in its many forms, is a huge factor in the lives and deaths of these children," Falconer said. "I very much worry that one of the forms racism takes in this city of Thunder Bay is that kids aren't necessarily safe at night by the rivers.

"Truthfully, it is a hard reality for us to face that there might be people out there, an evil out there, that would be prepared to put life at risk by throwing kids in the river, vulnerable kids who are intoxicated. I think the ruling of 'undetermined' says it all."[21]

SEVEN FALLEN FEATHERS

ON JANUARY 26, 2016, THE CANADIAN HUMAN RIGHTS Tribunal (CHRT) ruled that the Government of Canada had racially discriminated against the country's 163,000 Indigenous children. The tribunal stated that the Canadian government had failed to properly implement Jordan's Principle and that INAC willingly allowed Indigenous kids to fall victim to jurisdictional warfare.

The Canadian government was ordered to make it right. The new government of Justin Trudeau welcomed the ruling, and in March 2016 Ottawa announced a $71 million budget for child welfare and sent legal submissions to the tribunal to point out they had done what was asked of them. But the amount fell well short of the First Nations Caring Society's estimate of the $216 million that was needed to tackle the shortfall. Blackstock pointed out that the former Conservative government claimed in 2012 the actual shortfall was $108.1 million, which was still woefully short of her estimate for 2016.[1] The government said they were committed to setting aside hundreds of millions more, but the bulk of it wouldn't be released until after the next federal election in 2019.

More than a year later, after another three compliance orders had been served against the government, Cindy Blackstock and 163,000 children were still waiting for Ottawa to make good on its promise. Not only that, Ottawa had spent $707,000 in legal fees against a decision made by the Canadian Human Rights Tribunal that protects the rights of Indigenous children.[2]

The history of structural racism depends on three things, Blackstock explained. "Indian Affairs is not designed for anything other than colonialism," she said. "When a First Nations person like myself has to get a visitor's sticker to enter the building, we know what is going on, right? And at the top, the bureaucracy is completely white. You have them perpetrating the harms."[3]

Every generation has its whistleblowers; not just one or two, but many can be found both inside the bureaucracy and out. But their voices can sometimes be stifled or ignored. Dr. Peter Bryce is a largely unknown scientific figure from the turn of the last century who tried to raise warning flags about the treatment of children in the Indian residential schools.

Bryce, a white medical doctor who was an expert on tuberculosis and president of the American Public Health Association, was asked in 1904, by what was then known as Indian Affairs, to study the residential schools. What he discovered was alarming. The children were dying of tuberculosis, or the "white plague," at a rate of 24 percent per year. That rate rose to 42 percent over the next three years.[4]

"Medical science just knows what to do," Bryce wrote, saying Ottawa needed to improve ventilation in the schools and stop mixing sick kids with the healthy, and that children needed access to proper medical care.[5] His findings were ignored by the federal government, so he gave the story to the *Evening Citizen* newspaper in Ottawa. The story made front-page news.

Bryce was marginalized by the establishment. His funding was cut, and in 1921 he was pushed out of the civil service. In 1922 he published a book called *The Story of a National Crime: Being an Appeal for Justice to the Indians of Canada; the Wards of the Nation, Our Allies in the Revolutionary War, our Brothers-In-Arms in the Great War.* He was heavily persecuted for it.

Cindy Blackstock argues that the group that has always, throughout history, let Indigenous people down is the Canadian public. "The public has not responded to the whistleblowers. As musician Gord Downie says, we have been trained our entire lives to look away. When you look at this and you compare it to what happened in the civil rights movement in the United States, there was a mounting pressure to not look away, to stand up and fight," she says. "Not here."[6]

AFTER THE CONCLUSION OF the inquest in late 2016, the Office of the Independent Police Review Director announced it would carry out a "systemic review" of the Thunder Bay Police Service, looking for evidence of racism or discriminatory conduct. All Indigenous missing persons and death investigations would be under the microscope.

The systemic review would focus on the interactions between Indigenous people and the police, looking for any evidence that First Nations people are either "over-policed" or "under-policed" and evaluating whether investigations had been carried out in a discriminatory manner.[7] They would start with the death of Stacy DeBungee and they would also examine the "information and evidence" surrounding the deaths of the seven students.

Julian Falconer is quietly pleased that the OIPRD took notice of the inquest into the seven and that it has decided to scrutinize the Thunder Bay Police. Time and time again, Indigenous people have been getting the message that they are less than worthy victims. The DeBungee case was a particularly acute example of how police interests drop First Nations cases quickly and without explanation. It is the exact same complaint the families of Missing and Murdered Indigenous Women and Girls have had for decades.

"The quality of the investigations are, in my decades of practice, well below the standard of anything I have ever seen," Falconer said.

Police Chief Levesque issued a statement promising that Thunder Bay Police Services would fully comply with the systemic review: "Our service will co-operate fully in the review process and it is our hope that any recommendations arising from the process will assist us, and other police services in Ontario, to move forward towards meeting the needs of our diverse communities. We will continue to strive to work towards building a stronger relationship with the Indigenous community that we serve."

NORMA KEJICK SPENT EIGHT months in Thunder Bay attending the inquest. She wanted to bear witness to the proceedings on behalf of the NNEC and on behalf of all of their children. Every fibre of her being compelled her to sit and listen. But the grind of the court proceedings and the emotional upheaval of the testimony took its toll on Norma and on her marriage. Within the first four months of the inquest Norma's marriage disintegrated, and when the inquest wrapped up at the end of June 2016, her husband of more than thirty years left her. He accused her of loving the NNEC kids more than her own family — even though her children were all adults — and he told her he had found someone else.

Norma was devastated. She felt as if the foundation of her life, her marriage to her husband and their beautiful family, had been ripped away from her, this at a time when she'd been sitting in a courtroom listening to witness after witness recount the lives of the seven students. Psychologically, Norma was under incredible stress and was extremely fragile. So much so that she did the unthinkable one weekend when she was at her home in Lac Seul — she went to the bush with a rope to hang herself. The one person who championed suicide prevention in her community now wanted to die. She hopped into her suv, grabbed a cigarette, and drove into the forest. She hid her vehicle among the shrubs and the dense trees, then grabbed the rope and walked to a strong, thick tree.

Norma believes in the Creator — in one God, a higher spirit, whichever name he goes by. Her father was a medicine man and taught her all the sacred ways of her people. She stood by the tree and called the Creator. She knelt down on the ground and began to pray hard. She prayed to her father and to all of those she had loved and lost in her life, and she begged them to give her a sign. She prayed to them, imploring them to help her, to give her something.

"If you are really there, send me a sign, any sign," she said. "And if you don't I will finish what I came here to do."

Suddenly, a mallard duck, beautiful and strong with a bright green feathered head, whizzed by her head, almost touching her. Norma began to sob. She had asked for a sign and she had gotten one. She stood up, stumbled away from her chosen tree, found her hidden suv, and drove home.

Norma would come close to taking her life again that month, but again, she prayed hard, asked for a sign, and got one. But the suicidal thoughts kept coming back to her at odd times of the day. She knew she had to do something. She reached out to her niece. Shortly after, she began therapy and is now working hard to rebuild her psyche and her life.

That summer, she wanted to resign from NNEC because she couldn't take it anymore. She took her letter of resignation to the board of directors, but the board would not accept it. They begged her to stay. She was the institutional memory of NNEC and she was the one who was trying to hold it all together.

"Norma," they said to her, "you can't leave us. We are the most stable thing in your life."

That simple statement gave everyone a moment of levity, of laughter through tears. After everything they had gone through together with the loss of the seven, perhaps that moment would mark the ending of this devastating chapter.

MARYANNE PANACHEESE IS SITTING at her kitchen table, staring at the muddy, pale-grey road outside the front window of her trailer. She apologizes to her guests for the rusty nails that may be on her gravel driveway. The dogs got to the trash and have strewn items — broken plates, parts of a computer motherboard, plastic bottles — all over the front yard.

"I tried to pick the nails up," says the sixty-year-old grandmother. "I hope they don't get stuck in your tires."

Maryanne's long black-and-grey-streaked hair is tied back and she is absent-mindedly playing with the brown mole on the left side of her upper lip. She is thinking about Rule, her fourteen-year-old grandson. It is near the October break, a new initiative started by all Indigenous high schools in the north. All the students are now sent home for one week, plane and bus fares paid for, so they can reconnect with their families during that lonely period between September and December. This mandated one-week break was the result of the inquest into the death of Maryanne's son Paul and the six other students.

But Maryanne is distracted with worry. Rule left last month for his first year of high school at Pelican Falls. At first, NNEC told her Rule should go to Dennis Franklin but Maryanne refused. Rule is in a room with two other boys. He is having a hard time. He regularly tells his grandmother, his kokum, that he is homesick. He texts her and tells her he misses her.

The other day, she got a text that said *Come and get me.*

The words pierced her heart. Maryanne has been taking care of Rule all his life. His birth mother lives down the street from her, but as soon as Rule could walk, he went to his kokum's house and never left. And everyone accepted his choice.

When a mother gets that kind of message, she feels her child's agony and she desperately wants to comfort the child, to say something that will make it all better. But for Maryanne, who lost her son Paul, this was a different kind of torment. Layered into her grief is her own experience of being a residential school survivor. As soon as she got Rule's text, she grabbed the keys to her old grey pickup truck and ran for the door.

"I don't want him to feel lonely. It just comes back, what I went through with Paul and me trying to encourage him to stay…"

Then she took a deep breath and tried to calm herself down. She thought about it. She spoke to Rule. She eased his fears and his mind. She promised him she would see him very soon.

She had to remind herself, Rule was not her son Paul. Rule was only a few hours down the highway at Pelican

Falls. He was not in Thunder Bay by himself. He was safe in Sioux Lookout. Maryanne feared if Rule left school, there was a danger he wouldn't go back.

No, the answer was not for him to leave. Instead, she, along with her niece Melissa Skunk, who had a daughter in grade nine at Pelican, would drive down to Sioux Lookout a few days early and speak to the principal about how the kids from Mishkeegogamang were coping.

She put her keys away. She told Rule to try to stick it out until next year. Then, she let it slip that if he still felt this way then, she would move down to Sioux Lookout to take care of him.

She sat down heavily, crossed her legs underneath her, and crossed her arms over her chest — she was holding herself tight and she began to shake.

She looked out the window and cried. "It is like I am repeating what I did with my son." And this is what haunts Maryanne. "I had to go out, leave, for school. That is how I was. And that is what I did to my son too. Now I am trying to change that. I don't want my grandson to go through it. What if something happens to him when he is away? I don't want to push him. I know he needs his education. To be out there, to get to know other people. It is hard. They are so young."

Maryanne wants to know why the kids from Mish can't be bused to the public high school at Pickle Lake, thirty kilometres north up the highway.

"Do that at least until the end of grade ten," she says.

After the inquest, Maryanne approached Alvin Fiddler and asked him who would make sure the 145 recommendations were going to be implemented. Maryanne was tired, carrying six decades of pain and loss. She knew this was one burden she could not shoulder alone or solely with the women from Mish.

She saw the cycle starting again. With no end in sight.

SHORTLY AFTER ROBYN'S DEATH, Tina Harper flew to Thunder Bay to bring her daughter's remains back home. The night before she left Keewaywin, she was at church, sitting in a pew, trying to find comfort when there was none to be found. Her mind drifted to the conversation she had just had with her sister, Margaret Fiddler, who reported that a baby was on the way in her husband's extended family and the parents were young. Margaret told Tina the baby would be a boy and they spoke of how this was a new blessing, a new life.

Later, when she returned with her daughter and all her belongings, her sister brought the baby over to Tina's house to help cheer her up. Andrew, her husband, had been so quiet since Robyn's death that Tina welcomed the visitors, especially the sound of life. Margaret had a surprise: the baby was not a boy, it was a girl — and the parents had decided to name her Julia Robyn. As the days passed, the parents frequently brought the baby to Tina's, dropping her off for extended periods of time. Then one day, Julia Robyn just stayed. Her parents agreed that it was best for the baby if she stayed with Tina.

"That was ten years ago." She laughs.

Two years ago, Andrew died; she thinks it was of a broken heart. Her husband was never the same after

Robyn passed. He became quiet, withdrawn. He would sit in his chair for hours and stare. The loss of Andrew would have been almost unbearable if it weren't for Julia Robyn.

Tina takes a deep breath, then whispers through the phone, "She came to rescue me."

RICKI STRANG HAS A tattoo of the number 71 on his left forearm, his random favourite number. You can see it poking out of his sleeve when he adjusts his black LA Kings hockey cap on his head. His younger brother Reggie had a similar tattoo, but his was the number 21, his favourite random number. Reggie had another tattoo on his hand — the large emblem of the American metal band Mushroom Head. Reggie loved thrasher metal and he loved rap. Ricki now has all his brother's CDs. They aren't really his taste in music, but he listens to them all the time and he remembers his brother.

Strang lives in Poplar Hill. He has a four-year-old son named Reggie and a partner. He is living the stable life of a family man now that he is twenty-six years old. They live near Rhoda and see her often. He is her doting son, especially since she is no longer with Berenson. On this day, Ricki happens to be in Thunder Bay for a computer workshop. He doesn't often leave Poplar Hill, but today, he tells me, he feels strong enough to take a walk down by the McIntyre River. He wants to show me where he last saw his brother.

We park our rental car in the rear of the Shoppers Drug Mart parking lot and step out onto the pavement. The bike path is right there, about three metres from the store, and so is the May Street bridge. The spring runoff has turned the river a murky brown. The river is swollen but quiet, barely moving. It is nothing like the strength and might of the fast-moving Kaministiquia or the roar of Lake Superior. The McIntyre seems gentle, like a place where you go to feed the ducks. We haven't walked far before we see where the boys ended up drinking that night under the bridge. Faded garbage is tucked into the pebbles and stones. I'm surprised by how exposed it is, how close they were to the strip mall and the street.

I leave Ricki at the riverbank and turn up toward the parking lot to grab my camera from the trunk. It takes me a few minutes to adjust the settings for the bright sun. I shut the trunk and turn toward the river. Ricki is standing just to the right of the bridge on the riverbank. His head is bowed, his body heavy with emotion. I stand back and watch as Ricki throws some tobacco from his hand into the water, as an offering to his brother, before he slowly squats by the river's edge. He puts his arms around his knees and holds himself, staring into the water in silence. After a few minutes, he stretches his arms out wide in front of him, his palms hovering just above the still water. He puts his head down and embraces his brother.

CHRISTIAN MORRISSEAU'S MEMORIES ARE endless streams flowing from his mind. They come from deep inside. Once he starts to recount a tale, there is no stopping the words as they leap off the tip of his tongue.

Morrisseau now lives in Toronto. He sits on one of two black folding chairs that face the parking lot of an industrial mall. Used cigarette butts swim in a tar-coloured soup inside a plastic water bottle sitting at his feet. He watches the fancy cars pull up into the parking lot, people rushing in and out, too busy to notice the man with the long black hair pulled back in a ponytail staring at them.

The windows behind him are painted blue and white, fully carpeting the glass with slogans from an auctioneering company that buys and sells art online. His art. His father's art. People come and go all day. They come into the office, take some paintings, load them into Audis and Porsches, and drive away.

The door is propped open. Stale, cold air flows out, hitting a wall of sweltering heat.

Inside, spread across folding tables and propped up against the walls, are brightly coloured canvases in various stages of creation. The canvases are of all shapes and sizes, small ones the size of a poster and giant ones several tables long and wide.

In the corner of the office is a double bed, a pink couch, and an oversize flat-screen TV stuck on YouTube.

This is where Morrisseau is living for the next couple of months. He creates here. He paints. He sleeps. He smokes. He watches Alison Krauss sing soulfully about going down to the river to pray.

Every so often, someone parking their car will acknowledge Morrisseau. He'll wave back with a hand covered in paint, and smile.

One of the art dealers, an elderly man with thick white

hair, is inside staring at the large painting laid bare before him. He stares in awe at *Seven Fallen Feathers*. Everyone who sees it does.

The brightly coloured canvas spreads out across two long tables in the centre of the room. It demands your attention, the thick black lines of the Woodland style so famously brought to the world by his father. The black lines look like X-ray images that form characters filled with browns, purples, and yellows. The painting grabs you. It makes you feel as if you are gazing upon something holy, full of life and of pain.

The painting came out of Morrisseau's mind at 4:00 a.m. as he sat on his folding perch, staring into the dark parking lot. It was the night after the inquest into the seven's deaths was complete. After eight months of testimony, tears, and truths told, it was over.

Morrisseau thought he would feel a sense of relief or a sense of completion that the long journey was finally coming to a close. That the 145 recommendations read into the record at the conclusion of the inquest would mean something. Cause change.

Morrisseau didn't expect to feel empty. That old painful gnaw of grief that had taken up residence inside of him since they pulled Kyle's body out of the McIntyre River had not gone away. No, it had morphed into something else, something hollowing his soul. What was it telling him?

He needed to listen.

Don't forget me.

Yes. That was what the voice said.

He called the painting *Seven Fallen Feathers*. Each feather represents one of the seven dead students. Morrisseau was tired of hearing them being called that, "Seven dead students." People always referred to the kids like that. "The seven dead." As if they weren't anything else in life.

They had their own spirits. They were their own people.

Morrisseau couldn't stand hearing his son Kyle being called "one of the seven dead students" anymore, not by the news media, not by the lawyers, not by the people who meant well but found it easier to lump them all together as one.

Kyle was a fallen feather. They all were.

That night, when the painting came to him, he finished his cigarette, stood up, and spread out a giant blank canvas. He grabbed his brush, held it up high in his hand, and waited. He let the spirits guide him.

After days of non-stop painting, he was done. Finished. A massive canvas, as big as a king-size duvet.

A masterpiece. His requiem for his first-born son.

The painting shows each of the seven students in profile as they wait to pass on to the next world. On the far right is Kyle. He is the tallest of the brown figures. Their faces are all turned up toward the bright yellow drum, a sun, in the middle of the painting. The painting captures the moment when their hearts and spirits are passing on to their loved ones, who wait for them on the other side.

Kyle's grandfather Norval is painted in red, connected to both the drum and to Kyle by a thick red line. Norval is guiding his grandson to the afterlife.

EPILOGUE

ALVIN FIDDLER IS SURVEYING THE ROWS OF RECORDS AT Kops, a record store in downtown Toronto that buys and sells albums and boasts the "Best prices since 1965." He is upstairs in the country music section, flipping through album covers in protective plastic, dust flying as he hunts around in sections that are rarely perused.

He finds a Ralph Stanley album titled *Something Old, Something New and Some of Katy's Mountain Dew*, and he thinks he may have found a gem. Whenever he is in Toronto and has a free moment, he steals away to this store, looking for golden oldies to replenish his large collection of vinyl.

Every Saturday morning, Fidder chooses and then posts on Facebook one song taken from his musical library. He's like a Grand Chief deejay, spinning the most obscure old-time country tunes on hurtin' and losin'. He never misses a posting, no matter what he's doing or whatever happens to be going on. He takes the time to pick a song that expresses the groove he is feeling that day.

Music is Fiddler's happy place and spinning tunes connects him with his community in a friendly, personal way. His posts are moments of levity and, whether he knows it or not, some songs are received by his people with eye-rolling humour.

This musty old record store is his church, the place he comes to forget it all, for just a few precious moments.

He needs this brief respite — especially in light of recent events.

The events of the night of May 6, 2017, have psychologically and emotionally broken nearly everyone connected to the Seven Fallen Feathers — the families, NAN leadership, the lawyers, the police. It's as if the evil that lurks along Thunder Bay's riverbanks has suddenly emerged from the shadows.

After a six-year lull in which no Indigenous youth were found dead in the city's waterways, two teens disappeared on the same night and both of their bodies were found within two weeks of their disappearance.

Tammy Keeash, a seventeen-year-old artist and high school student, failed to make her curfew at her foster home that Saturday evening. And Josiah Begg, a fourteen-year-old boy who was visiting Thunder Bay with his father from the remote fly-in community of Kitchenuhmaykoosib Inninuwug, disappeared into thin air that same night. Begg and his father were staying at the Wequedong Lodge, where Dora Morris, Jethro Anderson's aunt, works. The two had come to town for Josiah's medical appointments. Josiah's image was captured on video that Saturday night near a bridge at the Neebing-McIntyre Floodway.[1]

The following day, at 1:28 p.m., Thunder Bay Police Service received a call from Tammy's foster home. Her guardians were concerned for her welfare and asked police to check an address where they thought she might be. Police drove to the location but could not find Tammy. One hour later, at 2:23 p.m., Tammy's guardian called police to report her missing.[2]

She would not be missing for long.

Alvin and the entire NAN leadership, all forty-nine NAN community chiefs, were on their way to Timmins for their annual spring meeting. As their flights landed at the Timmins Victor M. Power Airport and everyone settled into their hotel rooms, cell phones began ringing with the news that the body of Tammy Keeash had been found in shallow water in the Neebing-McIntyre Floodway.

Everyone was devastated and became increasingly worried about Josiah.

NAN's Deputy Grand Chief Anna Betty Achneepineskum and Fiddler did not wait for instruction from police. In between proceedings in Timmins, they began coordinating their own search for Josiah. The five foot five slender boy with dark eyes and a beautifully boyish smile had last been seen wearing a red hoodie and a red cap. Fiddler and Achneepineskum set up a search command centre at the EconoLodge on Memorial Avenue, which was later moved to Dennis Franklin Cromarty. Fiddler vowed to "turn Thunder Bay upside down" until Josiah was found. They had seen this before. Jethro. Curran. Reggie. Kyle. Jordan. And now Tammy.

Alvin and KI Chief James Cutfeet wanted every inch of every single riverbank in the city searched. They called on the Bear Clan, a group of Indigenous-led volunteer searchers, to mobilize along the water. The Bear Clan was first established in 1992 in Winnipeg, to patrol the streets looking for vulnerable Indigenous women and girls. In late 2016, during the inquest into the Seven Fallen Feathers, Deputy Grand Chief Anna Betty helped launch the clan in Thunder Bay. She wanted the patrol in place before the students returned after Christmas break.[3]

Fiddler and Achneepineskum made it clear to everyone: *Check the rivers.*

On Friday, May 12, Thunder Bay Police put out a press release regarding the investigation into Tammy's death. After an extensive search by the Criminal Investigations Branch, the police concluded, "There is no evidence to indicate criminality in this tragic death." Police further stated the results of the post-mortem indicated Tammy's death was "consistent with drowning."[4]

Fiddler could not believe what he was hearing. Police had quickly come to the same conclusion with regard to all the other boys whose bodies were found in the rivers — that there was no evidence of foul play and that the kids had died of accidental drowning.

Tammy was now the sixth Indigenous youth to be found in the water.

Like Jethro, Curran, Reggie, Kyle, and Jordan, Tammy was familiar with and grew up in a community surrounded by rivers and lakes. She was from North Caribou Lake First Nation, high up in the farthest northwest region of Ontario. She was also a Junior Canadian Ranger; this prestigious group of Indigenous youth in northern First Nations are trained to quickly mobilize and act as emergency search and rescue teams.

Tammy's death made headline news across the country. Fiddler and Nishnawbe Aski Nation were no longer the sole voices raising loud concerns about the safety of Indigenous youth in Thunder Bay. Grand Council Treaty No. 3, which encompasses twenty-eight First Nations communities, from west of Thunder Bay to north of Sioux Lookout and along the U.S. border to Manitoba, stood firmly behind Fiddler. The Assembly of First Nations National Chief Perry Bellegarde and Ontario Regional Chief Isadore Day also issued statements and spoke to national media about racism experienced by Indigenous people in Thunder Bay.

Stories of assaults that were never reported to police, or where no assailant was ever arrested and charged, began to appear on Facebook and Twitter under the hashtag #thisisthunderbay. The posts detailed accounts of Indigenous people being thrown in the river or assaulted with racial slurs or catcalling; some alleged mistreatment by police. And still fresh in everyone's minds was the brutal assault of Barbara Kentner, the Indigenous mother from Wabigoon Lake Ojibway Nation who was hit in the stomach by a trailer hitch that was thrown out of a moving car on January 29, 2017. Her sister Melissa, who was walking with Barbara at the time of the attack, heard someone in the car say, "I (expletive) got one of them." After the assault, Barbara was unable to leave the hospital. Her liver and kidneys were shutting down, and on July 4, 2017, she succumbed to her injuries.[5]

With another dead Indigenous teen and a missing child, the city and Thunder Bay Police were heaving under local and national pressure to address the issues of targeted racism and potential homicide against the Indigenous population. Posters of Josiah were put up all over the city. The search for Josiah became symbolic of the very fight going on inside Thunder Bay itself. So when, in an interview with CBC's Jody Porter, Thunder Bay Police insisted there was "no evidence" to suggest that Josiah was down by the river and actively discouraged people from searching the waterways — with one police officer going as far to say "everything points to" Josiah being found alive in the city — the Indigenous community and its allies said, *Enough.*[6]

None of the Indigenous searchers believed this claim. Instead, they asked the public to donate metal rakes and twine so they could make homemade dragging equipment. If the police wouldn't search the rivers, they would.

The chiefs of North Caribou and KI, along with NAN leadership, began discussing the idea of hiring private detectives. The community no longer trusted the Thunder Bay Police.

It would not be the first time the Indigenous community sought outside help. In February 2016, on behalf of NAN, the Provincial Advocate for Children and Youth, and Aboriginal Legal Services of Toronto, former Toronto Police Service homicide detective Dave Perry was hired to investigate Darryl Kakekayash's case. Perry concluded that what happened to Darryl could be called a "hate crime" and "attempt [*sic*]

murder." Perry was also hired to look into the death of Stacy
DeBungee. He discovered that Stacy's bank card was used hours
after his reported death. At the request of Thunder Bay Police,
who are currently under investigation by the OIPRD for systemic
racism, the Ontario Provincial Police have just finished a review
of Stacy's case. The results of the review are now with the police
in Thunder Bay but they have not made them public.

On Wednesday, May 17, Fiddler held a press conference
in the DFC gymnasium with Achneepineskum; Tammy's
mother, Pearl Slipperjack; KI Chief James Cutfeet; and
Josiah Begg's parents, Sunshine Winter and Rene Begg.

"Our community has no confidence in the police,"
Fiddler said. "Police have done no better investigating
Tammy's death, accepting drowning as the cause but fail-
ing to determine how she ended up in the water."[7]

Pearl Slipperjack clung to an eagle feather, a symbol
of strength, when she told the local media, "There are no
words to describe how I feel." And Sunshine Winter made
a direct appeal to Josiah: "Josiah, if you can hear this, we
want you to come back."[8]

The following day, May 18, lawyer Chantelle Bryson
looked out her office window and saw the OPP Underwater
Search and Recovery Unit on the McIntyre River. The OPP
began its search at the point where the McIntyre meets
Lake Superior, then slowly motored west. An OPP helicop-
ter flew overhead, swooping up and down the riverbanks,
searching for Josiah.

Late that afternoon, the OPP's sonar equipment detected
something in the water and the divers were called in.
People began to assemble along the riverbanks. Eventually,

the body of a young man was retrieved from the McIntyre's murky depths.

It would be days before a formal identification was made by the coroner's office in Toronto. But soon after the body was pulled out of the water, Josiah's parents knew: the body was clad in a red hoodie and a wallet was found on him. It was their son's.

Fourteen-year-old Josiah Begg was now the seventh Indigenous youth to have been found dead in one of Thunder Bay's rivers.

ON WEDNESDAY, MAY 31, Alvin Fiddler sat inside the wood-panelled Queen's Park press studio next to Grand Council Treaty No. 3 Ogichidaa Francis Kavanaugh, Rainy River First Nation Chief Jim Leonard, and Julian Falconer. On behalf of seventy-seven Northern Ontario chiefs, they demanded that the federal Royal Canadian Mounted Police be brought in to investigate the river deaths in Thunder Bay.

"It is our view the Thunder Bay police cannot fix this," Rainy River Chief Jim Leonard stated. "They have shown they are not able to come to any conclusion other than the deaths are non-suspicious and non-criminal, which doesn't hold any water with us. Today we are here to demand action immediately."9 He paused and then said that Thunder Bay is "a powder keg" waiting to go off.

As Fiddler, Kavanaugh, and Leonard spoke to the few members of the media assembled before them, members of the highest echelons of power in the Ontario government were watching on closed-circuit TV throughout the building. The provincial government knew they had a huge problem in Thunder Bay. Ontario Premier Kathleen Wynne was being briefed on the situation, and at the press conference it was announced the Ontario Civilian Police Commission would be appointing an investigator to look into the actions of the police board that oversaw the Thunder Bay Police Service. But due to municipal jurisdiction, the province could not override Thunder Bay Police and bring in the federal Mounties. The only way the RCMP could be brought in to take over the investigation was if Thunder Bay Police made the request themselves.

ON THURSDAY, JUNE 23, 2017, Ontario chief coroner Dr. Dirk Huyer stepped into the fray. As chief coroner, Huyer has overall responsibility for all death investigations in Ontario. That means he can request the assistance of any police service in Ontario to help with a death investigation or an inquest. Using this authority, he asked the York Regional Police to investigate the deaths of Tammy Keeash and Josiah Begg. He wanted them to work alongside the Nishnawbe-Aski Police Service and the Thunder Bay Police.

Huyer said that the York Regional Police would provide a "new perspective" on the deaths, and that they had experience in handling "complex death investigations."[10] York Regional Police employs 1,529 officers and serves 1.13 million people just north of Toronto in one of Canada's most diverse, fastest-growing communities.

While this was not the outcome Fiddler was looking for, it did offer a bit of hope.

IT HAS BEEN MORE than one year since the eight-month-long inquest into the deaths of the Seven Fallen Feathers released its 145 recommendations on June 28, 2016.

In some areas, there are signs of improvement.

The City of Thunder Bay has carried out a safety audit of problem areas along the riverbanks and the safety consultant hired to perform the audit is considering installing cameras — but a year out they are still debating which measures they should take.

Since the fall of 2016, Thunder Bay Police conduct daily foot patrols of known problem areas by the river and on recreational trails.

Thunder Bay Police also say they are working with the Matawa Learning Centre, DFC, the KO chiefs council, and the NNEC on missing persons protocols and contact information for their on-call workers. The police have asked for a set list of descriptors and identifiers for all First Nations students from the north attending Thunder Bay schools.

Nishnawbe Aski Nation has addressed each of the twenty-five inquest recommendations directed at them as far as their capacity allows. They are ready to set up a youth leadership program so teens can run summer, evening, and weekend activities for their peers — they are just waiting for the funding to be approved. They accept that no student should be denied access to high school programs for lack of space. But equitable funding for First Nations kids has to be ensured in order for many of the recommendations to actually be brought into being. And the NAN chiefs can't help but wonder about the Government of Canada's commitment to the inquest recommendations when it continues to throw up road-blocks to complying with the Canadian Human Rights Tribunal ruling. Like Cindy Blackstock and the 163,000 Indigenous kids, NAN is still waiting.

"We have gone as far as we can go and our hands are now tied," said Achneepineskum. "We need the political will of Canada and Ontario to address a myriad of issues, including jurisdictional ambiguity and the full implementation of Jordan's Principle. We remain optimistic that progress can be made, but in the meantime will do everything in our power to keep our youth safe."[11]

At the time of writing, Fiddler was hard at work securing an architect and hunting for funding from a number of different sources — both public and private, including the Gord Downie & Chanie Wenjack Fund — to build a safe student residence for northern children who attend high school in Thunder Bay.

"It would be nice if all of Canada could contribute to this," Fiddler said. In the coming days, he would be travelling to Ottawa to discuss a residence.

Yet the Government of Canada still refuses to comply with the CHRT ruling to provide equitable education, health care, and social services funding. On May 26, the tribunal slammed Ottawa for failing to follow their original January 2016 ruling, and said it had squandered any chance of preventing the suicides of two twelve-year-old Wapekeka First Nations girls, Jolynn Winter and Chantell Fox. Wapekeka had asked for emergency mental health funding from Canada after the remote Northern Ontario community discovered a youth suicide pact, but the request was denied. At the end of June, the federal government filed a judicial "review" of the CHRT ruling, asking for two areas to be quashed: that a request for services must be processed within twelve to forty-eight hours, and that such a request be processed without case-conferencing of health specialists. They were taking Cindy Blackstock and the First Nations Child and Family Caring Society of Canada to federal court.

Fiddler knows time is ticking. New students will be arriving in September. During the first week of July 2017, NAN would be holding an emergency meeting with its leadership to discuss the crisis every single community now faces — how to keep their high school students safe this coming school year. Everything is on the table, including the construction of the new DFC residence. Some of the chiefs will suggest that a quickly built temporary residence be set up for the kids in the meantime. They will also debate whether or not the students should be kept in their home communities for grades 9 and 10, as education reports suggested more than a decade ago, or whether arrangements should be made with the public school boards in Dryden, Kenora, and Ignace to take NAN kids.

"This isn't the kind of meeting we want to have," Fiddler told me. "But it is something we need to do, considering the current situation. They [parents] shouldn't be forced to send their kids to Thunder Bay."[12]

Fiddler was in his Thunder Bay office, working on setting up the meeting during the waning days of June. The Canada Day holiday approaches and the country prepares to celebrate its 150th birthday on July 1; for Alvin it will be a day of reflection. He will be at a powwow in Grand Council Treaty No. 3 territory with his family. He will be standing in a circle with all the nations surrounding him in ceremonial dance, and he will be thinking of the children before him decked out in their beautiful jingle dresses, their bright-coloured ribbons, and their feathers, and he will wonder about their future and what he can do to make sure they make it to the final prophecy — the eighth fire. Can the settlers and the Indigenous people come together as one and move forward in harmony? Fiddler hopes against hope that the colonial past will be overcome and that for the good of the country we call Canada, the Anishinaabe Nation will rise strong.

NOTES

PROLOGUE

1. Scott A. Sumner. "New Thunder Bay City Hall Makes a Positive Impression!," *Thunder Bay Business*, www.thunderbaybusiness. ca/article/new-thunder-bay-city-hall-makes-positive-impression-268.asp.

2. Thunder Bay history: http://www.thunderbay.ca/Living/Culture_ and_Heritage/tbay_history.htm#top.

3. Port of Thunder Bay: http://www.portofthunderbay.com/article/ port-of-thunder-bay-facilities-265.asp.

4. National Truth and Reconciliation Commission, Public Archives of Canada (Indian Affairs School Files). Constable D. Andersen, RCMP *Report: Patrol to Savanne IR — Assistance to Department of Indian Affairs*, October 27, 1930, http://nctr.ca/RBS_PDFS/ SCHOOL_SERIES/ON/c-7930-00785-00814.pdf.

CHAPTER 1: NOTES FROM A BLIND MAN

1. Description of Nishnawbe Aski Nation: http://www.nan.on.ca/article/about-us-3.asp.

2. Description of Assembly of First Nations across Canada: http://www.afn.ca/en/about-afn/description-of-the-afn.

3. Teaching of the Seven Fires Prophecy: http://www.wabanaki.com/seven_fires_prophecy.htm.

4. Ibid.

5. 2016 Thunder Bay Census Profile: http://www.thunderbay.ca/CEDC/Reports_and_Publications/Community_Profile_Facts_and_Statistics/Demographics.htm.

6. James Murray. "Stats Canada — Aboriginal Population of Thunder Bay Projected 15% by 2031," *Net News Ledger*, December 9, 2011, http://www.netnewsledger.com/2011/12/09/stats-canada-aboriginal-population-of-thunder-bay-projected-15-by-2031/.

7. Jody Porter. "Ten First Nations with More Than Ten Years of Bad Water," CBC *News*, September 8, 2014, http://www.cbc.ca/news/canada/thunder-bay/10-first-nations-with-more-than-10-years-of-bad-water-1.2755728.

8. Inquest exhibit: *Regional Education Strategic Plan 2015–2020*, Matawa First Nations, Advancing Education Excellence for All People in Matawa First Nations, p. 13.

9. "Former Girlfriend, Mother Testify as Life of Jordan Wabasse Examined at Student Inquest," *TBNewsWatch*, January 15, 2016, https://www.tbnewswatch.com/local-news/former-girlfriend-mother-testify-as-life-of-jordan-wabasse-examined-at-student-inquest-404160.

10. Jody Porter. "First Nations Student Deaths Inquest," CBC *News Live*, January 21, 2016, http://live.cbc.ca/Event/First_Nations_Student_Deaths_Inquest?Page=23.

11. Inquest exhibit: Thunder Bay Police Service, Police Investigation Summary of Officers' Actions — Jordan Wabasse, p. 1.

12. Porter. "First Nations Student Deaths Inquest."

13. Ibid.

14. Inquest exhibit: Thunder Bay Police Service, Police Investigation Summary of Officers' Actions — Jordan Wabasse, p. 7.

15. Ibid., p. 13.

16. James Murray. "Help Find Jordan Wabasse Awareness Walk — 500 km," *Net News Ledger,* March 7, 2011, http://www.netnewsledger.com/2011/03/07/help-find-jordan-wabasse-awareness-walk-500-km/.

17. Porter. "First Nations Student Deaths Inquest."

18. Ibid.

19. Inquest exhibit: Thunder Bay Police Service, Police Investigation Summary of Officers Actions — Jordan Wabasse, p. 16.

20. Ibid., p. 20.

21. Brandon Walker. "Body Recovered in Kam River," Thunder Bay *Chronicle Journal,* May 11, 2011, http://www.chroniclejournal.com/body-recovered-in-kam-river/article_3fa931de-1090-526d-8085-8753db8bd5b6.html.

22. Ibid.

23. "Former Girlfriend, Mother Testify."

24. Inquest exhibit: Thunder Bay Police Service, Police Investigation Summary of Officers Actions — Jordan Wabasse, p. 22.

25. Chantelle Bryson, interview with the author, May 2017; and Porter, Jody. "First Nations Student Deaths Inquest," CBC News Live, January 20, 2016, http://live.cbc.ca/Event/First_Nations_Student_Deaths_Inquest?Page=24.

26. Chantelle Bryson, interview with the author, May 2017.

27. Inquest exhibit: Thunder Bay Police Service, Police Investigation Summary of Officers' Actions — Jordan Wabasse, p. 25.

28. Inquest exhibit: Post-Mortem Report redacted, Jordan Wabasse, August 24, 2011, p. 4.

CHAPTER 2: WHY CHANIE RAN

1. Robert J. Surtees. *The Robinson Treaties (1850)*. Treaties and Historical Research, Indian and Northern Affairs Canada, 1986, https://www.aadnc-aandc.gc.ca/eng/1100100028974/1100100028976.

2. Ibid.

3. *Treaties Texts — Ojibewa Indians of Lake Superior*, Indigenous and Northern Affairs Canada, https://www.aadnc-aandc.gc.ca/eng/1100100028978/1100100028982.

4. Bob Joseph. "Indian Act and the Right to Vote," *Working Effectively with Indigenous People*, August 10, 2012, https://www.ictinc.ca/indian-act-and-the-right-to-vote.

5. "Canada and South Africa Share a Dark Past," Radio Canada International, http://www.rcinet.ca/english/archives/column/

the-link-africa/TruthandReconciliationCanadaSouthAfrica
ResidentialSchoolsAbuses/.

6. Truth and Reconciliation Commission of Canada. *Honouring the Truth, Reconciling the Future: Summary of the Final Report of the Truth and Reconciliation Commission of Canada*, p. 2, http://www.trc.ca/websites/trcinstitution/File/2015/Findings/Exec_Summary_2015_05_31_web_o.pdf.

7. Ibid., p. 5.

8. Donald J. Auger. *Indian Residential Schools in Ontario*. Nishnawbe Aski Nation and the Aboriginal Healing Foundation, 2010, p. 28.

9. Truth and Reconciliation Commission of Canada. *Honouring the Truth, Reconciling the Future*, p. 3, http://www.trc.ca/websites/trcinstitution/File/2015/Honouring_the_Truth_Reconciling_for_the_Future_July_23_2015.pdf.

10. Truth and Reconciliation Commission of Canada. Map of the schools identified by the Indian Residential School Settlement Agreement: http://www.myrobust.com/websites/trcinstitution/File/pdfs/2039_T&R_map_nov2011_final.pdf.

11. Auger. *Indian Residential Schools in Ontario*, p. 21.

12. National Centre for Truth and Reconciliation, Fort William Indian Residential School archives, Letter from J. D. McLean, assistant deputy and secretary of Indian Affairs, March 12, 1927.

13. Auger. *Indian Residential Schools in Ontario*, p. 30.

14. Ibid., p. 22.

15. Ibid., p. 24.

16. Ibid., 24.

17. "Number of Indian Residential School Student Deaths May Never Be Known: TRC," APTN National News, June 2, 2015, http://aptnnews.ca/2015/06/02/number-indian-residential-school-student-deaths-may-never-known-trc/.

18. Janet Carruthers. Foreword, *Tweedsmuir Community History Book*. Jaffray Women's Institute, 1945. Kenora Library article.

19. Auger. *Indian Residential Schools in Ontario*, p. 65.

20. Ibid., p. 65.

21. Ibid., p. 70.

22. Ibid., p. 66.

23. Ibid., p. 70.

24. Ibid., p. 70.

25. Ibid., p. 33.

26. Ibid., p. 70.

27. Ian Mosby, interviewed on *As It Happens*, CBC Radio, July 16, 2013, http://www.cbc.ca/radio/asithappens/wednesday-aboriginal-experiments-zetas-cartel-leader-obit-don-smith-1.2941800/food-historian-discovers-federal-government-experimented-on-aboriginal-children-during-and-after-wwii-1.2941801.

28. Auger. *Indian Residential Schools in Ontario*, p. 74.

29. Carruthers. Foreword, *Tweedsmuir Community History Book*. Kenora Library article.

30. Pearl Achneepineskum, interview with the author, August 2016.

31. Ibid.

32. Auger. *Indian Residential Schools in Ontario*, p. 73.

33. Truth and Reconciliation Commission of Canada. *Honouring the Truth, Reconciling the Future*, p. 105.

34. Ibid., p. 106.

35. Ian Adams. "The Lonely Death of Chanie Wenjack," *Maclean's*, February 1, 1967, http://www.macleans.ca/society/the-lonely-death-of-chanie-wenjack/.

36. Ibid.

37. Ibid.

38. Ibid.

39. *Coroner's Investigation Report of Charles (Chanie) Wenjack*, http://www.cbc.ca/thunderbay/interactives/dyingforaneducation/docs/charles_1966_5308.pdf.

40. Daisy Munro, interview with the author, September 2016.

41. Verdict of Coroner's Jury in death of Chanie Wenjack, November 17, 1966, http://www.cbc.ca/thunderbay/interactives/dyingforaneducation/docs/charles_1966_5308.pdf.

42. Ibid.

43. Adams. "The Lonely Death of Chanie Wenjack."

44. Brian Kelly. "School Survivor Forgives Assailant," *Sault Star*, August 5, 2012, http://www.saultstar.com/2012/08/05/school-survivor-forgives-assailant.

45. Adams. "The Lonely Death of Chanie Wenjack."

CHAPTER 3: WHEN THE WOLF COMES

1. Truth and Reconciliation Commission of Canada. *Canada's Residential Schools: The History*, vol. 1, part 2, 1939 to 2000, p. 47, http://www.myrobust.com/websites/trcinstitution/File/Reports/Volume_1_History_Part_2_English_Web.pdf.

2. Ibid., p. 48.

3. Northern Nishnawbe Education Council (NNEC) Holistic Student Services Program Parent/Student Guidebook.

4. NNEC Student Services Manual, 2007, p. 29.

5. Dennis Franklin Cromarty (DFC) High School. "What Every Student Needs to Know," pp. 51–2.

6. See the timeline on the J. R. Nakogee School, Attawapiskat First Nation: https://fncaringsociety.com/shannens-dream-timeline-and-documents.

7. Joanna Smith. "Bennett Stands by Promise to Remove 2-per-cent Funding Cap for On-Reserve Programs," *Toronto Star*, February 22, 2016, https://www.thestar.com/news/canada/2016/02/22/budget-to-remove-2-per-cent-funding-cap-for-on-reserve-programs-says-carolyn-bennett.html.

8. Truth and Reconciliation Commission of Canada. *Honouring the Truth, Reconciling the Future*, p. 148.

9. Ibid., p. 146.

10. Ibid., p. 148.

11. Paul Barnsley. "Auditor General Reports INAC Coming Up Short," *Windspeaker*, vol. 12, issue 1, 2004, http://ammsa.com/publications/alberta-sweetgrass/auditor-general-reports-inac-coming-short.

12. Tanya Talaga. "Thunder Bay High School Is Home Away from Home for First Nations Students, Inquest Told," *Toronto Star*, October 7, 2015, https://www.thestar.com/news/canada/2015/10/07/thunder-bay-high-school-is-home-away-from-home-for-first-nations-students-inquest-told.html.

13. "'My Heart Shattered': Mother to Testify at First Nations Student Deaths Inquest," *CBC News*, November 3, 2015, http://www.cbc.ca/news/canada/thunder-bay/my-heart-shattered-mother-to-testify-at-first-nations-student-deaths-inquest-1.3300519.

14. Dianne Hiebert and Marj Henirichs, with the People of Big Trout. *We Are One with the Land: A History of Kitchenuhmaykoosib Inninuwug*. Kelowna, B.C.: Rosetta Projects, 2007, p. 19.

15. Dora's memory of events is that she called Stella within twenty-four hours to tell her Jethro was missing. According to Stella's testimony, Dora called her two days after. "'My Heart Shattered': Mother to Testify at First Nations Student Deaths Inquest," CBC News, November 3, 2015, http://www.cbc.ca/news/canada/thunder-bay/my-heart-shattered-mother-to-testify-at-first-nations-student-deaths-inquest-1.3300519.

16. RCMP statistics on the 1,181 MMIWG: http://www.rcmp-grc.gc.ca/en/missing-and-murdered-aboriginal-women-national-operational-overview#sec3.

17. Andrew Bailey, David Bruser, Jim Rankin, Joanna Smith, Tanya Talaga, and Jennifer Wells. "Nearly Half of Murdered Indigenous Women Did Not Know or Barely Knew Killers *Star* Analysis Shows," *Toronto Star*, December 4, 2015, https://www.thestar.com/news/canada/2015/12/04/nearly-half-of-murdered-indigenous-women-did-not-know-killers-star-analysis-shows.html.

18. Jennifer Wells and Tanya Talaga. "No Rest, No Peace for Aboriginal Women Discarded by Killers," *Toronto Star*, December 5, 2015, https://www.thestar.com/news/canada/2015/12/05/no-rest-no-peace-for-aboriginal-women-discarded-by-killers.html.

19. Thunder Bay Police Media Release: http://www.falconers.ca/wp-content/uploads/2016/03/034-Thunder-Bay-Police-Media-Release-11NOV00.pdf.

20. Inquest exhibit: Bob Pearce, *Final Report for NNEC Board*, May 2001, p. 8.

21. Inquest exhibit: Garnet Angeconeb, "Seeking Solutions," In-School Program at the Dennis Franklin Cromarty High School, July 2001, p. 5.

CHAPTER 4: HURTING FROM THE BEFORE

1. November 2004 Report of the Auditor General of Canada, http://www.oag-bvg.gc.ca/internet/English/parl_oag_200411_05_e_14909.html#ch5hd3a.

2. Inquest exhibit: Jerry Paquette, "Support, Safety and Responsibility: A Review of the Secondary Student Support Program of the NNEC," November 2004, p. 133.

3. Ibid.

4. Ibid.

5. NAN suicide statistics: https://www.thestar.com/opinion/ editorials/2017/01/16/stop-the-tragic-suicides-on-reserves-editorial.html.

6. Nishnawbe Aski Nation. "Backgrounder: Communities in Crisis," http://www.nan.on.ca/upload/documents/backgrounder-communities-in-crisis.pdf.

7. Ontario Ministry of the Solicitor General. "Verdict of Coroner's Jury" on the death of Selena Sakanee, http://www.fixcas.com/ scholar/inquest/sakanee.pdf.

8. "Aboriginal Youth Suicides Cascading," *TBNewsWatch*, June 30, 2015, https://www.tbnewswatch.com/local-news/aboriginal-youth-suicides-cascading-study-finds-401835.

9. Raziye Akkoc. "2004 Boxing Day Tsunami Facts," *The Telegraph*, December 19, 2014.

10. "Disaster Relief: Canada's Rapid Response Team," CBC *News*, first posted January 13, 2010; updated March 14, 2011, http://www. cbc.ca/news/canada/disaster-relief-canada-s-rapid-response-team-1.866930.

11. Ibid.

12. White Feather Forest Initiative: http://www.whitefeatherforest. ca/our-first-nation/.

13. Ecology and Society: http://www.ecologyandsociety.org/vol18/ iss3/art9/.

14. Stephen Lambert. "Hope Returning to Pikangikum," *Toronto Star*, January 8, 2007, https://www.thestar.com/news/2007/01/08/ hope_returning_to_pikangikum.html.

15. Laura Eggertson. "Children as Young as Six Sniffing Gas in Pikangikum," *CMAJ*, vol. 186, no. 3. February 18, 2014, http://www. cmaj.ca/content/186/3/171?related-urls=yes&legid=cmaj;186/3/171.

16. Office of the Chief Coroner (Ontario). *The Office of the Chief Coroner's Death Review of the Youth Suicides at the Pikangikum First Nation 2006–2008*, p. 15, https://provincialadvocate.on.ca/documents/en/Coroners_Pik_Report.pdf.

17. Eggertson. "Children as Young as Six Sniffing Gas in Pikangikum."

18. National Institute on Drug Abuse. *What Are the Short- and Long-Term Effects of Inhalant Use*, https://www.drugabuse.gov/publications/research-reports/inhalants/what-are-short-long-term-effects-inhalant-use.

19. Christie Blatchford. "Hope and Sadness at an Aboriginal School So Unlike Any Other," *National Post*, October 7, 2015, http://news.nationalpost.com/full-comment/christie-blatchford-hope-and-sadness-at-an-aboriginal-school-so-unlike-any-other.

20. Inquest exhibit: Missing Persons Report, Curran Strang.

21. Inquest exhibit: Extracts from NNEC Report on Curran Strang Incident, notes of Donna Fraser, Secondary Student Support Worker, September 26, 2005.

22. Jody Porter. "Homicide Ruling Recommended in Death of First Nations Student in Thunder Bay," *CBC News*, May 26, 2016, http://www.cbc.ca/news/canada/thunder-bay/homicide-first-nations-death-inquest-1.3600214.

23. Inquest exhibit: Ontario Drowning Report 2015 Edition. http://www.lifesavingsociety.com/media/216840/98drowningreport2015ontario_web.pdf.

24. "Fire Destroys Reserve's Only School, Sparks Support Movement," CBC News, July 24, 2007, http://www.cbc.ca/news/canada/fire-destroys-reserve-s-only-school-sparks-support-movement-1.659874.

25. The Office of the Chief Coroner's Death Review of the Youth Suicides at the Pikangikum First Nation 2006–2008, p. 15.

26. Ibid., p. 13.

CHAPTER 5: THE HOLLOWNESS OF NOT KNOWING

1. Hiebert and Heinrichs with the People of Big Trout. We Are One with the Land, p. 20.

2. Dianne Hiebert and Marj Heinrichs with the People of Mishkeegogamang. Mishkeegogamang: The Land, the People & the Purpose. Kelowna, B.C.: Rosetta Projects, 2009, p. 110.

3. Inquest exhibit: Community Backgrounder on Mishkeegogamang.

4. Jon Thompson. "Unresolved Trauma Destabilizing Life in Mishkeegogamang," TBNewsWatch, March 8, 2016, https://www.tbnewswatch.com/local-news/unresolved-trauma-destabilizing-life-in-mishkeegogamang-404877.

5. Alicja Siekierska and Jesse Winter. "Where Are the Girls, Part 2," Toronto Star, February 24, 2017, http://projects.thestar.com/first-nations/first-nations-communities-struggle-with-fire-safety/.

6. Government of Canada. Hourly Data Report for February 13, 2014, obtained at http://climate.weather.gc.ca/historical_data/search_historic_data_e.html.

7. "Pickton Trial Timeline," CBC News, first posted July 30, 2010; updated November 1, 2016, http://www.cbc.ca/news/canada/pickton-trial-timeline-1.927418.

8. "'In His Own Words': Serial Killer Robert Pickton Selling Book on Amazon that Claims He's Innocent," National Post, February 21, 2016, http://news.nationalpost.com/news/canada/in-his-own-words-serial-killer-robert-pickton-selling-book-on-amazon-that-claims-hes-innocent.

9. The Office of the Provincial Advocate for Children and Youth. "Our Dreams Matter Too: First Nations Children's Rights, Lives, and Education," p. 11, https://fncaringsociety.com/sites/default/files/OurDreams-June2011_0.pdf.

10. Ibid., p. 8.

11. Ibid., p. 74.

12. Jody Porter. "First Nations Student Deaths Inquest: 'Help Us,' Mom Pleads," CBC News, October 9, 2015, http://www.cbc.ca/news/canada/thunder-bay/first-nations-student-deaths-inquest-help-us-mom-pleads-1.3265316.

13. Inquest exhibit: Paul Panacheese Autopsy Report, November 11, 2006.

14. Inquest exhibit: Transcript of May 21, 2015, letter from Dr. Toby Rose, Ontario Deputy Chief Forensic Pathologist.

15. Inquest exhibit: Transcript of testimony of Dr. Toby Rose, April 7, 2016, p. 13.

16. Ibid., p. 14.

17. Ibid., p. 15.

CHAPTER 6: WE SPEAK FOR THE DEAD TO PROTECT THE LIVING

1. Transcript: Inquest Concerning the Deaths of Jethro Anderson, Reggie Bushie, Robyn Harper, Kyle Morrisseau, Paul Panacheese, Curran Strang, and Jordan Wabasse, October 29, 2015, pp. 52–3.

2. Ibid., p. 50.

3. Ibid., p. 10.

4. Ibid., p. 10.

5. Ibid., pp. 10, 26.

6. Ibid., pp. 10–11.

7. Ibid., pp. 10, 15.

8. Ibid., pp. 10, 39.

9. Ibid., pp. 10, 39.

10. Ibid., pp. 10, 40.

11. Jody Porter. "First Nations Student Deaths Inquest: On-call Support Worker Testifies." CBC News, October 28, 2015, http://www.cbc.ca/news/canada/thunder-bay/first-nations-student-deaths-inquest-on-call-support-worker-testifies-1.3292436.

12. Inquest exhibit: Superior North EMS and Thunder Bay Fire Rescue Crew Reports, January 13, 2007.

13. Keewaywin First Nation website gallery, "Summer students and employees 2006: Robyn Harper," http://keewaywin.firstnation.ca/?q=gallery&g2_itemId=13090.

14. Office of the Chief Coroner, "Death Investigations," https://www. mcscs.jus.gov.on.ca/english/DeathInvestigations/office_coroner/ coroner.html.

15. Inquest exhibit: Office of the Chief Coroner, "Guidelines and Directives," p. 21.

16. "Ontario's Chief Coroner Testifies at First Nations Student Deaths Inquest," CBC News, October 30, 2016, http://www.cbc.ca/news/ canada/thunder-bay/ontario-s-chief-coroner-testifies-at-first-nations-student-deaths-inquest-1.3296114.

17. "First Nations Student Deaths Inquest: Testimony from Robyn Harper's Mother," CBC News, October 27, 2015, http://www.cbc.ca/ news/canada/thunder-bay/first-nations-student-deaths-inquest-testimony-from-robyn-harper-s-mother-1.3290518.

18. Robyn Harper Post-Mortem Report, January 14, 2007.

19. Ibid.

20. Centers for Disease Control and Prevention. *Morbidity and Mortality Weekly Report*, http://www.cdc.gov/mmwr/preview/ mmwrhtml/mm6353a2.htm?s_cid=mm6353a2_w.

21. Porter. "Homicide Ruling Recommended in Death of First Nations Student in Thunder Bay."

22. Inquest exhibit: Office of the Chief Coroner, "Guidelines and Directives," memorandum from Dr. Barry McLellan, February 28, 2007, p. 35.

23. Inquest exhibit: Office of the Chief Coroner, "Guidelines for Death Investigations," relaxed guidelines on showing up to death investigations, April 12, 2007, p. 49.

CHAPTER 7: BROTHERS

1. Information about Jordan Anderson's death and the establishment of Jordan's Principle: https://www.ncbi.nlm.nih.gov/pmc/articles/PMC2603509/.

2. Assembly of First Nations and First Nations Child & Family Caring Society of Canada Human Rights Complaint against Indian and Northern Affairs Canada, https://fncaringsociety.com/sites/default/files/fnwitness/HumanRightsComplaintForm-2007.pdf.

3. United Nations Declaration on the Rights of Indigenous Peoples, http://www.un.org/esa/socdev/unpfii/documents/DRIPS_en.pdf.

4. Ibid.

5. Kristy Kirkup. "Isolation a Barrier to Exposing Sexual Abuse in Remote Indigenous Communities: Bellegarde," *Toronto Star*, November 13, 2016, https://www.thestar.com/news/canada/2016/11/13/isolation-a-barrier-to-exposing-sexual-abuse-in-remote-indigenous-communities-bellegarde.html.

6. United Nations Declaration on the Rights of Indigenous Peoples.

7. United Nations. "General Assembly Adopts Declaration on Rights of Indigenous Peoples; 'Major Step Forward' Towards Human Rights for All, Says President," meetings coverage and press releases, September 13, 2007, https://www.un.org/press/en/2007/ga10612.doc.htm.

8. Further background on Jordan's Principle available at: https://fncaringsociety.com/sites/default/files/jordans-principle/docs/PictouLanding-background-JP-June2011.pdf.

9. Inquest exhibit: Office of the Chief Coroner, Bureau Summons to Witness re: Inquest into Reggie Bushie. Documentation of Raymond Albert.

10. Jody Porter. "Brother Hopes for 'Truth, Justice' at First Nations Student Deaths Inquest," CBC News, November 29, 2015, http://www.cbc.ca/news/canada/thunder-bay/brother-hopes-for-truth-justice-at-first-nations-student-deaths-inquest-1.3340455.

11. Inquest exhibit: Testimony of Ricki Strang, Thursday, November 26, p. 36.

12. Ibid., p. 37.

13. "Thunder Bay Was Only Choice for Reggie Bushie to Receive High School Education, Inquest Hears," TBNewsWatch, November 24, 2015, https://www.tbnewswatch.com/local-news/thunder-bay-was-only-choice-for-reggie-bushie-to-receive-high-school-education-inquest-hears-403628.

14. "NAN Welcomes Inquest into First Nation Student Death," Nishnawbe Aski Nation news release, June 8, 2008, http://www.nan.on.ca/upload/documents/com-2008-06-06-bushie-inquest-june-6-08.pdf.

15. Julian Falconer letter to Dr. David Eden, March 6, 2008, http://www.falconers.ca/wp-content/uploads/2015/11/March-6-08-ltr-to-Dr-David-Eden-from-Falconer-Charney-re-Deaths-of-NAN-Youth.pdf.

16. News release on Inquest into Reggie Bushie's Death, June 6, 2008, https://news.ontario.ca/archive/en/2008/06/06/Inquest-Into-The-Death-Of-Reggie-Bushie-Announced.html.

17. Donovan Vincent. "Case Headed to the Supreme Court of Canada Will Tackle Native Jury Roll Complaints," Toronto Star,

July 1, 2014, https://www.thestar.com/news/canada/2014/07/01/case_headed_to_the_supreme_court_of_canada_will_tackle_native_jury_roll_complaints.html.

18. Julian Falconer letter to Ontario Attorney General Chris Bentley, September 10, 2008.

19. Charlie Angus. "The Bravery and the Tragedy of Shannen Koostachin," *Maclean's*, August 20, 2015, http://www.macleans.ca/news/canada/were-not-going-to-quit-the-bravery-and-tragedy-of-shannen-koostachin/.

20. Shannen Koostachin's quote during her speech on Parliament Hill available at: https://fncaringsociety.com/shannens-dream-learn-more.

21. Indigenous and Northern Affairs Canada. "Statement of Apology to Former Students of Indian Residential Schools," https://www.aadnc-aandc.gc.ca/eng/1100100015644/1100100015649.

CHAPTER 8: RIVER, GIVE ME MY SON BACK

1. Canadian Public Health Association. "TB and Aboriginal People," http://cpha.ca/en/programs/history/achievements/02-id/tb-aboriginal.aspx.

2. Carmen L. Robertson. *Mythologizing Norval Morrisseau: Art and the Colonial Narrative in the Canadian Media*. Winnipeg: University of Manitoba Press, 2016, p. 15.

3. Inquest exhibit: Report card for Kyle Morrisseau, October 28, 2009.

4. Inquest exhibit: Thunder Bay Police Services Chronology/Notes — Kyle Morrisseau, p. 14.

5. Ibid., p. 13.

6. Ibid., p. 12.

7. Ibid., p. 12.

8. Ibid., p. 12.

9. Ibid., p. 2.

10. Ibid., p. 2.

11. Ibid., p. 10.

12. Porter, Jody. "First Nations Student Deaths Inquest," CBC *News Live*. December 14, 2015, available at: http://live.cbc.ca/Event/ First_Nations_Student_Deaths_Inquest?Page=10.

13. Inquest exhibit: Thunder Bay Police Services Chronology/Notes — Kyle Morrisseau, p. 13.

14. Inquest exhibit: PowerPoint presentation by Dr. Toby Rose, deputy chief forensic pathologist, and Karen Woodall, Ph.D., forensic toxicologist.

CHAPTER 9: LESS THAN WORTHY VICTIMS

1. Court of Appeal Judgement. *Pierre v. McRae*, March 10, 2011, pp. 26–27, http://www.falconers.ca/wp-content/uploads/2015/07/Eden-COA-Judgment-March-10-2011.pdf.

2. Jody Porter. "20 Cases Delayed by Ontario's Jury Roll Problem," CBC *News*, January 2, 2015, http://www.cbc.ca/news/canada/thunder-bay/20-cases-delayed-by-ontario-s-jury-roll-problem-1.2865727.

3. Transcript: Inquest Concerning the Deaths of Jethro Anderson, Reggie Bushie, Robyn Harper, Kyle Morrisseau, Paul Panacheese, Curran Strang, and Jordan Wabasse, October 29, 2015, p. 30.

4. Oliver Sachgau. "Hamilton, Thunder Bay Had Highest Rates of Hate Crime in Canada in 2013," *Globe and Mail*, June 9, 2015, https://www.theglobeandmail.com/news/national/hamilton-thunder-bay-had-most-hate-crime-in-canada-in-2013/article24885875/.

5. "Editorial: Thunder Bay Police Don't Understand Why Joking About an Aboriginal Murder Victim Is Grotesque," *Globe and Mail*, September 19, 2012, http://www.theglobeandmail.com/opinion/editorials/thunder-bay-police-dont-understand-why-joking-about-an-aboriginal-murder-victim-is-grotesque/article4555037/.

6. Tanya Talaga. "One Rape. A Hate Crime. Thunder Bay's Simmering Divides Come to Light," *Toronto Star*, December 8, 2015, https://www.thestar.com/news/canada/2015/12/08/one-rape-a-hate-crime-thunder-bays-simmering-divides-come-to-light.html.

7. Tanya Talaga. "'Systemic Racism' Toward Natives in Justice System, Frank Iacobucci Finds," *Toronto Star*, February 26, 2013, https://www.thestar.com/news/canada/2013/02/26/systemic_racism_toward_natives_in_justice_system_frank_iacobucci_finds.html.

8. Tanya Talaga. "Ontario's Justice System in a 'Crisis' for Aboriginals: Frank Iacobucci Report," *Toronto Star*, February 26, 2013. https://www.thestar.com/news/canada/2013/02/26/ontarios_justice_system_in_a_crisis_for_aboriginals_frank_iacobucci_report.html.

9. Ibid.

10. Jody Porter. "Coroner Rules on Scope of First Nation Student Death Inquest," *CBC News*, May 8, 2015, http://www.cbc.ca/news/canada/thunder-bay/coroner-rules-on-scope-of-first-nation-student-death-inquest-1.3065722.

11. Transcript: Inquest Concerning the Deaths of Jethro Anderson, Reggie Bushie, Robyn Harper, Kyle Morrisseau,

Paul Panacheese, Curran Strang, Jordan Wabasse; testimony of Detective Allan Shorrock, November 5, 2015, p. 30, http://www.falconers.ca/wp-content/uploads/2016/03/NOV.5.2015.SHORROCK.TRN_.pdf.

12. Julian Falconer, interview with the author.

13. Ibid.

14. Wayne Rivers. "Lawyer at Thunder Bay Inquest Introduces Possibility Some Students Murdered," *APTN National News*, October 7, 2015, http://www.falconers.ca/wp-content/uploads/2015/10/Lawyer-at-Thunder-Bay-inquest-introduces-possibility-some-students-murdered-APTN-National-NewsAPTN-National-News.pdf.

15. Dr. Toby Rose on pathology and homicide: http://www.falconers.ca/wp-content/uploads/2017/05/Page-135-Seven-Youth-Inquest-Transcript-Examination-of-Dr.-Rose-October-6-2015.pdf.

16. Jonathan Rudin quotes reported by Jody Porter: live.cbc.ca/Event/First_Nations_Student_Deaths_Inquest?Page=52.

17. Closing Submissions of Nishnawbe Aski Nation given by Julian Falconer available at http://www.falconers.ca/wp-content/uploads/2016/05/Video-Closing-Submissions-of-Nishnawbe-Aski-Nation.mp4.

18. Tanya Talaga. "Coroner's Inquest into Deaths of Indigenous Students Provides Recommendations but Few Answers," *Toronto Star*, June 28, 2016, https://www.thestar.com/news/canada/2016/06/28/inquest-jury-on-aboriginal-youths-deaths-says-3-died-accidentally-4-undetermined.html.

19. Ibid.

20. Ibid.

21. Ibid.

CHAPTER 10: SEVEN FALLEN FEATHERS

1. Cindy Blackstock. "One Year Later, Liberals Still Discriminate Against First Nations Children," *Ottawa Citizen*, October 17, 2016, http://ottawacitizen.com/opinion/columnists/blackstock-one-year-later-liberals-still-discriminate-against-first-nations-children.

2. Tanya Talaga and Alex Ballingall. "Ottawa Spent $707,000 in Legal Fees Fighting Decision That Protects Indigenous Children," *Toronto Star*, June 2, 2017, https://www.thestar.com/news/canada/2017/06/02/ottawa-spent-707000-in-legal-fees-fighting-a-rights-decision-that-protects-indigenous-children.html.

3. Cindy Blackstock, interview with the author.

4. Cindy Blackstock. "The Long History of Discrimination Against First Nations Children," *Policy Options*, October 6, 2016, http://policyoptions.irpp.org/magazines/october-2016/the-long-history-of-discrimination-against-first-nations-children/.

5. Ibid.

6. Cindy Blackstock, interview with the author.

7. Tanya Talaga. "Ontario Police Watchdog Widens Probe of Thunder Bay Police," *Toronto Star*, November 3, 2016, https://www.thestar.com/news/canada/2016/11/03/ontario-police-watchdog-widens-probe-of-thunder-bay-police.html.

EPILOGUE

1. Josiah's image was captured on video that Saturday night. He was near a bridge at the Neebing-McIntyre Floodway. See Jody Porter, "'No Evidence' Missing Indigenous Teen Went into the River, Thunder Bay Police Say," CBC News, May 15, 2017, http://www.cbc.ca/news/canada/thunder-bay/josiah-begg-river-search-1.4116105.

2. Thunder Bay Police Service. Press release, Friday, May 12, 2017, http://www.thunderbaypolice.ca/news/tammy-keeash-investigation-update.

3. "Thunder Bay Bear Clan Patrol to Be Set Up." CBC News, December 14, 2016, http://www.cbc.ca/news/canada/thunder-bay/thunder-bay-bear-clan-1.3895623.

4. Tanya Talaga. "Tammy Keeash's Death 'Consistent with Drowning According to Post Mortem,'" Toronto Star, Friday, May 12, 2017.

5. Peter Edwards. "Trailer Hitch Attack on First Nation Woman Called Hate Crime," Toronto Star, March 28, 2017, https://www.thestar.com/news/canada/2017/03/28/trailer-hitch-attack-on-first-nations-woman-called-hate-crime.html.

6. Jody Porter. "'No Evidence' Missing Indigenous Teen Went into the River," CBC News, May 15, 2017, http://www.cbc.ca/news/canada/thunder-bay/josiah-begg-river-search-1.4116105.

7. "Thunder Bay Police Under Fire Over Handling of Death and Missing First Nations Youth," APTN National News, May 17, 2017, http://aptnnews.ca/2017/05/17/thunder-bay-police-under-fire-over-handling-of-death-and-missing-first-nations-youth/.

8. Tanya Talaga. "First Nations Family Rejects Thunder Bay Explanation for Teen's Death," *Toronto Star*, May 17, 2017, https://www.thestar.com/news/canada/2017/05/17/first-nations-family-rejects-thunder-bay-police-explanation-for-teens-death.html.

9. Tanya Talaga. "First Nations Leaders Call for RCMP to Take Over Thunder Bay Teen Death Cases," *Toronto Star*, May 31, 2017, https://www.thestar.com/news/canada/2017/05/31/first-nations-leaders-call-for-rcmp-to-take-over-thunder-bay-teen-death-cases.html.

10. Tanya Talaga. "York Regional Police Now Investigating Thunder Bay Indigenous Teen Deaths," *Toronto Star*, June 23, 2017, https://www.thestar.com/news/canada/2017/06/23/york-regional-police-now-investigating-thunder-bay-indigenous-teen-deaths.html.

11. Nishnawbe Aski Nation press release: "NAN Releases Progress Report on Seven Youth Inquest Recommendations," June 28, 2017.

12. Alvin Fiddler, interview with the author, June 2017.

SUGGESTED READING

Auger, Donald J. *Indian Residential Schools in Ontario*. Thunder Bay, ON: Nishnawbe Aski Nation, 2005.

Heinrichs, Marj, and Dianne Hiebert, with the People of Mishkeegogamang. *Mishkeegogamang: The Land, The People and The Purpose*. Kelowna, B.C.: Rosetta Projects, 2009.

Hiebert, Dianne, and Marj Heinrichs, with the People of Big Trout Lake. *We Are One with the Land: A History of Kitchenuhmaykoosib Inninuwug*. Kelowna, B.C.: Rosetta Projects, 2007.

King, Thomas. *The Inconvenient Indian: A Curious Account of Native People in North America*. Toronto: Anchor Canada, 2013.

King, Thomas. *The Truth About Stories: A Native Narrative*. CBC Massey Lectures. Toronto: House of Anansi Press, 2003.

Lake of the Woods Museum, NeChee Friendship Centre, and Lake of the Woods Ojibway Cultural Centre. *Bakaan nake'ii ngii-izhi-gakinoo'amaagoomin: We Were Taught Differently: The Indian Residential School Experience*. Exhibition pamphlet. Lake of the Woods, ON, 2014.

National Centre for Truth and Reconciliation, University of Manitoba. Winnipeg, MB. http://umanitoba.ca/nctr/.

Robertson, Carmen L. *Mythologizing Norval Morrisseau: Art and the Colonial Narrative in the Canadian Media*. Winnipeg, MB: University of Manitoba Press, 2016.

Truth and Reconciliation Commission of Canada. http://nctr.ca/reports.php.

Villeneuve, Jocelyne. *Nanna Bijou, the Sleeping Giant*. Newcastle, ON: Penumbra Press, 1979.

ACKNOWLEDGEMENTS

There are so many people to thank. This book is the result of many, many hands. All the failings of fact, accuracy, and anything else are purely my own and I apologize.

This book would not have been possible if it weren't for the support of Nishnawbe Aski Nation Grand Chief Alvin Fiddler and Tesa Fiddler. Alvin and Tesa, you opened up your memories to me, your teachings, and your home. You have both dedicated your lives to bringing equity, justice, and truth to all Indigenous people in the north and beyond. You are examples to everyone and you have always made the time for me and for this I am grateful. Deputy Grand Chief Anna Betty Achneepineskum, your words of wisdom are needed and always welcome, thank you.

To the families of the Seven Fallen Feathers — my one hope is to bring honour to the lasting memories of your children, and that their lives are never dismissed or forgotten. I tried to tell their stories, and without your participation in this book I could never have done so. Chi-miigwetch for sharing the stories of the Seven Fallen Feathers.

Dora Morris, you are strength, eloquence, and inspiration. I am grateful for the late-night coffee and talks. Bernice Jacob, thank you for taking my countless phone calls and just listening. Pearl Achneepineskum, you are a pure delight — empathetic and whip smart, and you possess a beautiful mind. Your words gave me the guidance that shaped this book. Daisy Munro, thank you for your wise words and for all the time you shared with me when I showed up unannounced at your school. To Elder Sam Achneepineskum — you have shown infinite patience in sharing your story and the story of our Nish. Thank you for Donald Auger's book. It has been my go-to. I will buy you a triple-triple anytime.

Maryanne Panacheese, you have always been on the other end of the phone. Thank you for inviting me to your home and telling me about your sister Sarah Skunk. I hope one day you find her and peace. Melissa Becky, you have guided me well, and Mishkeegogamang is so lucky to have you in its corner.

Tina Harper, your grace, quiet strength, and love are inspirational. Thank you for always spending time with me and for telling me about Robyn.

Ricki Strang, you shared with me the most devastating moments of your young life. You have strongly served your brother Reggie's memory. You honour him and in doing so, your son,

Reggie. I look forward to our next pasta dinner. Rhoda King, your determination and questions made the inquest happen.

Christian Morrisseau, I am in awe of your talent. You think in endless, lyrical streams of thought and every word you say always carries meaning. You are a true artist and a wonderful father. Thank you for sharing Kyle's story. A special thank you for the painting that graces the cover of this book and for inspiring its title. Robbie Kakegamic, thank you for the story of Kyle breakdancing.

Norma Kejick, you are the needle and thread that stitched this book together and you continue to be the strength that so many count on. Please know that you are adored and thank you for agreeing to let me in so I could tell your important story.

Shawon Wavy and Darryl Kakekayash, you are both so brave and you both freely told me your stories without any fear, only with hope for change. Miigwetch. James Benson, you were a good friend to Curran, thank you for sharing.

To Elder Thomas White — thank you for your big black case of photographs and books and your tips about where to look.

I first heard Cindy Blackstock speak at an education conference at Fort William First Nation six years ago and she opened my eyes to the inequities right before me. Blackstock is a champion of children's human rights and history will judge her to be so. I am honoured to know her. Canada needs more Cindy Blackstock. She should be embraced and treasured, not fought against.

Retired Supreme Court Justice Frank Iacobucci, your report *First Nations Representation on Ontario Juries* was groundbreaking, and thank you for sharing your experiences with me. To CBC reporter Jody Porter, your reporting of social issues in the north and of the inquest is the best example of what public service journalism is and should be.

Thank you to the Office of the Chief Coroner for Ontario and to the Thunder Bay Police Service.

It is no exaggeration to say that without the support, knowledge, and listening ear of Chantelle Bryson, I could not have completed this book. Chantelle, you have always been on the other end of the phone and I have so much to thank you for that I actually don't know where to start. But I'll say this — your instincts are bang on and your heart is always in the right place. You are a passionate lawyer and an ally, and I know you will continue to fight like hell to make the world a better place for all our children. My immense thanks also go out to the Office of the Provincial Advocate for Children and Youth, and, especially, Irwin Elman. Don't stop. The kids need you.

John Cutfeet, you have saved me more times than I can recall and you selflessly help every time I ask. I am grateful to call you my emissary in the northwest, my friend.

Meaghan Daniels, you are incomparable and you lived, breathed, and felt every moment of the inquest every day and you represented Nishnawbe Aski Nation with bravery and honour. I can't thank you enough for your legal mind and for reviewing this manuscript with an eagle eye.

I've known Julian Falconer for nearly two decades and I'm constantly astounded by the passion he brings to defending and improving the human rights of every single person in this country. Julian, you discovered the north and it changed your life — the north does that. All of us owe you a debt of gratitude for your decision to open an office in Thunder Bay and for your strong focus on Indigenous issues. You are the Anishinaabe's best champion, a natural ally.

Michael Heintzman, you have always helped me out when I'm on deadline, in dire need, or when I just need someone to talk to and decompress with. Thank you for always making everything happen. You are the best at what you do.

Christa Big Canoe, thank you for everything. You were my first stop on this journey. After the inquest was over, I sat in your Toronto office and spoke to you about writing this book and you listened, as you always do, and then steered me in the right direction.

Ian Adams, I have not met you. I tried to find you to tell you that the article you wrote in 1967 for *Maclean's* was a remarkable feat of journalism in an era when no one cared to pay any attention to Indigenous issues. You trail-blazed for all of us and without your work on Chanie Wenjack, we couldn't do what we do now.

My journalistic home for more than two decades has been the newsroom at the *Toronto Star*. I walked through the door at the *Star* as an intern in 1995 and never looked back. The *Star* has nurtured me through various stages in my career and it wholeheartedly supported this book. Our newsroom is blessed to have John Honderich standing up for us, constantly believing in what our editorial staff is capable of achieving. John, you read the Truth and Reconciliation Commission's *Calls to Action* and you took them to heart — especially numbers 84 through 86. Lynn McAuley, you taught me how to use my voice and always believed in me. You are both my mentor and my friend. Michael Cooke, you make it all happen every day and you never hold back — the paper is better for it.

To my best friend, Michelle Shephard — you made the introduction to Janie Yoon after telling me for years to just do it, just write it down. You have brought so much to my life — laughter, love, and support. Jim Rankin, thank you for sharing her. Patty Winsa, thank you for the coffees and for listening to me ramble. To Jennifer Quinn, thank you for everything — from the couch to the laughter. To Rita Daly, you lovingly pushed us all along.

This book has been a partnership between Janie Yoon, the editorial director at House of Anansi, and myself. Janie had the vision to get this book done and I couldn't ask for a more intellectual, talented, and supportive editor. I am in awe of you and of how you always see what is beyond and know exactly how to get us there. To House of Anansi publisher Sarah MacLachlan, you believe in female writers and without your confidence and support, we couldn't do it.

Without the support and love of my mother, Sheila Van Sluytman, this book would not have been. She always believed we could do better and that there was a place for us in this world. My mother's family is her everything, and she has sacrificed and lived through more than I can say.

William, my son, you'll be happy to note I made it past page three. You are my strength, my heart. Natasha, my beautiful girl, you are loving, full of glorious wonder, and your patience knows no bounds. You two are the next generation: remember who you are and carry the stories forward.

Toronto
June 2017

INDEX

TANYA TALAGA has been a journalist at the *Toronto Star* for twenty years, covering everything from general city news to education, national health care, foreign news, and Indigenous affairs. She has been nominated five times for the Michener Award in public service journalism. In 2013, she was part of a team that won a National Newspaper Award for a year-long project on the Rana Plaza disaster in Bangladesh. In 2015, she was part of a team that won a National Newspaper Award for *Gone*, a series of stories on Missing and Murdered Indigenous Women and Girls. She is the 2017–2018 Atkinson Fellow in Public Policy. Talaga is of Polish and Indigenous descent. Her great-grandmother, Liz Gauthier, was a residential school survivor. Her great-grandfather, Russell Bowen, was an Ojibwe trapper and labourer. Her grandmother is a member of Fort William First Nation. Her mother was raised in Raith and Graham, Ontario. Talaga lives in Toronto with her two teenage children.

A portion of each sale of *Seven Fallen Feathers* will go to the Dennis Franklin Cromarty Memorial Fund, set up in 1994 to financially assist Nishnawbe Aski Nation students' studies in Thunder Bay and at post-secondary institutions.

Further donations can be made to:
http://www.cromartyfund.ca.